Clean Apex Code

Software Design for Salesforce Developers

Pablo Gonzalez
Foreword by Paul Battisson

Clean Apex Code: Software Design for Salesforce Developers

Pablo Gonzalez
Dublin, Ireland

ISBN-13 (pbk): 979-8-8688-1410-5   ISBN-13 (electronic): 979-8-8688-1411-2
https://doi.org/10.1007/979-8-8688-1411-2

Copyright © 2025 by Pablo Gonzalez

This work is subject to copyright. All rights are reserved by the Publisher, whether the whole or part of the material is concerned, specifically the rights of translation, reprinting, reuse of illustrations, recitation, broadcasting, reproduction on microfilms or in any other physical way, and transmission or information storage and retrieval, electronic adaptation, computer software, or by similar or dissimilar methodology now known or hereafter developed.

Trademarked names, logos, and images may appear in this book. Rather than use a trademark symbol with every occurrence of a trademarked name, logo, or image we use the names, logos, and images only in an editorial fashion and to the benefit of the trademark owner, with no intention of infringement of the trademark.

The use in this publication of trade names, trademarks, service marks, and similar terms, even if they are not identified as such, is not to be taken as an expression of opinion as to whether or not they are subject to proprietary rights.

While the advice and information in this book are believed to be true and accurate at the date of publication, neither the authors nor the editors nor the publisher can accept any legal responsibility for any errors or omissions that may be made. The publisher makes no warranty, express or implied, with respect to the material contained herein.

Managing Director, Apress Media LLC: Welmoed Spahr
Acquisitions Editor: Aditee Mirashi
Development Editor: James Markham
Editorial Assistant: Jacob Shmulewitz

Cover designed by eStudioCalamar

Cover image designed by Pexels

Distributed to the book trade worldwide by Springer Science+Business Media New York, 1 New York Plaza, New York, NY 10004. Phone 1-800-SPRINGER, fax (201) 348-4505, e-mail orders-ny@springer-sbm.com, or visit www.springeronline.com. Apress Media, LLC is a Delaware LLC and the sole member (owner) is Springer Science + Business Media Finance Inc (SSBM Finance Inc). SSBM Finance Inc is a **Delaware** corporation.

For information on translations, please e-mail booktranslations@springernature.com; for reprint, paperback, or audio rights, please e-mail bookpermissions@springernature.com.

Apress titles may be purchased in bulk for academic, corporate, or promotional use. eBook versions and licenses are also available for most titles. For more information, reference our Print and eBook Bulk Sales web page at http://www.apress.com/bulk-sales.

Any source code or other supplementary material referenced by the author in this book is available to readers on GitHub. For more detailed information, please visit https://www.apress.com/gp/services/source-code.

If disposing of this product, please recycle the paper

To my wife and daughter.

Thank you for your patience.

Table of Contents

About the Author xv

About the Technical Reviewer xvii

Foreword xix

Acknowledgments xxi

Introduction xxiii

Chapter 1: Refactoring Apex Code: First Steps 1
    1.1 What Is Clean Apex Code 2
    1.2 Fixing the Formatting 6
    1.3 Fixing the Method Signature 9
    1.4 Using Better Names 11
    1.5 Clarifying the Boolean Logic 13
    1.6 Making Code Reusable 17
    1.7 Don't Repeat Yourself (Too Much) 19
    1.8 Putting It All Together 23
    1.9 Conclusion 26

Chapter 2: Naming: Simple Techniques for Better Software Design 27
    2.1 Collection Names 28
        2.1.1 The Problem 28
        2.1.2 A Better Way 29
        2.1.3 Closing Thoughts 31

TABLE OF CONTENTS

- 2.2 Hide Boolean Logic 31
  - 2.2.1 The Problem 31
  - 2.2.2 A Better Way 33
  - 2.2.3 Closing Thoughts 35
- 2.3 Be Intentional 36
  - 2.3.1 The Problem 36
  - 2.3.2 A Better Way 37
  - 2.3.3 Closing Thoughts 37
- 2.4 Exactly the Same but Totally Different 38
  - 2.4.1 The Problem 38
  - 2.4.2 A Better Way 39
  - 2.4.3 Closing Thoughts 40
- 2.5 Keeping Code Relevant 40
  - 2.5.1 The Problem 40
  - 2.5.2 A Better Way 41
  - 2.5.3 Closing Thoughts 42
- 2.6 Context Isn't Enough 42
  - 2.6.1 The Problem 42
  - 2.6.2 A Better Way 43
  - 2.6.3 Closing Thoughts 43
- 2.7 Use Different Names for Variables and Classes 44
  - 2.7.1 The Problem 44
  - 2.7.2 A Better Way 45
  - 2.7.3 Closing Thoughts 47
- 2.8 Use Pronounceable Names 47
  - 2.8.1 The Problem 47
  - 2.8.2 A Better Way 48

TABLE OF CONTENTS

2.9 Use Searchable Names 48
    2.9.1 The Problem 49
    2.9.2 A Better Way 49
    2.9.3 Closing Thoughts 50

2.10 Use Problem Domain Names 50
    2.10.1 The Problem 50
    2.10.2 A Better Way 51
    2.10.3 Closing Thoughts 51

2.11 Not All Names Should Be Treated Equally 52
    2.11.1 The Problem 52
    2.11.2 A Better Way 53
    2.11.3 Closing Thoughts 53

2.12 Magic Numbers 53
    2.12.1 The Problem 54
    2.12.2 A Better Way 55
    2.12.3 Closing Thoughts 55

2.13 Conclusion 56
    2.13.1 Make It a Team Sport 56
    2.13.2 If You Can't Name It… 56
    2.13.3 Names Are Important, but Not *That* Important 56

2.14 Conclusion 57

Chapter 3: Doing One Thing: Abstraction, Boolean Parameters, and Design Patterns 59

3.1 Why Should Methods Do One Thing 59

3.2 Mixing Different Levels of Abstraction 61

3.3 Causing Duplication 64
    3.3.1 Testability 64

3.4 What Is "One Thing"? 65

vii

TABLE OF CONTENTS

   3.5 Boolean Parameters 67
   3.6 Alternatives to Boolean Arguments 70
   3.7 Multiple Boolean Parameters 72
   3.8 Enums and Switch Statements 76
   3.9 Replacing the Switch Statement with a Design Pattern 84
   3.10 Conclusion 92

Chapter 4: How Long Should Methods Be: Length, Depth, and Subtasks 95
   4.1 Short Methods 95
   4.2 The Clean Code Philosophy 96
   4.3 Very Short Methods 100
      4.3.1 To Explain 100
      4.3.2 To Hide Information 101
      4.3.3 To Simplify the API 102
      4.3.4 To Give the Action a Name 103
   4.4 Longer Methods 104
   4.5 Deep vs. Shallow Modules 106
   4.6 Smaller Methods Increase Coupling 107
   4.7 Not All Methods Are the Same 108
   4.8 Subtasks Should Be Separate Methods 109
   4.9 Conclusion 113

Chapter 5: Comments Don't Lie, Developers Do 115
   5.1 Everybody Lies 115
   5.2 Self-documenting Code 118
   5.3 Version Control Comments 120
   5.4 Aha! Comments 122
   5.5 Why Comments 122

TABLE OF CONTENTS

5.6 Dead Code 125

5.7 Funny Comments 127

5.8 ApexDoc Comments 128

5.9 To-Do Comments 129

5.10 Reference Comments 133

5.11 Implementation Comments 134

5.12 Conclusion 134

Chapter 6: Null, Validations, and Guard Clauses 135

6.1 Null 135

6.2 Safe Navigation Operator 136

6.3 Null Coalescing 139

6.4 Empty 141

6.5 Validating Strings 142

6.6 Validating Booleans 142

6.7 Validating Maps 144

6.8 Validating If Lists Are Empty 145

6.9 Validating If Lists Are Null 150

6.10 Guard Clauses and Multiple Returns 153

6.11 Should You Return Null 159

6.12 Clean Validations 162

6.13 Conclusion 163

Chapter 7: Cascading Failures in Trigger Boundaries 165

7.1 The Exception Dilemma 165

7.2 Business Process Boundaries and Atomic Operations 170

7.3 Avoid Using Triggers for Cross-Object Operations 174

7.4 Decoupling in Trigger Frameworks 176

TABLE OF CONTENTS

7.5 Async Processing to Avoid Cascading Failures 177
    7.5.1 Using Queueable Apex to Isolate Failures 178
    7.5.2 Using Change Data Capture to Isolate Failures 179
    7.5.3 Using Platform Events to Isolate Failures 182
7.6 Triggers Should Be Able to Stop All Exceptions..184
7.7 Conclusion 189

Chapter 8: Object-Oriented Programming in Apex 191
8.1 A Bit of History 192
8.2 What Is an Object? 194
8.3 Challenges with the Object Model 195
8.4 Class vs. Instance 198
8.5 Objects in Apex 200
8.6 Encapsulation 202
    8.6.1 Encapsulation in Apex 205
8.7 About Polymorphism 207
8.8 Inheritance 208
    8.8.1 Inheritance in Apex Programming 212
    8.8.2 When to Use Inheritance in Apex 215
8.9 Interfaces 217
    8.9.1 Interfaces in Apex 221
8.10 Abstract Classes 223
8.11 Why We Need Polymorphism 229
8.12 Conclusion 231

x

TABLE OF CONTENTS

Chapter 9: Software Design Principles 233
9.1 What Are Design Principles? 233
9.2 SOLID 234
9.2.1 Single Responsibility Principle 235
9.2.2 The Open/Closed Principle 238
9.2.3 The Liskov Substitution Principle 241
9.2.4 The Interface Segregation Principle 243
9.2.5 The Dependency Inversion Principle 245
9.3 DRY 252
9.4 YAGNI 254
9.5 Design Errors Out of Existence 255
9.6 Conclusion 256

Chapter 10: Modularity, Coupling, and Cohesion 257
10.1 Modularity 257
10.2 Properties of Modular Software 259
10.3 Modularity in Our Daily Work 262
10.4 Better Together or Apart 266
10.5 Coupling 268
10.6 Cohesion 271
10.7 Cohesion in Salesforce Development 275
10.8 Conclusion 280

Chapter 11: Dependency Injection and Boundaries 281
11.1 What Is Dependency Injection (DI)? 282
11.2 Not All Coupling Is Eliminated by DI 285
11.3 DI Works with Modular Design 287
11.4 What Is a Dependency? 287
11.5 Not All Dependencies Are Equal 289

xi

TABLE OF CONTENTS

    11.6 Boundaries 294

    11.7 Better Injected or Better Hard-Coded 298

    11.8 Late Binding 300

    11.9 Inversion of Control 304

    11.10 Conclusion 304

Chapter 12: Unit Tests, Stubs, and Mocking the Salesforce Database 305

    12.1 Why Bother with Testing 307

    12.2 Nobody Knows What a Unit Test Is 308

        12.2.1 Unit As a Method 310

        12.2.2 Unit As a Unit of Work 310

        12.2.3 Unit As a Unit of Behavior 311

        12.2.4 Unit As Unit of Code 312

        12.2.5 Which One Is It? 313

    12.3 Properties of a Good Unit Test 314

    12.4 Integration Tests and Interactions with the Database 315

        12.4.1 Salesforce Tests Are Integration Tests by Default 315

        12.4.2 Integration Tests Are Not Evil 319

        12.4.3 Salesforce Is a Database-Driven System 322

        12.4.4 Integration Tests Are Slow 323

    12.5 Mocking DML Operations 324

        12.5.1 Brute Force 325

        12.5.2 Testing the Internals Without the Database 326

        12.5.3 Simple Context-Aware Wrapper 328

        12.5.4 Dependency Injection 329

        12.5.5 Test Doubles and the Stub API 331

TABLE OF CONTENTS

12.6 Libraries for Mocking DML Operations 336
12.6.1 General-Purpose Mocking Libraries 337
12.6.2 Drop-In Replacements for the Database Class 337
12.7 Mocking DML Statements Affect SOQL Queries 338
12.8 Mocking SOQL Queries 338
12.8.1 How to Mock SOQL Queries 341
12.8.2 Moving SOQL into Methods 341
12.8.3 Use a SOQL Wrapper 342
12.9 Should You Mock the Database? 345
12.10 Conclusion 346

Chapter 13: The Apex Well-Architected Framework 347
13.1 A FFLIB Recap 348
13.2 The Challenges with FFLIB 351
13.2.1 Narrow View of the Platform 352
13.2.2 Selectors Are Shallow Modules 353
13.2.3 Over-engineering 355
13.2.4 Not Built for Salesforce 355
13.3 Gratitude 357
13.4 What's the Alternative? 357
13.5 Apex Well-Architected Framework 358
13.6 Use Salesforce DX Folders 360
13.7 Where to Place Business Logic 362
13.7.1 What Is Business Logic? 364
13.7.2 Business Logic Should Be Written from the Inside Out 364
13.7.3 Concrete Guidelines for Business Logic 367
13.8 Filtering Logic in Trigger Handlers 368
13.9 Domain Classes 371

xiii

TABLE OF CONTENTS

13.10 Internal Libraries 374

    13.10.1 Trigger Handlers 375

    13.10.2 Apex Logging and Observability 375

    13.10.3 Continuous Delivery with Feature Flags 376

    13.10.4 Selector Classes 378

    13.10.5 General Utilities 378

13.11 Other Principles 379

13.12 Conclusion 380

Index **381**

About the Author

Pablo Gonzalez started his career as a Salesforce developer and later moved into product management, where he focuses on building tools that make life easier for developers. He's worked on Salesforce DevOps products like HappySoup, Salto, and AutoRABIT, blending his technical skills with his love for solving practical problems.

He's passionate about good software engineering practices and believes the best way to get the most out of Salesforce is to approach it with an engineering mindset. Pablo's goal is to give Salesforce engineering teams the tools and knowledge they need to succeed—and enjoy their work more.

Originally from Costa Rica, Pablo now lives in Ireland with his wife and daughter. He loves trying new foods and sharing good meals with family and friends.

About the Technical Reviewer

Venkata Karthik Penikalapati is a seasoned software developer with more than a decade of expertise in designing and managing intricate distributed systems, data pipelines, and AI/ML applications. Armed with a master's degree in Computer Science from the University at Buffalo, his knowledge spans the realms of machine learning, data engineering, and workflow orchestration. Venkata thrives in the realm of distributed systems, continually pushing the boundaries of innovation.

Currently, Karthik is a valuable member of the Salesforce team within the Search Cloud division. Here, he's at the forefront of cutting-edge developments, spearheading the integration of the latest advancements in artificial intelligence (AI).

Foreword

Programs are meant to be read by humans and only incidentally for computers to execute.

—Donald Knuth

I remember quite clearly my first days learning about the Salesforce platform, about objects, fields, relationships, and metadata. About the power of the platform to build quick and simple applications to help businesses move faster. About formula fields and workflow rules, and then triggers, Visualforce, and Apex. In the 15 years since, the platform has grown tremendously and has taken on various new clouds, products, and features (and names). Still, one technology has remained constant as the beating heart of the platform's automation power, Apex.

I have written two books on Apex, the first trying to help those beginning their journey (*Learning Salesforce Development with Apex*) and the second to help those looking to truly come to grips with the various features of the language (*Mastering Apex Programming*). It was through this second book and Pablo discussing it with me that we first met. Since then, we have often caught up at conferences across continents, as well as discussed each other's public work on social media, where we both regularly espouse our views on all things Salesforce.

Having written two books on the subject and delivered countless hours of training, I feel I can say I know Apex pretty well. One skill that requires constant honing however is ensuring that I write clean Apex. Apex that can be reworked, extended, updated, and refactored. Most importantly though, Apex that another developer can read and understand with confidence.

FOREWORD

In their book *The Elements of Programming Style,* authors Brian Kernighan and P. J. Plauger start the preface to the first edition by stating clearly "Good programming cannot be taught by preaching generalities." This book does not preach generalities but will show you, the reader, how you can, through clear explanations and well-composed examples, begin to write cleaner Apex code. Pablo may be best known for his work in the DevOps space, but this book will help you write code that makes it possible for you to adopt such practices within your organization.

I wish this book had been available 15 years ago when I started, to help me in structuring the code I was writing. I was fortunate that when I first started with Apex I was working in a very structured code base environment with an experienced team, and as such, many of these practices were learned through osmosis. When I moved into the consulting space, I quickly noticed that not everyone was as thorough. This book would have helped me immensely in promoting and enforcing good behaviors.

In the time since I started, the complexity of the work delivered on the platform has grown exponentially. You, the reader, are now more likely to be working in an org with 5+ years of legacy development, code, flows, process builders, and all other manner of automation and fixes. It can be very daunting to even think about how you can improve such environments to be more robust. I encourage you to read this book, take your time to think about the advice Pablo gives, and begin to apply it little by little in your own work, and you will see the benefits. When starting a new project, make it your goal to follow the patterns and principles shared in this book from the start. If everyone who reads this work makes the code they work with just 10% better, the entire industry will feel a huge benefit. Good luck, and happy reading.

Paul Battisson
Salesforce MVP Hall of Fame
CEO, Groundwork Apps
Cloudbites.tv

Acknowledgments

I couldn't have written this book without the help of my contributors, who joined me in this journey by the power of social media. They helped me refine my arguments, ensure I was pragmatic, and, most importantly, provided me with endless support and encouragement. I'm endlessly thankful to the following individuals:

- Prateek Kumar
- Andrii Sukhetskyi
- Luke Buthman
- Tzhe'ela Trooper
- Dhiraj Prajapati
- Manuel Guerrero
- Akshi Boojhawon
- Chandler Anderson
- Keith Rogers
- Jorge Teo
- Sumanth Naik
- Alejandro Ruz Carrasco

ACKNOWLEDGMENTS

Additionally, the following individuals helped me indirectly through conversations, feedback, and general advice:

- Mitch Spano
- James Simone
- Jonathan Gillespie
- Paul Battisson
- Robert Baillie

Thank you all.

Introduction

This book is not for beginners, and it is not an adaptation of *Clean Code* by Robert C. Martin. I start with those two statements because they are the most common questions I get about this book. I will address both these questions shortly.

I wrote this book because I have seen too many Apex code bases filled with unnecessary complexity. If you have been developing in Salesforce for a while, I am sure you have come across plenty of bad code, sometimes the kind that feels like a nightmare. My goal is to help you write code that is easier to understand, maintain, and extend. In turn, this should make your life as a developer much easier.

Who This Book Is For

This book is for Salesforce developers who know Apex well and have **at least five years of experience** working with it. It does **not** teach general or basic Apex concepts. Readers are expected to know the language well and be comfortable reading the developer documentation to learn new things.

However, even experienced Salesforce developers can lack skills in software design, since this is not something that is traditionally taught in any official Salesforce resource nor is it something that is naturally learned in the field.

To truly understand software design, you must study a broad range of topics that, when put together, give you a framework for thinking about software in new ways. In a way, it is like learning to play the piano at home versus taking professional lessons later in life. Learning at home will only get you so far.

INTRODUCTION

With that said, this book is for experienced Salesforce developers who want to take their skills to the next level and stand out among their peers. Once you learn and apply the teachings in this book, you will never be the same developer again.

Not a *Clean Code* Rehash

Because of the name of this book, some people have asked if it is just a rehash or adaptation of *Clean Code* by Robert C. Martin. If you have read *Clean Code*, you might even wonder why you should read this.

This book is not an adaptation of Martin's work. While his teachings have inspired me and thousands of developers, this book is not based on his principles.

There are only two things this book has in common with *Clean Code*: there is a chapter dedicated to naming programming constructs, and the book title itself. Other than that, the content is completely different, and in many cases, I actually disagree with Martin and present alternative views.

Finally, this is the book I wish existed when I first read *Clean Code* and many other books. It takes multiple paradigms and software design concepts from different domains and applies them to Apex development in a way that has never been done before.

What This Book Is About

This book is about software design. Software design is the process of designing your code with the intention of reducing complexity. I've realized that it's very hard to explain what software design is in simple words. In a way, you have to go through the book to *experience* software design. However, let me try to give you an example of what this book is really about.

INTRODUCTION

A traditional Apex book would focus on teaching you which Apex features to use, such as Queueable vs. Future; Apex best practices; and how to work within governor limits. This book assumes you already know all that. Instead, it focuses on concerns such as

- Are your variable and method names good enough?
- Are the responsibilities of classes and methods well defined?
- Is your code modular?
- Does your code achieve a good balance between coupling and cohesion?
- Are you making the most out of object-oriented programming?
- Are your tests optimized for speed? Are you using advanced techniques such as mocks and stubs?
- Does your code follow SOLID, DRY, and other common design principles?
- Are you aware of the business process boundaries between your Apex trigger handlers?

These questions all have a common goal. When applied well, they help reduce complexity.

I have made each chapter title as descriptive as possible so that you know what to expect just by browsing the table of contents. I encourage you to do so before moving further.

INTRODUCTION

Do Not Expect Perfect Code

Because of the book's title and audience, some readers may expect every code sample to be perfect. That is neither possible nor desirable because the examples are **optimized for teaching and learning, not for running in production.**

With that in mind, you will see plenty of code without exception handling, dependency injection, or other things that you would normally expect in production code. You may also notice that some examples do not pass static analysis tools like PMD. That is intentional.

Static analysis tools are useful for enforcing consistency and catching mistakes, but they are not a substitute for learning software design. If I had to ensure that every example passed PMD, the code would be filled with annotations, boilerplate, and formatting tweaks that add no real value to the lesson. Worse, it would distract from the actual concept being taught.

Additionally, some formatting choices in this book are due to **the constraints of a book format, not because I would format my code this way in a real-world project.** Line breaks, indentation, and spacing are sometimes adjusted for readability on a printed page rather than an IDE. If an example appears formatted strangely, assume it was done for clarity within the book layout.

If a chapter focuses on naming variables and methods, I do not want to clutter the examples with design patterns or dependency injection. Likewise, in a chapter about modularity and coupling, I may not focus as much on naming. The priority in each chapter is to make sure the core idea is clear.

By the end of the book, I introduce the Apex Well-Architected Framework, which brings all these concepts together. When you follow the framework, you can expect *your* code to be well-structured, maintainable, and designed with intention. And of course, if you want to make every line of your code PMD-compliant, you are free to do so.

CHAPTER 1

Refactoring Apex Code: First Steps

Any fool can write code that a computer can understand. Good programmers write code that humans can understand.

—Martin Fowler

This chapter is a quick introduction to clean Apex code. We'll start by looking at some sample code and then gradually improve it step by step.

A word of caution before we start: Do not expect perfectly clean code by the end of this chapter. We will not talk about dependency injection, mocks, modularity, or any advanced patterns. The purpose of this chapter is simply to get us into the right mindset. If you are very experienced, you may find this basic and common sense. I still recommend you go through it so that you understand the tone of the book and some of the topics that will be covered in greater depth later on. I guarantee the book will become more advanced very quickly.

CHAPTER 1   REFACTORING APEX CODE: FIRST STEPS

1.1 What Is Clean Apex Code

Let's start by defining what clean code is. Clean code is

- Easy and pleasant to read
- Clear in its intention
- Easy to maintain
- Easy to test

Even with this definition, what actually constitutes clean code can be somewhat subjective. Just like in real life, where one person's messy living room might seem tidy to someone else, the same goes for code. The perception of cleanliness can vary from one person to another.

With that in mind, the easiest way to understand clean code is to compare it to not-so-clean code. Let's look at an example:

> **Note**   I'm separating the method signature from the body to prevent too much indentation, which can make the code difficult to read in a book format.

Method Signature

```
@future(callout=true)
public static void createTasks(Set<Id> ids)
```

Method Body

```
List<Account> acctRecs = [SELECT Id,
Name, OwnerId, is_supplier__c, verification__c, AnnualRevenue
FROM Account WHERE Id IN :ids];

List<Task> tks = new List <Task>();
```

```
for(Account rec: acctRecs){
    if(rec.is_supplier__c != false && rec.verification__c ==
    'Completed' && rec.AnnualRevenue > 100{
            Task paTk = new Task();
        paTk.WhatId = rec.Id;
        paTk.Subject = 'Call for new Partner account';
        paTk.category__c = 'Partner';
        paTk.OwnerId = rec.OwnerId;
        tks.add(paTk);
    }else if (rec.is_supplier__c != true && rec.AnnualRevenue
     < 100) {
        Task caTk = new Task();
        caTk.category__c = 'Customer';
        caTk.WhatId = rec.Id;
        caTk.Subject = 'Call for new Customer account';
        caTk.OwnerId = rec.OwnerId;
        tks.add(caTk);
    }else{
        Task dfTk = new Task();
        dfTk.WhatId = rec.Id;

        dfTk.Subject = 'Call for new standard account';
        dfTk.OwnerId = rec.OwnerId;
        tks.add(dfTk);
    }

    if(rec.is_supplier__c == true && rec.verification__c ==
    'Completed' &&
        rec.AnnualRevenue > 100){
        String accountJson = JSON.serialize(rec);
        HttpRequest req = new HttpRequest();
        req.setEndpoint('https://api.netsuite.com/partners');
        req.setMethod('POST');
```

CHAPTER 1   REFACTORING APEX CODE: FIRST STEPS

```
        req.setHeader('Content-Type', 'application/json');
        req.setBody(accountJson);

        Http http = new Http();

        try {
            HttpResponse res = http.send(req);
        } catch (System.CalloutException e) {
            Logger.error('Callout error: '+ e.getMessage());
        }
    }
}
insert tks;
```

This isn't the worst code in the world. In fact, I'm sure you recognize the structure: a few `if` statements, a few `for` loops, and eventually a DML statement at the end. Every org I've worked with had methods that looked just like this one.

Now, how confident are you that you fully understand this code? Here are a few things that jump out at me when I read it:

- The method name `createTasks` doesn't tell us much. Is this a general-purpose method for creating tasks? Why does it take an Id list as a parameter? Can this be used to create tasks in any situation? We don't really know. We are forced to read the entire method in order to understand where and when it can be used.

- The name of the account list `acctRecs` isn't clear. We can guess it stands for "account records," but that's just a guess. It could mean anything. Is it some naming convention we're not aware of?

- After the first `if` statement, we create a task with the variable name `paTk`. What does `paTk` stand for? Is it "partner account task"? Maybe, maybe not. This pattern repeats in the other task creation blocks. We don't know what these names imply. We could be missing some important context.

- We are repeating the logic for creating a task three times. The only difference is the content of the `subject` and `category__c` fields. If we need to change the logic for creating a task, we must change it in three places. That's the three places where bugs can hide.

- Before the HTTP callout, we repeat the first `if` statement we saw earlier in the method. We still don't know what this condition represents, but assuming it represents the same concept in two different places, we again have to change the code in multiple places if the requirement changes.

- What is this HTTP callout for? What's its purpose? There's nothing in the code to help us make an educated guess.

- The formatting seems inconsistent. Occasionally, we have spaces before a new block of code starts, while other times we don't. The indentation isn't consistent either.

- Finally, we try to insert the tasks without handling any exceptions that might occur.

Now, let's go through a scenario where I refactor this code to make it cleaner. Refactoring involves changing the internal structure of the code without affecting its external behavior—in other words, the code will function the same but be much easier to read. We will talk about refactoring in more detail in future chapters.

I'll do this step-by-step, without fixing everything in one go. If you notice I skip something you'd like to see fixed, be patient; I'll likely address it by the end of the chapter. Finally, don't pay too much attention to the logic and whether it makes sense from a business point of view; this is merely an example to illustrate the concepts we will cover in the book.

1.2 Fixing the Formatting

The first step I'm tackling is fixing the formatting. I've chosen to start here because it's the simplest way to enhance the cleanliness of this code. Here's a breakdown of the changes I'll implement:

- I'll insert a space between blocks of code. Whenever I open an `if` or `for` loop, there will be a space before the next block of code.
- I'll ensure there's a space between closing parentheses and opening brackets.
- I'll group related concepts closer together.
- I'll incorporate general spacing throughout to provide breathing room for the mind.

Here's the updated version:

Note I've stacked the conditions inside each `if` statement vertically because the book does not allow enough horizontal space. In real life, I wouldn't do this.

```
List<Account> acctRecs = [SELECT Id,
Name, OwnerId, is_supplier__c, verification__c, AnnualRevenue
FROM Account WHERE Id IN :ids];

List<Task> tks = new List <Task>();

for (Account rec: acctRecs) {

    if(
        rec.is_supplier__c != false &&
        rec.verification__c == 'Completed'
        && rec.AnnualRevenue > 100
    ) {

        Task paTk = new Task();
        paTk.WhatId = rec.Id;
        paTk.Subject = 'Call for new Partner account';
        paTk.category__c = 'Partner';
        paTk.OwnerId = rec.OwnerId;
        tks.add(paTk);

    } else if (
        rec.is_supplier__c != true
        && rec.AnnualRevenue < 100
    ) {

        Task caTk = new Task();
        caTk.category__c = 'Customer';
        caTk.WhatId = rec.Id;
        caTk.Subject = 'Call for new Customer account';
        caTk.OwnerId = rec.OwnerId;
        tks.add(caTk);

    } else {
```

```
        Task dfTk = new Task();
        dfTk.WhatId = rec.Id;
        dfTk.Subject = 'Call for new standard account';
        dfTk.OwnerId = rec.OwnerId;
        tks.add(dfTk);
    }

    if (rec.is_supplier__c == true
        && rec.verification__c == 'Completed'
        && rec.AnnualRevenue > 100
    ) {

        String accountJson = JSON.serialize(rec);

        HttpRequest req = new HttpRequest();
        req.setEndpoint('https://api.netsuite.com/partners');
        req.setMethod('POST');
        req.setHeader('Content-Type', 'application/json');
        req.setBody(accountJson);

        Http http = new Http();

        try {
            HttpResponse res = http.send(req);
        } catch (System.CalloutException e) {
            Logger.error('Callout error: '+ e.getMessage());
        }

    }
}
insert tks;
```

Take a moment to flip through the pages and compare this version to the original one. You'll likely notice that even if you don't fully understand what the code is doing or why, it's easier to read now. That's because the spacing provides our mind with a break, allowing us to absorb each concept before moving on to the next. This is a practice that's often overlooked, yet it's simple to implement and offers immediate benefit. Let's continue.

1.3 Fixing the Method Signature

Let's continue by making the method name clearer. The name `createTasks` doesn't tell us much about what type of tasks we are creating and why.

After reading the code, I figured out this is called from the account trigger handler, and it's meant to notify account owners of a new account that has been created for them. The fact that tasks are being used for that notification is just an implementation detail (in the future, they could be notified via an instant message, etc.). With this new context, I made the following changes to the method signature:

Before

```
@future(callout=true)
public static void createTasks(Set<Id> ids)
```

After

```
@future(callout=true)
public static void notifyAccountOwners(Set<Id> newAccountIds)
```

This reads a lot better because now I know why this method exists. Before I could tell what it did, but not why. Also, if in the future we change how account owners are notified, the method name is still relevant. Finally, I now know that the Ids belong to new accounts and are not meant to be generic sObject Ids.

CHAPTER 1   REFACTORING APEX CODE: FIRST STEPS

Following this change, I can now make the intent of the SOQL query clearer as well:

Before

```
List<Account> acctRecs = [SELECT ...
FROM Account WHERE Id IN :ids];
```

After

```
List<Account> newAccounts = [SELECT ...
FROM Account WHERE Id IN :newAccountIds];
```

Finally, I can make the for loop variable clearer:

Before

```
for (Account rec: acctRecs) {
    if(
        rec.is_supplier__c != false &&
        ...
    ) {
```

After

```
for (Account newAccount: newAccounts) {
    if(
        newAccount.is_supplier__c != false &&
        ...
    ) {
```

Now, we understand more about this method. We know it's used to notify account owners, and we use the Ids of newly created accounts. Notice how much information we provided to the reader simply by using better names. Speaking of which…

CHAPTER 1　REFACTORING APEX CODE: FIRST STEPS

1.4 Using Better Names

Looking further down at the code, I'm concerned about the names we are using for the task variables.

```
if(...) {

    Task paTk = new Task();
    paTk.WhatId = newAccount.Id;
    paTk.Subject = 'Call for new Partner account';
    paTk.category__c = 'Partner';
    paTk.OwnerId = newAccount.OwnerId;
    tks.add(paTk);

} else if (...) {

    Task caTk = new Task();
    caTk.category__c = 'Customer';
    caTk.WhatId = newAccount.Id;
    caTk.Subject = 'Call for new Customer account';
    caTk.OwnerId = newAccount.OwnerId;
    tks.add(caTk);

 } else {

    Task dfTk = new Task();
    dfTk.WhatId = newAccount.Id;
    dfTk.Subject = 'Call for new standard account';
    dfTk.OwnerId = newAccount.OwnerId;
    tks.add(dfTk);
  }
```

CHAPTER 1   REFACTORING APEX CODE: FIRST STEPS

We see `paTk`, `caTk`, and `dfTk`. The issue with these names is that not only are they uncommon, but I also don't know if they have a specific meaning that I should be aware of. Maybe `paTk` is an internal acronym for a special type of task record, or perhaps it's a term that is well recognized by the business. If I replace `paTk` with `partnerTask`, will I change the meaning of this logic? I'm not sure.

Or perhaps it's just what the developer thought of in the moment as a short version of "partner account task." How do I know which is correct? These uncertainties discourage me and other developers from modifying this code. Code that discourages other developers from changing it is not clean code.

Alright, assuming I did some research and concluded that these aren't internal business names, I made the following changes:

```
Task taskPartnerAccount = new Task();
taskPartnerAccount.WhatId = newAccount.Id;

...

Task taskCustomerAccount = new Task();
taskCustomerAccount.category__c = 'Customer';

...

Task defaultTask = new Task();
defaultTask.WhatId = newAccount.Id;
```

This reads a lot better. Yes, the names are much longer, but now, we can tell immediately how one task is different from the others. Our intention is clear.

1.5 Clarifying the Boolean Logic

Let's look at the boolean logic inside the `for` loop.

```
if(
    newAccount.is_supplier__c != false &&
    newAccount.verification__c == 'Completed'
    && newAccount.AnnualRevenue > 100
)  {
  ...
} else if (
    newAccount.is_supplier__c != true
    && newAccount.AnnualRevenue < 100
)
...
```

There are several concerns I have about this code. First, the use of double negatives makes it hard to read. For example:

`newAccount.is_supplier__c != false`

I find myself reading this out loud to make sense of it: "If the supplier field is not false." Wouldn't it be easier to just say, "If the supplier field is true?" Similarly, in the second `if` statement, we say, "if the supplier field is not true," which would be clearer as "if the supplier field is false." This kind of double negative logic can quickly become difficult to follow, especially when combined with additional boolean logic. For example, "if the supplier field is not false and the verification is completed and the annual revenue is more than 100." Let's make this logic easier to understand by checking if the field *equals* `true` and `false`, respectively:

13

```
if(
    newAccount.is_supplier__c == true &&
    newAccount.verification__c == 'Completed'
    && newAccount.AnnualRevenue > 100
)   {
    ...
} else if (
    newAccount.is_supplier__c == false
    && newAccount.AnnualRevenue < 100
)
...
```

That's better, but it's not quite there yet. The following expression is redundant:

```
newAccount.is_supplier__c == true
```

Because the is_supplier__c field is a check box, it already has either a true or false value. So, we can simply use the field itself as the evaluation criteria, like this:

```
if(
    newAccount.is_supplier__c &&
    newAccount.verification__c == 'Completed'
    && newAccount.AnnualRevenue > 100
)   {
    ...
} else if (
    !newAccount.is_supplier__c
    && newAccount.AnnualRevenue < 100
)
...
```

CHAPTER 1   REFACTORING APEX CODE: FIRST STEPS

Notice that in the second `if` statement, I'm using the `!` operator to negate the boolean, which is the same as say "if the supplier field is false." This is a lot more succinct. There's less code to read and it gets straight to the point.

The second concern I have is why we're mixing the account supplier field with the verification status and the annual revenue field. What do these three fields have in common? Why are they used together inside the `if` statement? What is the condition we are evaluating here? I see the fields being evaluated, but I don't understand the business context. I don't understand how these three fields together represent a higher concept that needs to be true before we can proceed.

After some digging, I learned that the annual revenue determines the tier of the account and that we only need to create tasks for certain tiers. Additionally, accounts that are tagged as suppliers are considered partner accounts, but only if the verification status is completed. Could you have guessed all this context from reading this code? I wouldn't have. Most developers would address this by adding a comment with the ticket number of the requirement that led to the creation of this code, like this:

```
//https://myorg.atlassian.net/browse/FC-1220
//create tasks for accounts based on tier
if(
    newAccount.is_supplier__c &&
    newAccount.verification__c == 'Completed'
    && newAccount.AnnualRevenue > 100
)
```

While this isn't so bad, wouldn't it be better if the code itself was the documentation? Why rely on a third-party system of record for that? Let's try that; I'm going to start by extracting the boolean logic to their own variables:

15

CHAPTER 1   REFACTORING APEX CODE: FIRST STEPS

```
Boolean isPartnerAccount = (newAccount.is_supplier__c &&
newAccount.verification__c == 'Completed');

Boolean isCustomerAccount = !newAccount.is_supplier__c;

Boolean isGoldTier = newAccount.AnnualRevenue > 100;

Boolean isSilverTier = newAccount.AnnualRevenue < 100;
```

By moving the boolean expressions out of the `if` statements and into specific variables, I'm able to give them a name. Once I have the boolean logic extracted to variables, I can reuse these variables in the `if` statement to construct something like this:

```
if (isPartnerAccount && isGoldTier) {
   ...
}
else if (isCustomerAccount && isSilverTier) {
   ...
}
else {
   ...
}
```

Again, this works because both `isPartnerAccount` and `isGoldTier` are booleans, so I can combine them to create another boolean expression. Doesn't this read like pure plain English? I can even read it out loud: "If this is a partner account and it's a gold tier account, do this…"

Also note that I no longer need to stack the conditions on top of each other. You can easily read this even in a book format.

CHAPTER 1   REFACTORING APEX CODE: FIRST STEPS

1.6 Making Code Reusable

Now, if the distinction between partner and customer accounts is so important, surely, we have logic all over our code base that needs to differentiate between a partner and a customer account. The same is true for the boolean logic that determines the account tier. It's great that we extracted this logic into boolean variables, but those variables can't be easily reused by other classes. Let's fix this by moving this logic to a domain class called `AccountDomain`

```
public with sharing class AccountDomain {

    public static Boolean isPartnerAccount(Account account) {
        return account.is_supplier__c
        && account.verification__c == 'Completed';
    }

    public static Boolean isCustomerAccount(Account account) {
        return !account.is_supplier__c;
    }
...
```

   Now, this logic can be reused by any other class. Also, because we have methods instead of simple variables, we can add as much logic as we want inside of them. For example, if the requirements change in the future (and they will) on how we determine that an account is a gold tier one, we can simply modify this method, and automatically, all other code that depends on it will start using the new logic without even "knowing."

   It's worth noting that these new methods assume the `account` variable was created by querying all the necessary fields. If the variable doesn't have all the fields, you will get the dreaded error `SObject row was retrieved via SOQL without querying the requested field`.

CHAPTER 1   REFACTORING APEX CODE: FIRST STEPS

This is one reason for using selector classes[1] to query records, so that you can ensure consistency on which fields are queried. Alternatively, you could pass the account Id and query the necessary fields, but then, you couldn't stop another developer from using this method inside a for loop, which could cause the SOQL governor limit to be exceeded. For this reason, passing the account reference is a better design choice.

Anyway, let's see what our boolean logic looks like now with the new methods:

```
Boolean isPartnerAccount = AccountDomain.
isPartnerAccount(account);

Boolean isCustomerAccount = AccountDomain.isCustomerAccountAcco
unt(account);

Boolean isGoldTier = AccountDomain.isGoldTier(account);
Boolean isSilverTier = AccountDomain.isSilverTier(account);

if (isPartnerAccount && isGoldTier) {
    ...
}
else if (isCustomerAccount && isSilverTier) {
    ...
}
else {
    ...
}
```

---

[1] Selector is a design pattern where queries are encapsulated inside of methods so that they can be reused consistently. We will explore this pattern later in the book.

CHAPTER 1 REFACTORING APEX CODE: FIRST STEPS

Your initial reaction may be "that looks nice but now you have a ton more variables and classes!" And you're right, I get it. Clean code can often result in more code than the quick-and-dirty code. But let's review the benefits so far:

- The boolean logic now reads like plain English.

- We've made the code self-documenting. We understand the relationship between account tiers and account types without having to reference old ticket numbers.

- We've made some of this logic reusable in other parts of our code base, and in doing so

- We've introduced a new concept into our code base: the concept of tiers and account types. This makes our code base more language-rich.

But we're not done yet.

1.7 Don't Repeat Yourself (Too Much)

Moving on, we can see that the code for creating tasks is almost identical in all three places:

```
if(isPartnerAccount  && isGoldTier) {

    Task taskPartnerAccount = new Task();
    taskPartnerAccount.WhatId = newAccount.Id;
    taskPartnerAccount.Subject = 'Call for new Partner account';
    taskPartnerAccount.category__c = 'Partner';
    taskPartnerAccount.OwnerId = newAccount.OwnerId;
    tks.add(taskPartnerAccount);
```

19

```
} else if (isCustomerAccount && isSilverTier) {
    Task taskCustomerAccount = new Task();
    taskCustomerAccount.category__c = 'Customer';
    taskCustomerAccount.WhatId = newAccount.Id;
    taskCustomerAccount.Subject = 'Call for new Customer
    account';
    taskCustomerAccount.OwnerId = newAccount.OwnerId;
    tks.add(taskCustomerAccount);
} else {
    Task defaultTask = new Task();
    defaultTask.WhatId = newAccount.Id;
    defaultTask.Subject = 'Call for new standard account';
    defaultTask.OwnerId = newAccount.OwnerId;
    tks.add(defaultTask);
}
```

The only thing that differs is how we populate the `subject` and `category__c` fields. However, notice that in the third condition, we aren't populating the `category__c` field. Why not? Is this by design? Is this a bug? Was there a requirement that this field only needed to be populated for accounts of a certain tier? Such a simple omission can lead to many questions, and not having clear answers to these questions makes the code hard to reason about and hard to change. I did some (fictitious) research and found out that no one knows why this field is even there and why it's not populated for this condition. I don't have a solution to this problem, so I'll have to leave this logic as is for now.[2]

---

[2] I included this example to show that writing clean code is also about not causing confusion and uncertainty for future developers who need to read it (which can also be your future self).

Moving on, the next problem is that aside from these two fields, the logic for creating a task is the same. If we need to change this logic, we must update it in three different places. What if we forget to update one of the blocks? That's probably what happened when the previous developer added the category__c field. We can fix this by simply extracting this logic into a private method called getBaseTask(). Like this:

```
if (isPartnerAccount && isGoldTier) {

    Task partnerAccountTask = getBaseTask(newAccount);
    partnerAccountTask.category__c = 'Partner';
    partnerAccountTask.Subject = 'Call for new Partner
    account';
    tasks.add(partnerAccountTask);
}
else if (isCustomerAccount && isSilverTier) {

    Task customerAccountTask = getBaseTask(newAccount);
    customerAccountTask.category__c = 'Customer';
    customerAccountTask.Subject = 'Call for new Customer
    account';
    tasks.add(customerAccountTask);
}
else {

    Task defaultTask = getBaseTask(newAccount);
    defaultTask.Subject = 'Schedule call for new standard
    account';
    tasks.add(partnerAccountTask);
}
```

The getBaseTask() method generates a task with default fields, but we can still incorporate specific logic inside each condition. This way, we can reuse some logic while still maintaining some control over it.

CHAPTER 1   REFACTORING APEX CODE: FIRST STEPS

We can clean this up even further by wrapping the block for each task type into their own methods, while still reusing getBaseTask(), for example:

```
private static Task createPartnerAcccountTask(Account account) {
    Task task = getBaseTask(account);
    task.category__c = 'Partner';
    task.Subject = 'Call for new Partner account';
    return task;
}
private static Task createCustomerAcccountTask(Account account) {
    Task task = getBaseTask(account);
    task.category__c = 'Customer';
    task.Subject = 'Call for new Customer account';
    return task;
}
```

With this change, the code would now look like this:

```
if (isPartnerAccount && isGoldTier) {
    tasks.add(createPartnerAccountTask(newAccount));
}
else if (isCustomerAccount && isSilverTier) {
    tasks.add(createCustomerAccountTask(newAccount));
}
else {
    tasks.add(createDefaultTask(newAccount));
}
```

CHAPTER 1   REFACTORING APEX CODE: FIRST STEPS

At this point, however, I worry that I may have gone too far. Did I really need to create the `getBaseTask()` method and then a specific method for each type of task? On one hand, the code is much easier to read. On the other hand, understanding the end-to-end flow now requires drilling down into several small methods. Knowing when to abstract a piece of logic into its own method is a balancing act, often more art than science, combined with experience.

In this particular case, having one method per task type would be beneficial if we anticipate changes in how each task is created. For example, if a new requirement mandates modifying how partner tasks are created, I would only need to update the `createPartnerAccountTask()` method without worrying about anything else. Without such a method, I'd have to go through the code to find where partner tasks are created.

Also, let's assume the organization heavily uses tasks. Does it make sense for the `getBaseTask()` logic to be buried inside this class? Presumably, we need this logic in many more places. How do we know whether this method belongs here or if it should be in a different Apex class? This is not a trivial question to answer and will be explored in more detail in future chapters.

1.8 Putting It All Together

I'm going to skip some of the other improvements to the code because they are simple variations of the principles we just went over. After refactoring the entire method, here's what I ended up with:

```
List<Task> tasks = new List<Task>();

for (Account newAccount : newAccounts) {

    Boolean isPartnerAccount =   AccountDomain.
    isPartnerAccount(newAccount);
```

23

```
    Boolean isCustomerAccount = AccountDomain.isCustomerAccount
    Account(newAccount);

    Boolean isGoldTier = AccountDomain.isGoldTier(newAccount);

    Boolean isSilverTier = AccountDomain.
    isSilverTier(newAccount);

    if (isPartnerAccount && isGoldTier) {
        tasks.add(createPartnerAccountTask(newAccount));
    }
    else if (isCustomerAccount && isSilverTier) {
        tasks.add(createCustomerAccountTask(newAccount));
    }
    else {
        tasks.add(createDefaultTask(newAccount));
    }

    if (isPartnerAccount) {
        syncAccountWithNetsuite(newAccount);
    }
}
try {
    insert tasks;
} catch (Exception e) {
    Logger.logError(tasks,e);
}
```

Read this from top to bottom a few times. You'll see it reads in plain English, almost as if someone were verbally explaining what the code does. In fact, let's try that. I can read this out loud as

CHAPTER 1   REFACTORING APEX CODE: FIRST STEPS

- To create new tasks for accounts, we loop over the new accounts.

- We determine whether the accounts are partner or customer accounts and their tier.

- If the account is a partner and gold tier, we create a partner account task.

- If the account is a customer and silver tier...

Do you know what else this reads like? It reads just like the acceptance criteria of a user story. This is what clean code looks like.

Except…look at the `syncAccountWithNetsuite()` method. Why is this code here? How is creating tasks related to syncing partner accounts with NetSuite? Well, it turns out, it actually has nothing to do with it. What probably happened is that the developer received two requirements at the same time, both triggered by checking if the account is a partner account. So, the code was added here since they were already checking the account type. What's worse is that now, every time we call the `notifyAccountOwners()` method, we make API calls to NetSuite.

This is known as a *side effect*, and this one is particularly nasty. The main code claims to do one thing (notify account owners) but *also* does something completely different. We will explore this anti-pattern in more detail in future chapters.

In this case, the correct solution would be to extract this completely out of this method and add it somewhere else in the trigger handler class, while also reusing our domain class, like this:

```
//somewhere in the trigger handler class
if (AccountDomain.isPartnerAccount(account)) {
    syncAccountWithNetsuite(account);
}
```

25

An even better design would be to encapsulate the logic that deals with the NetSuite API into its own class:

```
//somewhere in the trigger handler class
if (AccountDomain.isPartnerAccount(account)) {
    NetSuiteAPI.syncPartnerAccount(account);
}
```

I saved this one for last on purpose to make the point that clean code isn't just about readable names and spacing; it's also about the design of our software: how loosely coupled it is, whether it's modular, and whether it has cohesion. These are concepts we will explore in future chapters.

1.9 Conclusion

I hope you enjoyed this exercise. We covered several principles of clean code at a high level, but there's still *much more* to explore. We also witnessed the process of gradually refining legacy code without making drastic changes. In the new version of the code, the purpose of every variable and method is evident, leaving no room for ambiguity or uncertainty. When modifications are needed, it's straightforward to pinpoint where those changes should occur.

There's still more we could've done to make this code cleaner and modular; as I said at the beginning, this was just a brief introduction. In the upcoming chapters, we'll go deeper into the principles behind some of the decisions I made while refactoring this code. Specifically, in the next chapter, we'll explore one of the most crucial aspects of clean code: choosing good names.

CHAPTER 2

Naming: Simple Techniques for Better Software Design

> *There are only two hard things in Computer Science: cache invalidation and naming things.*
>
> —Phil Karlton

Developing on the Salesforce platform involves naming many metadata elements: custom fields, objects, validation rules, flows, Apex classes, methods, and variables. A significant part of understanding what's going on inside a Salesforce org is deciphering the meaning behind these names.

For instance, if a validation rule is called `Prevent_update_when_-_lead_is_inactive`, you can safely assume it contains logic to throw an error if a set of fields determines the lead is inactive. In contrast, a validation rule named `prevent_update` doesn't provide the same clarity; you would have to open it to understand its purpose.

In the previous chapter, we saw multiple examples of how better names added clarity and intention to our code. However, I didn't explain why I made some of the choices I made. In this chapter, we will explore several principles that will help us decide how to name our programming constructs—such as classes, methods, and variables.

CHAPTER 2   NAMING: SIMPLE TECHNIQUES FOR BETTER SOFTWARE DESIGN

> **Note** For brevity, I will refer to all these elements as "programming constructs" throughout this chapter.

To explain each of the principles, I will use the following format:

- **Context**: A brief explanation of the scenario or context in which a specific pattern is useful

- **The Problem**: Why the traditional way of solving this scenario is problematic

- **A Better Way**: My recommendation for how to use a better name, given the context

- **Closing Thoughts**: Additional information

2.1 Collection Names

Apex programming is all about bulk processing. The List, Set, and Map collection types are probably the most commonly used as we process records in bulk. And equally common is seeing variables with names that include their collection type, such as accountList or opportunityMap. Should we do this?

2.1.1 The Problem

It's very common to see variables of List and Set type where the name includes the type, for example:

```
Set<Account> accountSet;
List<Account> accountList;
Map<Id,Account> accountMap;
```

The argument for doing this is typically that it makes it immediately obvious that you are dealing with a specific collection type. For example, if you know you are dealing with a map, then you know you can use the `keySet()` method. However, this is only true if the following conditions are also true:

- The variable is still a `Map`. Perhaps it used to be a `Map` but was later changed to a `Set` and no one bothered to change the name (`clear()`, `isEmpty()` and other methods are available in both `Map` and `Set` collections).
- If it is indeed a `Map`, it is a map of what it says it is, in this case a map of Ids to Account records.
- Your team is following all the guidelines we will explore in this chapter, such as consistency, relevancy, avoiding misinformation, etc.

If any of these aren't true, then you can't solely rely on the name of a variable to assume its type.

An argument *against* this practice is that any modern IDE will show you the variable declaration just by clicking on it, so there's no need to pollute the variable name with its type; it's unnecessary.

Something I find interesting is that we mostly follow this practice for collection types. Rarely have I seen a boolean variable named `isAccountActiveBoolean` or a string variable named `caseSubjectString`. I think most developers would agree that those aren't good names, so why are we happy to do the opposite for collection types?

2.1.2 A Better Way

A better pattern is to name your variables based on what they represent or what they mean in a given context, not what type of data they contain (except for `Map` variables, more on this later).

CHAPTER 2   NAMING: SIMPLE TECHNIQUES FOR BETTER SOFTWARE DESIGN

For collection types, I recommend you simply use the plural form of the type, such as `accounts`, `leads`, and `opportunities`. Whether the collection is a `List` or a `Set` shouldn't really matter; it's an implementation detail that has little effect on the business logic. This also means you can later change your mind and use a different collection type, and it won't affect the name of the variable; the name will remain relevant.

Of course, if you are working with multiple variables of the same type, make sure that their names are different and that they convey their intention clearly. For example, in a single class, you may have `partnerAccounts` and `inactiveAccounts`. Similarly, if you are using a `Set` because your business logic requires unique values in the list, then using a name like `uniqueAccounts` may be beneficial.

For `Map` collections however, I do recommend keeping their structure in mind when naming them. I like using the following convention:

`[collection]by[key]`

So, if we have a map of Ids to accounts, such as `Map<Id,Account>`, I would name this `accountsById`. This basically means that this is a collection of accounts sorted/organized by their record Id. If you are using a more complex `Map` like `Map<Id,Map<Id,Contact>>`, I recommend the name `contactsByIdByParentAccount`. Yes, that's a very long name, but it accurately represents what the variable holds and makes it easier to reason about any complex operations that the code may be doing on that map.

That said, some developers approach maps differently. While writing this section, several contributors highlighted that they prefer naming their maps using the singular form of the collection type. Thus, they would use `accountById` instead of `accountsById` (noting the latter uses "accounts" in plural). Their rationale is that since a map represents a one-to-one mapping of keys and values, the singular form appears more logical. For instance:

```
//this will only ever retrieve 1 account
Account relatedAccount = accountById.get(recordId);
```

To emphasize, the argument here is that the `get` method retrieves a single account, so the map should not be named using the plural form. Personally, I like using the plural name of the collection because a map is a collection, and I think of it as "a collection of accounts, sorted by their Id." After a lot of back-and-forth, we concluded both options are valid. If there's disagreement among your developers regarding this, you must pick the one with the most votes and ensure everyone uses it consistently.

2.1.3 Closing Thoughts

To summarize, I recommend you use the plural name of the sObject type when dealing with `Set` and `List` variables. When you are using `Map` variables, use a name that represents the collection type and the key by which they are organized. And most importantly, be consistent.

2.2 Hide Boolean Logic

Boolean variables and logic are at the heart of programming. We are almost always checking if some condition is true before we proceed with the next action. It is thus important that our booleans are properly named too.

2.2.1 The Problem

To understand the challenge with boolean logic in Apex, let's think about formula fields for a moment. Think of a formula field of type check box; you implement some complex logic, and the result is either the check box is on, or it is off. For example, you may have a formula check box that is ticked if the contact's birthdate is today, as follows:

CHAPTER 2   NAMING: SIMPLE TECHNIQUES FOR BETTER SOFTWARE DESIGN

```
IF(
    MONTH(TODAY()) = MONTH(Birthdate) &&
    DAY(TODAY()) = DAY(Birthdate),
    true,
    false
)
```

How would you imagine such a field would be named? Probably something along the lines of Is_Contact_Bday_Today__c; and that's an accurate, contextual name. When we see the field, we don't have to think too much about it, we just know that the field will tell us if the contact's birthdate is today. We are allowed to think of the field as a concept, and we don't need to be concerned with the details.

Imagine how bizarre it would be if instead of showing the field label in a page layout, we showed the entire formula syntax for all our users to see. They would have to parse the boolean logic in their heads before they can make sense of it, and once they understand it, they can determine if the contact's birthdate is indeed today. This would not be a good user experience.

What does this have to do with Apex? Formula fields treat boolean logic as a concept, and what we see in a page layout is the concept, not the details of how that concept is calculated. If we can agree that hiding boolean logic is useful to our users, then how come we are perfectly happy to write logic in Apex that looks like this:

```
if ((!String.isBlank(acc.Website)
&& !String.isBlank(acc.Industry)
|| acc.IsActive && acc.NumberOfEmployees > 0)
&& (acc.BillingCountry == 'United States'
|| acc.BillingCountry == 'Canada'
|| acc.Custom_Field__c)
```

```
       && acc.LastModifiedDate.daysBetween(System.today()) <= 30) {
           //do something interesting
       }
       else {
           //do something less interesting
        }
```

Why are we ok to show this to our users? Now, you may be thinking "but users will never see this code!" **The users of your code are not your end users but your future self and the rest of your development team**. You and they will have to read this code in the future, and you will have a very hard time deciphering what this logic does. This is not any different than showing the entire boolean logic of a formula field for your end users in a page layout.

2.2.2 A Better Way

To fix this problem, we can draw inspiration from formula fields and give our boolean logic a name that describes a concept. We do this by wrapping the boolean logic with a method, like this:

```
private static boolean isEligibleForSync(Account acc) {
     return ((!String.isBlank(acc.Website)
     && !String.isBlank(acc.Industry)
     || acc.IsActive && acc.NumberOfEmployees > 0)
     && (acc.BillingCountry == 'United States'
     || acc.BillingCountry == 'Canada'
     || acc.Custom_Field__c)
     && acc.LastModifiedDate.daysBetween(System.today()) <= 30)
}
```

CHAPTER 2   NAMING: SIMPLE TECHNIQUES FOR BETTER SOFTWARE DESIGN

Then, we can use this boolean logic in different places in our code:

```
if (isEligibleForSync(account)) {
    //do something interesting
}
```

This way, when others read this code, they don't need to worry about the details of how we determined that this account is eligible for sync (or whatever concept you are working with).

While this is an improvement, the boolean logic itself is still complex. We could break this logic into sub-boolean statements to help our readers easily make sense of it. For example:

```
Boolean requiredFieldsAreNotNull = (!String.isBlank(acc.Website)
        && !String.isBlank(acc.Industry));

Boolean isNorthAmerica = (acc.BillingCountry == 'United States'
        || acc.BillingCountry == 'Canada');

Boolean otherCriteria = //more logic here

//combine all the booleans to determine if the
//account is eligible for sync

return (requiredFieldsAreNotNull && isNorthAmerica && otherCriteria);
```

Now, we know that to determine if an account is eligible for sync, we first need to check if the required fields are populated, whether the account is in North America, and whether other criteria is true. This, along with the method name, makes this logic very easy to understand. We can simply read the variable names without having to dig into the details.

We can also do this for much simpler logic. For example, in a trigger handler, where it's common to check if field values have changed during transactions, you could have the following logic:

```
Boolean hasNameChanged = (newAccount.Name != oldAccount.Name);

if (hasNameChanged) {
    //do something interesting
}
```

Finally, as we saw in the previous example and in Chapter 1, we can combine multiple named boolean variables to make the logic even easier to understand.

```
if(isPartnerAccount && isGoldTier) {
    ...
}
else if (isCustomerAccount && isSilverTier) {
    ...
}
else {
    ...
}
```

2.2.3 Closing Thoughts

We've learned how easy it is to give our boolean logic a name that describes the concept it is calculating. This can make your code much easier to read; I like to think that it reads in plain English "if this is true, do this, otherwise, do that."

What's missing is agreeing on a naming convention for the boolean variables or methods. There are different schools of thought here, and there's no right or wrong answer. For example, the following are all valid names for a boolean variable:

```
Boolean hasNameChanged;
Boolean didNameChange;
Boolean nameHasChanged;
```

Personally, I like to name my booleans in the form of a question, so from the examples above, I would use `nameHasChanged`. When you use the variable inside of an `if` statement, it reads in almost plain English. Which variation you use is up to you and your team, but I do recommend you agree on one variation and then use it consistently throughout the code base.

2.3 Be Intentional

Part of crafting a good name is ensuring that a name reveals the intention of the variable, method, or class.

2.3.1 The Problem

When we use names that don't reveal intentions, we force the reader to guess what the code does. Consider the following example:

```
String cs = 'Active'
```

The name of this variable doesn't reveal anything about its intended use. `cs` could mean anything here, and the only way to find out is by reading all the code around it. Then, we can make an educated guess, but still a guess. Sometimes developers add comments to try to clarify a poorly chosen name, like this:

```
//set conversion status
Strings cs = 'Active';
```

2.3.2 A Better Way

Use names that reveal the intention of the class, method, or variable. The name should answer all the questions you may have about it. Rather than using a comment to explain what cs means, give it a descriptive name that reveals the intended use, such as

`String conversionStatus;`

There could be other variations of this. For example, perhaps the variable stores the Lead conversion status at the beginning of the Apex transaction, so you could name it:

`String initialConversionStatus;`

Just adding the word `initial` reveals that this was the starting point and that perhaps we are going to change the conversion status at some point during the method execution.

The same is true for method names:
`createTasksForLeads(List<Lead> convertedLeads)` is more descriptive and intuitive than `createTasks(List<Lead> ls)`.

2.3.3 Closing Thoughts

Obviously, not everything can be explained with a simple method or variable name. Sometimes, the name of a variable only makes sense in the context of a particular Apex class or method. The point of this principle is to be conscious when naming your code. I recommend asking yourself, "In the distant future, will I be able to read this variable or method name and quickly understand its intention?" If your gut says "no," then use a better name.

2.4 Exactly the Same but Totally Different

Another variation of the previous guideline is ensuring that constructs of the same type have names that explicitly state how they are different. A good example is `oldLeads` vs. `newLeads`. Using the words "old" and "new" makes a meaningful distinction between the variables.

2.4.1 The Problem

When we don't make meaningful distinctions, code that is otherwise clean can become very hard to understand. Consider the following code:

```
public static Boolean hasPriorityChanged(
  Opportunity o1,
  Opportunity o2
) {
  return o1.Priority__c != o2.Priority__c;
}
```

This is a reasonable piece of code. The name of the method clearly tells us that it evaluates if the priority has changed, and the return statement makes use of the implicit boolean expression, making the code short and succinct. However, the variable names for the Opportunity records `o1` and `o2` don't provide any meaningful information on how they are *different*. They don't answer questions such as

- Do they represent the *same* opportunity in different trigger contexts?
- Are they meant to represent two completely *different* opportunities?

CHAPTER 2   NAMING: SIMPLE TECHNIQUES FOR BETTER SOFTWARE DESIGN

> **Note**   Using longer names such as `opportunity1` and `opportunity2` won't make a difference here. We still don't understand how they are different, if at all.

2.4.2 A Better Way

Let's see how much different this code reads when we use better names:

```
public static Boolean hasPriorityChanged(
  Opportunity oldOppty,
  Opportunity newOppty
) {
  return oldOppty.Priority__c != newOppty.Priority__c;
}
```

   Now, it's clear that this method is comparing the values of the same opportunity in different trigger contexts. We know this because the words `old` and `new` have a strong meaning in Apex triggers. But the whole meaning can change if we use different names yet again:

```
public static Boolean hasPriorityChanged(
  Opportunity childOppty,
  Opportunity parentOppty
) {
  return childOppty.Priority__c != parentOppty.Priority__c;
}
```

   Now, it appears that we are checking if the priority has changed between a parent and a child opportunity. This is a completely different use case from the previous two examples, and we made it clear just by using better names.

2.4.3 Closing Thoughts

The lesson here is to consider how different variables of the same type are different and to make sure we give them proper names that make that distinction obvious to the reader. This also applies to method names. Consider the following example:

```
DataFactory.insertLeads()
vs
DataFactory.createLeads()
```

What is the difference between the two? It's impossible to know just by looking at the names. You'd have to go look at the code to understand how they are different.

2.5 Keeping Code Relevant

Code is not static; it changes over time as business and technical requirements change. This means sometimes our methods and variables also change and their responsibility increases. How do we ensure names stay relevant as time goes on?

2.5.1 The Problem

Imagine we have a trigger handler that retrieves all the contacts related to a parent Account, like this:

```
List<Contact> allContacts = [SELECT Name FROM Contact WHERE AccountId IN :parentAccountIds];
```

Suppose later the requirement changes, and we only need to get the contacts for accounts created in the past 7 days, so the developer changes the query to this:

```
List<Contact> allContacts = [SELECT Name FROM Contact WHERE AccountId IN :parentAccountIds];
```

Spend a few seconds spotting the differences between the queries.

If you feel confused, it is because the query hasn't changed at all. This is because the developer simply changed the logic that populates `parentAccountIds` so that it *only* includes accounts created in the past 7 days. And this indeed satisfies the business requirement.

The problem, however, is that now the variable names `allContacts` and `parentAccountIds` are not relevant and accurate. We aren't dealing with all the contacts anymore. Our code says it does one thing, but it does another. Those few seconds of confusion you just experienced is the same a developer will experience when reading code that does not evolve with the requirements.

2.5.2 A Better Way

As business requirements evolve, so should the names of our programming constructs. In this scenario, the best solution would be to also update the variable names to reflect the new requirement. Our new query would look like this:

```
List<Contact> recentlyCreatedContacts = [SELECT Name FROM Contact WHERE AccountId IN :accounts7DaysOld];
```

We can read this query without having to read any code above it and immediately understand that we are dealing with a subset of contacts.

2.5.3 Closing Thoughts

Keeping our names relevant over time is an easy way to maintain clean code. It only takes a few seconds. You have two choices: spend those few seconds updating the names to ensure they remain relevant, or spend those few seconds being confused by outdated names.

2.6 Context Isn't Enough

Sometimes, no matter how well we name our programming constructs, they don't make sense to outsiders or new developers. Often, you need context to understand why particular name or terminology is being used. Context is not an excuse to use poorly thought-out names though.

2.6.1 The Problem

When I was discussing this book with another Salesforce developer, they showed me some of their open source work. In one of their projects, I found this Apex class:

```
public with sharing class File_t extends DomainBuilder {
    public File_t() {
        super(ContentVersion.SObjectType);
        name('file');
        path('/document.pdf');
        body('content');
    }

    public File_t name(String value) {
        return (File_t) set(ContentVersion.Title, value);
    }
//more code below
```

The first time I saw this, my immediate reaction was: "What does that _t stand for in the class name? Does it mean test? type? or Tom?" There was no way for me to know. I decided to ignore this and kept inspecting the rest of the code, but my brain wouldn't let it go. Every few seconds, I would start thinking what kind of mysterious context I must be missing. Surely that _t represents something important!

So, I discussed this with the developer, and they explained to me that with this Domain Builder library you can create classes that represent custom objects. For example, if you have a custom object called `Product_Master__c`, then you could create a corresponding class called `ProductMaster`. However, you can't create an Apex class with the name of a standard object, such as `Account` or `Opportunity`, or in this case, `File`, because those are the names of standard objects and are reserved.

Their solution was to append the letter t to those classes, which stands for "test." How could I have known this? The only way I could know this was by speaking to them, and that conversation provided the context that I needed.

2.6.2 A Better Way

Relying solely on context is not good idea. We must ensure our Apex construct names are clear and unambiguous.

After some healthy back-and-forth, we decided that using the suffix `Standard` may be a better choice, such as `AccountStandard` or `FileStandard`. This way it's clearer to the user that this represents a standard object. The word "standard" has a strong meaning in the Salesforce platform, so it is a good choice.

2.6.3 Closing Thoughts

If context is so important, then the question becomes, which class naming convention inherently adds more context? Even after understanding the Domain Builder problem space, `File_t` offers little additional context to the solution space. Each time you read _t, you have to translate it. "Oh yeah, it means this because of that." On the other hand, given the same established context, `FileStandard` "bakes in" context, as we know Standard here applies to standard objects. Each time I read `Standard`, I know not just the solution but the intent behind the solution.

If a developer does not have a fundamental contextual grounding, then all bets are off, and the answer about which code is cleaner can only be "it depends." Once context has been established, the more the chosen convention adds relevant context, the cleaner the code is.

The moral of the story is that context alone is not enough. Good names alone aren't enough either. We must use names that *reinforce* and enrich the context of our application.

2.7 Use Different Names for Variables and Classes

It's common for variables and classes to share the same name. For example, `lead` is a perfectly valid name for a variable, and "lead" is also the name of a built-in sObject type. How do you tell the difference between variables and classes?

2.7.1 The Problem

Using the same name for variables and classes can sometimes lead to confusing or unexpected behavior. Consider the following code:

```
Lead Lead = new Lead(LastName = 'a', Company = 'b');
insert Lead;
```

This is perfectly valid code. It compiles and it successfully inserts the Lead record. But it is a little strange to look at. How does Apex know that `insert Lead` means insert the variable `Lead` and not the sObject type `Lead`? Regardless, it works.

However, the same isn't true for custom data types. Consider the following:

```
global class TwilioAPI {

    public static TwilioRestClient getDefaultClient() {
        //more code here
    }
}
```

The method `getDefaultClient` is static, so if I call it using the following code, Apex throws an error because you can't call a static method from a nonstatic context:

```
TwilioAPI api = new TwilioAPI();
api.getDefaultClient();//cannot call a static method on an
                        instance
```

If I call the method directly from the class, it works:

```
TwilioAPI.getDefaultClient();//static context
```

But here's where things get a little strange. What if I do the following:

```
TwilioAPI TwilioAPI = new TwilioAPI();
//is this the class or the instance?
TwilioAPI.getDefaultClient();
```

Suddenly, this fails with an error stating it cannot call a static method from a nonstatic context. The compiler assumes you are calling `getDefaultClient` on the instance, not the class.

2.7.2 A Better Way

To avoid some of these strange behaviors and confusing-looking code, adopt the following guidelines.

Camel Case

Use camel case for variable and method names. Camel case is where the first letter starts in lower case and subsequent words start with upper case. For example:

`Lead lead = new Lead();`

`searchById();`

Pascal Case

For class names, use Pascal case, which means every word starts with upper case. Valid examples include

`TwilioAPI`, `DMLOptions`, and `UnitOfWork`.

Avoid Reusing Class Names

For custom types, avoid instantiating variables with the same name as the type. For example, prefer

`TwilioAPI api = new TwilioAPI();`

Over

`TwilioAPI TwilioAPI = new TwilioAPI();`

And here's another example:

`//starts with upper case. Is this a list or a class?`
`Contacts.add(contact);`

If we stick to the guideline of starting class names with upper case letters, it becomes unclear what `Contacts` refers to. Is it a variable of type `List<Contact>`, or is it an actual class named `Contacts`? Some developers actively create domain classes with plural names of sObjects, such as

CHAPTER 2   NAMING: SIMPLE TECHNIQUES FOR BETTER SOFTWARE DESIGN

`Accounts, Opportunities`, etc. This convention is often used by those who have adopted the `fflib` library, also known as Apex Enterprise Patterns. While the names sound nice for domain classes, they also sound like list variables, so I personally recommend avoiding this convention.

> **Note**   I will discuss the pros and cons of the Apex Enterprise Patterns and the `fflib` library later in the book.

2.7.3 Closing Thoughts

This guideline might appear obvious to experienced developers, but it's not uncommon to come across variable and method names using upper or Pascal case. When I encounter such situations, I find myself getting confused and needing to pause. I then must inspect the variable to determine if it's truly a variable or possibly a class. Sticking to naming conventions avoids this hassle and makes the code easier to follow.

2.8 Use Pronounceable Names

It's common for developers to talk about their code. This can be during a standup meeting, a troubleshooting session, etc. We also think a lot about our code; we think about the variables and methods we are using, whether we are using them correctly, and so on. Given we spend so much time talking and thinking about our code, it makes sense to use names we can easily remember and pronounce.

2.8.1 The Problem

If we don't use names that can be easily remembered and pronounced, we can't effectively communicate our ideas. Consider the following code:

CHAPTER 2   NAMING: SIMPLE TECHNIQUES FOR BETTER SOFTWARE DESIGN

```
public static void crt(List<OpportunityLineItem> olis) {
    for (OpportunityLineItem oli : olis) {
        Date oliCrtDt = oli.CreatedDate;
        Date syMDStamp = oli.SystemModstamp;
        //more code here...
    }
}
```

Imagine talking to your colleagues about how there's a bug in the `crt` method whenever the `syMDStamp` is different from the `oliCrtDt`. This would be a strange conversation to listen to.

2.8.2 A Better Way

Choose names that are pronounceable, like `lineItemCreatedDate` and `lineItemSystemModStamp`. Yes, they may be longer, but they're easy to use in conversation and remember. As Keith Rogers (contributor for this book) expressed, "If you are talking to a nontechnical person and giving a demo, what would you describe this as?" This sentiment encapsulates the essence of selecting clear and understandable names.

2.9 Use Searchable Names

Apart from talking and thinking about our code, we often write code on top of it. Sometimes, we need to find where a particular piece of logic is written so that we can extend it or fix something that is broken. What if we can't find that piece of logic? What if there isn't a single place where that logic is defined?

2.9.1 The Problem

Consider the scenario where your org has an integration with NetSuite. You make API calls to NetSuite both from Apex and Flows. NetSuite allows you to specify the maximum number of retries in case an API call fails, and your architect has defined that limit to be 5. Imagine that the number is used everywhere throughout your code base, as follows:

```
syncWithNetSuite(accounts,5)
...
retrieveLatestFinancialRecords(5)
...
createInvoice(records,5)
```

What if you now had to increase this limit from 5 to 10? How could you find that number in the code base? Searching for the number 5 in your code editor would bring hundreds if not thousands of results.

2.9.2 A Better Way

A better solution would be to wrap this limit in a constant that can be reused throughout the code base, such as

```
public class NetSuiteGlobals {
    public static final MAX_API_RETRIES = 5;
        ...
}
```

Then, when the time comes to change this limit, you can simply search for the word `MAX_API_RETRIES`. The number of search results will be significantly less, and it'll be much easier to know where to make the change.

2.9.3 Closing Thoughts

Using constants is a pretty well-known practice. This guideline isn't about that. The example merely uses constants to help drive the point home. And the point is that we should use names that we can *easily search* in our IDE. This is also very much related to using pronounceable names; if we use the name ntsutApLmt in a variable, not only it will be hard to pronounce, but it will also be very hard to search.

2.10 Use Problem Domain Names

While Apex code can satisfy requirements from almost any business domain, we are all bound by the limits of the Salesforce platform. The platform comes with its own set of problems that we all need to deal with such as governor limits, async and batch processing, DML operations, etc. When dealing with Salesforce-specific problem domains, we must use well-known names and terminology.

2.10.1 The Problem

Consider this code:

```
public with sharing class AccountRecordsProcessor {
    public static void processAfterModification(
        Map<Id, Account> nAccts, Map<Id, Account> oAccts) {
        //some processing here
```

What do you think this method does? Was it immediately obvious that this is an Account trigger handler? Probably not. What if I showed you the same code, but with better names?

```
public with sharing class AccountTriggerHandler {

    public static void afterUpdate(
        Map<Id, Account> oldAccounts, Map<Id, Account> newAccounts) {

        //some processing here
```

This is the exact same logic. There's no difference between the two examples, except in the second one, I'm using well-known names for the problem domain of Apex triggers. With the original code, there was simply no way of knowing we were dealing with a trigger context, and it just looked like a generic piece of code.

2.10.2 A Better Way

It's best to stick to well-known names. Why use `AccountRecordsProcessor` instead of `AccountTriggerHandler`? The former one is technically correct, but it uses a fancy name instead of the standard convention.

Also, we renamed the method from `processAfterModification` to `afterUpdate`, which now makes it extra clear that this method is called during the after update trigger event.

2.10.3 Closing Thoughts

This example might seem trivial and even silly, but the point is: we should avoid reinventing platform or domain-specific names. We should resist any temptation to appear overly clever by inventing new or innovative names for things that most developers are already familiar with. It's preferable to stick to what developers are already accustomed to.

2.11 Not All Names Should Be Treated Equally

A common side effect that developers experience after learning about clean code is they think all names must be perfectly crafted; I remember when I went through that phase. We'll see, however, that not all names are equally important.

2.11.1 The Problem

Consider the following code:

```
Integer comparisonNumber = 10;

for (Integer variableToIncrement = 0; variableToIncrement < comparisonNumber; variableToIncrement++) {
    System.debug(variableToIncrement+1);
}
```

In case you can't tell, this is a traditional for loop. It's very hard to read because we took the learnings from this chapter to an extreme and gave every variable a meaningful name. However, such a simple for loop should be written like this:

```
for (Integer i = 0; j = 0; i < 10; i++) {
    System.debug(i+1);
}
```

This is a lot easier to read. The only caveat here is we don't know what the number 10 represents here. This can sometimes become an antipattern that is known as a "magic number," which we will explore next.

2.11.2 A Better Way

Why is it ok for these variables to have not-so-great names? It's because their lifespan is very short. If the variable has a very short lifespan, its name doesn't have to be the greatest name ever; a simple short name will do. In this case, using the letter i in a `for` loop is a standard convention, which is another reason to use that instead of trying to come up with a clever name.

However, some variables with a short lifespan can greatly influence the behavior of your application. Consider the following code:

```
Boolean a = true;
Database.insert(leads,a);
```

In this example, a is actually very important, as it will fail the entire batch of records if a single error occurs. The impact of such a small variable is considerable. In this case, something like this would read better:

```
Boolean allowsPartialSuccess = false;
Database.insert(leads,!allowsPartialSuccess);
```

2.11.3 Closing Thoughts

Use your judgement when deciding how important the name of a variable or method should be. Always do your best to use meaningful names, but remember there will always be exceptions.

2.12 Magic Numbers

When we mix business logic with mathematical calculations, it isn't always obvious what the numbers represent and how they are relevant to the specific logic.

2.12.1 The Problem

Every Salesforce developer should know that the governor limit for SOQL queries in a synchronous transaction is 100. If you are executing multiple queries in a single transaction, your code might look like this to ensure you don't exceed the limit:

```
if (Limits.getQueries() < 100) {
    queryAccountFields(recordIds);
}
```

Here, we use the `Limits` class to get the number of queries issued so far and compare it against the limit of 100 queries per transaction. But would everyone understand what the number 100 represents here? What if this code is in a Queueable apex class, where Salesforce increases the limit to 200? Suddenly, the number 100 doesn't make much sense.

As the reader of this code, you might wonder, "Did the developer intend to run only one 100 queries, or were they trying to avoid exceeding the limit, whatever that limit was, depending on whether the transaction was synchronous or asynchronous?" Really, there's no way to know.

The reason it's hard to tell the intention of the previous developer is that the number 100 has no inherent meaning; it could mean anything. This antipattern is known as a magic number. Another example of this antipattern is

```
for (Integer i = 0; i < 27; i++) {
    NetSuiteAPI.retrySync(accountRecord);
}
```

Here, we call the NetSuite API a maximum of 27 times. But why? What does 27 mean? Is it the maximum number of API calls we can issue per transaction? Is it some limit in NetSuite? Again, there's no way to know.

2.12.2 A Better Way

Avoid using magic numbers by wrapping them in variables that clearly convey their meaning and intention. Here's what the examples above would look like if we follow this guideline:

```
for (Integer i = 0; i < NetSuiteAPI.HOURLY_LIMIT; i++) {
    NetSuiteAPI.retrySync(accountRecord);
}
```

It's immediately clear why we limit the number of API calls to the value specified by `NetSuiteAPI.HOURLY_LIMIT`. Going back to the original example where we compared the number of queries against 100, a better solution would be

```
if (Limits.getQueries() < Limits.getLimitQueries()) {
    queryAccountFields(recordIds);
}
```

With this approach, it's clear that we don't care about issuing exactly 100 queries. What matters is that we don't execute more queries than allowed in a specific transaction, which will be different depending on whether the transaction is synchronous or asynchronous.

2.12.3 Closing Thoughts

If numbers are part of your business logic, make sure to wrap them in variables that clearly express their meaning and intended use. Having magic numbers in the code base can make the code hard to understand. Code that is hard to understand is code that is hard to change, and therefore, it isn't clean.

2.13 Conclusion

Naming things in programming is hard. Just go back a few pages and see how many principles we covered in this chapter. Many factors influence how we should name programming constructs, and good names in one context can be poor names in another.

Here are three more guidelines I would encourage you to consider when thinking about names.

2.13.1 Make It a Team Sport

Coming up with important names should be a team effort. If you're trying to name something critical that everyone will use, share the name with your team to get feedback.

2.13.2 If You Can't Name It...

Sometimes, difficulty in naming things can indicate that the design is flawed. If you can't name it (and if you can't draw a diagram of it), the concept itself might be muddled and needs rework.

2.13.3 Names Are Important, but Not *That* Important

When I first learned about clean code, I thought names were the most important thing in the world. I would obsess over whether I had chosen the perfect name for my classes. I'd even spend a whole day thinking: "Did I use the best name possible?" This is a waste of time; don't be like me. If you can't decide on a good name for more than one hour, pick the best name you can think of and move on. Sometimes, what's more important is consistency and a shared understanding among your development team.

This isn't to say everything we've covered here is optional. It isn't. But what is more important than just the names is the design of your software. Bad names usually reflect bad design. If you focus on crafting a good design, your names are likely to be good.

2.14 Conclusion

Before we move on, here's what you should remember.

- Take a few seconds to think about the names of your variables and methods. A little effort today can save you hours later when trying to understand your code.
- Agree with your team on how to name maps, as you will be using them every day.
- Be consistent. However, avoid consistently using bad names.
- Don't go too far; names like `leadsThatWereConvertedInPast15Days` are too long.
- If you can't think of a good name, move on and come back to it later.

CHAPTER 3

Doing One Thing: Abstraction, Boolean Parameters, and Design Patterns

Functions should do one thing. They should do it well. They should do it only.

—Robert C. Martin

Common wisdom suggests that clean methods have two traits: they do one thing and they are short. However, these characteristics are merely the end result of various design principles. Applying these ideas without understanding the underlying principles won't help you learn how to properly think about methods.

3.1 Why Should Methods Do One Thing

Before we define what "one thing" is, let's first explore why methods should do one thing. Consider the following example:

CHAPTER 3　DOING ONE THING: AB STRACTION, BOOLEAN PARAMETERS, AND DESIGN PATTERNS

```
public static User createUser(String firstName, String
lastName, String username){

...

//throws exception if any of the parameters are missing
validateParams(firstName, lastName, username);

List<User> existingUsers = [SELECT Id FROM User WHERE Username
= :username];

if (!existingUsers.isEmpty()) {

    //we'll discuss why in chapter 5
    throw new PortalException('User already exists: ' + username);
}
else {
    //set default profile, alias, timezone, etc
    User newUser = setUserDefaults(firstName, lastName, username);

    //no exception handling here
    //wait for chapter 5
    insert newUser;

    String chars = '12345abcdefghijklmnopqrstuvwxyz';
    String password = '';
    while (password.length() < 8) {
        Integer i = Math.mod(
                    Math.abs(Crypto.getRandomInteger()),
                    chars.length());
        password += chars.substring(i, i+1);
    }

    System.setPassword(newUser.Id,password);

    return newUser;
```

CHAPTER 3   DOING ONE THING: AB STRACTION, BOOLEAN PARAMETERS, AND DESIGN PATTERNS

How many things do you think this method does? Let's count them:

- It validates parameters.
- It queries users from the database.
- It throws an exception if the user already exists.
- If it doesn't exist, it creates a new one while setting all the default fields.
- It generates a password from a random string.
- It resets the user password.
- It returns a new user.

Clearly, this method does more than one thing. And that in and on itself isn't bad; the problem arises from the consequences of doing more than one thing. Let's explore these consequences.

3.2 Mixing Different Levels of Abstraction

The first problem with methods that do more than one thing is that they can often mix different levels of abstraction. Abstraction is a big topic that we will cover in detail in future chapters. For now, we can define abstraction as a mental model we use to understand concepts.

For example, when you drive a car, you are operating it at a higher level of abstraction, which includes the steering wheel, pedals, and other controls. You are not concerned about the internals of the car and how moving the steering wheel actually makes the wheels turn. These details are hidden from you because exposing them would make driving a car much more complicated.

CHAPTER 3   DOING ONE THING: ABSTRACTION, BOOLEAN PARAMETERS, AND
            DESIGN PATTERNS

In contrast, these details are crucial for a car mechanic who is inspecting a fault in the car. The mechanic operates at a lower level of abstraction. The higher the level of abstraction, the fewer details we are exposed to; the lower the level of abstraction, the more details and complexity will be visible.

Another example of abstraction is when you see a map in a zoo or amusement park. That map isn't an accurate representation of the actual distances between attractions; it's a simple mental model to help you find where you are and figure out the path to the next attraction. Such a map would be useless to an architect tasked with expanding the park.

Likewise, if you were provided with an architectural map to find your way in the park, you'd probably have a hard time reading it because it exposes too many details that are unnecessary to you. The amusement park map is at a higher level of abstraction compared to the architectural map.

What does this have to do with methods? Let's look at our previous example. In the same method where we create a user using simple DML logic, we also have complex logic to generate a random string using the `Crypto` and `Math` classes. While generating a password might be part of creating a user, the logic for generating a random string is at a much **lower level of abstraction** than the simple DML logic.

When we mix different levels of abstraction, we make it harder for other developers to understand the code. To fully understand how a user is created, we force them to understand the complex logic for generating random strings. It's like driving a car while simultaneously being responsible for making sure the oil circulates through the engine.

Mixing different levels of abstraction also causes unnecessary coupling between our logic. Every time we need to change how a password is generated, we have to change the `createUser()` method. And an arbitrary change inside `createUser()` could break our password generating logic.

In this case, the right solution would be to extract this logic to its own class so that it is completely independent. For example:

```
public class Password {

    public static String generatePassword() {

        String chars = '12345abcdefghijklmnopqrstuvwxyz';
        String password = '';

        while (password.length() < 8) {

            Integer i = Math.mod(
                    Math.abs(Crypto.getRandomInteger()),
                    chars.length());
            password += chars.substring(i, i+1);
        }

        return password;
    }
}
```

Note The Site class has some methods for resetting password. This use case is simply an illustration and not an encouragement to re-create existing logic from the Apex library.

Then, in our method, we can reuse this logic like this:

`insert newUser;`

`System.setPassword(newUser.Id,`**`Password.generatePassword()`**`);`

`return newUser;`

Now, when other developers read the code inside createUser(), they don't need to worry about how the password is generated. They can simply ignore that unless it's relevant to their current task. Just like you can ignore the mechanics of the car engine while you are driving.

CHAPTER 3 DOING ONE THING: ABSTRACTION, BOOLEAN PARAMETERS, AND DESIGN PATTERNS

We can conclude that one reason methods should do one thing is so that they don't mix different levels of abstraction.

3.3 Causing Duplication

Another reason methods should do one thing is because the more things a method does simultaneously, the more chances for duplication to exist in our code base.

Let's go back to the previous example where the random password logic was embedded in the `createUser()` method. In that scenario, it was impossible to reuse that logic anywhere else in the code base. If there isn't a main class responsible for generating passwords, developers will be encouraged to re-create this logic over and over again.

This isn't to say that all logic should be reusable, but if we break down a method into smaller parts, the more chances exist for some of those smaller parts to be useful somewhere else.

We can conclude that another reason methods should do one thing is to encourage deduplication of code.

3.3.1 Testability

If methods do one thing, they also become easier to test. Following the example above, I can now write a test for `Password.generatePassword()` that is completely disconnected from `createUser()`:

```
@IsTest
static void testGeneratePassword() {
    Integer defaultPasswordLength = 8;
    Integer actualLength = Password.generatePassword().length();

    Assert.areEqual(defaultPasswordLength, actualLength);
}
```

Without isolating this logic into its own method, I would have to test it in the presence of other logic that is unrelated, or worse, logic that is on a different level of abstraction.

Breaking down methods so they focus on one thing means we can also focus on testing one thing.

3.4 What Is "One Thing"?

In the previous section, we established three benefits for why methods should do one thing. Let's review them:

- It encourages separation of different levels of abstraction.
- It encourages reusability.
- It encourages testability.

Now, the challenge is defining what "one thing" means. One could argue that creating a user is one thing. One could also argue that making a cup of tea is one thing. But is it? To make a cup of tea, you have to

- Find tea
- Boil water
- Find a cup
- Put the tea in the cup
- Add the boiling water

And to boil water, you have to

- Have access to water
- Have a source of heat
- Have a container to connect the source of heat to the water

CHAPTER 3   DOING ONE THING: AB STRACTION, BOOLEAN PARAMETERS, AND
            DESIGN PATTERNS

And to have a source of heat, you may need many other components, such as electrical wiring, etc. It appears that we are back where we started: abstraction.

Doing one thing means **doing one thing at the same level of abstraction**. When a method mixes different levels of abstraction, it certainly does multiple things. And so, we can also say that a method *can* do multiple things, as long as they are all in the same level of abstraction. Let's see again the sample method with the changes we made:

```
validateParams(firstName, lastName, username);

List<User> existingUsers = [SELECT Id FROM User WHERE Username = :username];

if (!existingUsers.isEmpty()) {
    throw new PortalException('User already exists: ' +
    username);
}
else {
    User newUser = setUserDefaults(firstName, lastName,
    username);

    insert newUser;

    System.setPassword(newUser.Id,Password.generatePassword());

    return newUser;
}
```

The method does multiple things because creating a user involves multiple steps. But as a developer reading this code, I'm only concerned with a high level of abstraction. I'm not worried about **how** we determine the if parameters are invalid or which are the default fields or how we generate a password. I'm dealing with these concepts through a higher abstraction that lets me focus on the bigger picture without getting bogged down in the details.

My final recommendation is not to obsess about whether a method does one thing. Sometimes, you really have to do multiple things to achieve a task, and that's okay. A better approach is to always be conscious of not mixing different levels of abstraction. Better yet, as you write a new method, run all of its logic through this simple checklist:

- Is this at a different level of abstraction?
- Should this be reusable?
- Can I easily test it?

Focusing on these three principles will naturally lead you to write methods that do one thing.

3.5 Boolean Parameters

The use of boolean parameters is cause for a lot of debate on the Internet. The main criticism is that a boolean parameter makes a method do more than one thing. A common example of this is the `insert` method of the `Database` class from the standard Apex library. One of the versions of this method has the following signature:

```
insert(sObject[] recordsToInsert, Boolean allOrNone)
```

The `allOrNone` parameter determines whether an error should cause the entire operation to fail or whether we want to allow for partial success. By definition, those are two different things. For illustration purposes, this is how the parameter is used:

```
//allows partial success
Database.insert(newAccounts,false);
```

CHAPTER 3   DOING ONE THING: AB STRACTION, BOOLEAN PARAMETERS, AND
            DESIGN PATTERNS

```
//atomic, a single failure causes the entire batch to fail
Database.insert(newAccounts,true);
```

We can't see what the code looks like inside of the `Database.insert()` method, but we can imagine it looks something like this:

```
Database.SaveResult[] insert(sObject[] recordsToInsert, Boolean allOrNone) {
    //some general logic here

    if (allOrNone) {
        //some logic here
        //that throws an exception if the insert fails
    }
    else {
        //some logic here
        //that wraps failures inside the SaveResult object
        //and does not throw an exception
    }
}
```

The split that occurs inside of the if statement is where two different things happen. And that's what boolean parameters do: "if this is true, do **this**, otherwise, do **that**."

We already agreed that you should avoid doing multiple things in a single method; however, boolean parameters do have their place. They can be useful constructs provided that the following conditions are met:

- They enhance the main behavior of the method.

- They operate at the same level of abstraction.

- There's only one boolean parameter. If more are needed, an alternative technique must be used (we'll get to this shortly).

CHAPTER 3   DOING ONE THING: AB STRACTION, BOOLEAN PARAMETERS, AND DESIGN PATTERNS

Let's see if the `allOrNone` parameter meets these criteria.

First, the parameter enhances the behavior of the DML operation by determining how errors should be handled; it isn't a completely unrelated option. It fits the story. For example, I could say out loud "I want to insert accounts and handle failures gracefully" and it makes sense. This means that the parameter operates at the same level of abstraction as the method being enhanced.

Finally, this is the only boolean parameter that you can pass to the `insert()` method. If you need to pass more, you have to use the `DMLOptions` class, which we will discuss soon. In short, the `allOrNone` parameter has the characteristics of a well-defined boolean parameter.

To understand what a poorly designed boolean parameter looks like, let's imagine this fictional parameter:

```
insert(sObject[] recordsToInsert, Boolean writeToDebugLog)
```

In this example, the `writeToDebugLog` parameter determines whether the operation details are written to the debug log. This option doesn't enhance the behavior of the DML operation; writing to the debug log is an unrelated concern. Furthermore, whether the operation writes to the debug log or not should not be a concern of the method calling `Database.insert()`.

Writing to the debug log is at a much lower level of abstraction than the general details of the DML operation.

Finally, if we were to need more options, the following method signature would also be problematic:

```
Database.SaveResult[] insert(
        sObject[] recordsToInsert,
        Boolean writeToDebugLog,
        Boolean allOrNone
)
```

69

The inclusion of two boolean parameters means the method is now doing many more things at different levels of abstractions.

3.6 Alternatives to Boolean Arguments

Some argue that boolean parameters shouldn't be used at all and that, instead, you should create one method for each of the behaviors you want to provide. In that scenario, we would see the following methods in the Database class:

`//instead of these`

`//Database.insert(newAccounts,false);`

`//Database.insert(newAccounts,true);`

`//we would have these`

`Database.insertPartial(newAccounts);`

`Database.insertAtomic(newAccounts);`

Rather than having the boolean parameter determine how failures are handled, we split the logic into two *meaningfully* different methods. I believe this is easier to read. You can read the words "insert partial," and you can mostly assume what the method does. When you read the `insert()` method with the `allOrNone` parameter, it isn't immediately obvious what that parameter does (I always find myself looking at the documentation to make sure I remember its default value).

Part of the reason this isn't immediately obvious with the `allOrNone` parameter is that the name of the parameter isn't ideal. When we read the words out loud "all or none," it doesn't immediately make us think about atomic vs. partial operations. I believe this parameter should have been called `allowPartialSuccess`, which would make the method signature much more intuitive and clear:

CHAPTER 3   DOING ONE THING: AB STRACTION, BOOLEAN PARAMETERS, AND DESIGN PATTERNS

```
insert(sObject[] recordsToInsert, Boolean allowPartialSuccess)
```

This brings us to the fourth rule of boolean parameters: If you are going to provide a boolean argument, make sure that the name clearly explains how it will enhance the main functionality of the method. All the guidelines we explored in Chapter 2 for good names apply to boolean parameters as well.

Going back to the topic of whether it is better to split the logic into different methods, the answer is: it depends. If `insert()` was the only method of the `Database` class that supported partial vs. atomic operations, then I believe splitting the logic into two methods would make sense and it would improve the readability of the code. However, the `Database` class contains dozens of overloaded methods. For example, these are all overloaded versions of the `insert()` method:

```
insert(recordToInsert, allOrNone)
insert(recordsToInsert, allOrNone)
insert(recordToInsert, dmlOptions)
insert(recordsToInsert, dmlOptions)
insert(recordToInsert, allOrNone, accessLevel)
insert(recordsToInsert, allOrNone, accessLevel)
insert(recordToInsert, dmlOptions, accessLevel)
insert(recordsToInsert, dmlOptions, accessLevel)
```

If there were two versions of each of these methods (atomic and partial success), it would double the amount of methods in the `Database` class. And this is only when we look at the `insert` operation. There are many more DML operations in that class such as `update`, `delete`, `convertLead`, etc. The developers of the Apex language probably made the trade-off to use a simple boolean argument instead of having twice the amount of methods per DML operation.

CHAPTER 3 DOING ONE THING: AB STRACTION, BOOLEAN PARAMETERS, AND DESIGN PATTERNS

The key takeaway here is that whether to split logic into two different methods or use a boolean parameter depends entirely on the use case and how either decision will impact future users of the code. I will talk more about when (and when not to) to split methods in the next chapter.

3.7 Multiple Boolean Parameters

Sometimes, a method will take more than one boolean parameter in ways that aren't immediately obvious. We can again look at the `Database` class for examples. One of the overloaded versions of the `insert()` method looks like this:

```
insert(List<SObject> recordsToInsert, Boolean allOrNone, System.AccessLevel accessLevel)
```

The third parameter, `accessLevel`, is not a boolean but an Enum of the type `System.AccessLevel`. Here's what the documentation says about this parameter:

*The accessLevel parameter specifies **whether** the method runs in system mode (`AccessLevel.SYSTEM_MODE`) **or** user mode (`AccessLevel.USER_MODE`).*

The use of the word "or" clearly shows that the operation will do either of two things, depending on what access level is specified. In other words, the method can do two *different* things. But again, we go back the trade-offs we explored earlier. The alternative would be to create a method that looks like this:

```
insertAtomicAdminMode(newAccounts);
```

This is clearly not a good name for a method, and in the case of the `Database` class, we would end up with many more methods, one per access level. This is another reason boolean parameters should be used

72

CHAPTER 3   DOING ONE THING: ABSTRACTION, BOOLEAN PARAMETERS, AND DESIGN PATTERNS

with caution; they force the reader of the code to have intimate knowledge about what the parameter does. Consider the following code:

```
Database.insert(accounts,false,AccessLevel.USER_MODE);
```

It isn't immediately obvious what `false` represents here. The same is true for `AccessLevel.USER_MODE`. You must understand the *order* in which these parameters are passed and what exactly they do. In these scenarios, a better approach could have been to allow developers to create different DML operations using the fluent interface pattern, like this:

> **Note**   I will build this later in the chapter and explain more about how it works.

```
DML dmlOperation = new DML()
    .withPartialSupport()
    .withAdminAccess()
    .setRecords(newAccounts)
    .setOperation(DML.OPERATION.INSERT);

dmlOperation.execute();
```

This reads better than many boolean parameters being part of the method signature. You also don't need to know what each parameter does, because the method that takes that parameter will tell you so.

Talking about multiple boolean parameters, the `Database` class methods do in fact allow for multiple parameters, by using the `DMLOptions` class. The `DMLOptions` class is a simple wrapper object for multiple boolean parameters that can be passed to most of the methods in the `Database` class. And to make matters worse, some of the options have child options that can be specified. For example:

CHAPTER 3 DOING ONE THING: AB STRACTION, BOOLEAN PARAMETERS, AND DESIGN PATTERNS

```
Database.DMLOptions dmlOptions = new Database.DMLOptions();

dmlOptions.EmailHeader.triggerAutoResponseEmail = true;

Case newCase = new Case(subject='Plumbing Problems');

Database.insert(newCase, dmlOptions);
```

Now, the `insert()` method will also look at `EmailHeader.triggerAutoResponseEmail` to determine whether it should send emails. This is yet another thing that the method must do.

Passing an options object is a very common pattern when multiple boolean parameters can be passed.

While each individual parameter may operate at a different level of abstraction, the concept of "options" is at the same level of abstraction as the method. This pattern is also very common in JavaScript and Node. js programs. For example, when using the fetch API to make API calls in LWC, you can pass an options parameter to the fetch function:

```
export default class DataFetcher extends LightningElement {
    fetchData() {
        const url = '<https://api.example.com/data>';
        const options = {
            method: 'GET',
            headers: {
                'Content-Type': 'application/json'
            }
        };
        fetch(url, options)
```

With this rather long essay about the `Database` class, I'm not trying to say that it is poorly designed. Instead, what we are seeing here is that

CHAPTER 3   DOING ONE THING: AB STRACTION, BOOLEAN PARAMETERS, AND DESIGN PATTERNS

sometimes multiple boolean parameters are unavoidable. Sometimes, like in the case of DML operations, we really do need to be able to provide multiple options that specify how the operation should behave.

Whether we provide those options as multiple boolean parameters, using the fluent interface pattern, or in an object wrapper, it ultimately means that the method will indeed do many things.

And so, we come to the realization that the "methods should do one thing" rule is more of a guideline than a rule. We must always work toward creating methods that do one thing, but in certain domains where complex operations are involved, doing one thing may involve doing many other things, and that's to be expected.

Let's summarize the learnings from this section.

- You can use boolean parameters when they enhance the main logic and they operate at the same level of abstraction.

- Boolean parameters should be named properly.

- If the boolean parameter only affects one method, consider splitting the logic into two methods instead.

- If you need to pass multiple boolean parameters, use the fluent interface pattern, the builder pattern, or a wrapper object.

- Sometimes, multiple boolean parameters are unavoidable, and sometimes, they are indeed desirable.

I want to finish this section by showing you an example of the `SObject.clone()` method of the standard Apex library. Here's an example from the official documentation:

CHAPTER 3   DOING ONE THING: AB STRACTION, BOOLEAN PARAMETERS, AND DESIGN PATTERNS

```
Account originalAccount = new account(Name = 'Acme',
Description = 'Acme Account');

Account clonedAccount = originalAccount.clone(false, false,
true, false);
```

I will leave it to you as an exercise to decide if the method does one thing and whether Salesforce did a good job in its design.

3.8 Enums and Switch Statements

Enums and switch statements usually go together to define boolean logic with multiple possible paths. Enums in Apex define a finite collection of constants. A common use case in Apex is to use a switch statement on the `Trigger.OperationType` enum to decide what logic to call in different trigger contexts:

```
trigger AccountTrigger on Account (before insert, after insert) {
    switch on Trigger.operationType {
        when BEFORE_INSERT {
            AccountDomain.validateAddresses(Trigger.new);
        }
        when AFTER_INSERT {
            SalesNotifications.notifySalesReps(Trigger.new);
        }
    }
}
```

The `Trigger.OperationType` enum defines what trigger operations are possible; you can't add or remove values from it. These makes enums popular for conditional logic, as seen in the example above.

CHAPTER 3   DOING ONE THING: AB STRACTION, BOOLEAN PARAMETERS, AND DESIGN PATTERNS

However, to truly understand when to create your own Enums and when to pair them with the switch statement, we need to dig deeper.

We will do this by continuing to explore the previous example of a fluent interface-style class that makes DML code easier to reason about. Here's the code that we want:

```
DML dmlOperation = new DML()
                .setOperation(DML.Operation.INSERTS)
                .setRecords(accounts)
                .setAllowPartialSuccess(false);

dmlOperation.execute();
```

The fluent interface is a design pattern that allows you to chain method calls together in a readable and intuitive way. Each method in the chain returns the current instance (`this`), which allows you to chain multiple method calls in a single statement. It's beyond the scope of this book to explore this pattern extensively, but it is a good example for exploring complex conditional logic. The following is how you would create a basic version of this:

```
public without sharing class DML {

    //private -- the attributes of a DML operation

    private List<SObject> records;
    private Boolean allowPartialSuccess;
    private String operation;

  //setter methods for the private variables

    public DML setOperation(String operation) {
        this.operation = operation;
        return this;
    }
```

77

CHAPTER 3   DOING ONE THING: AB STRACTION, BOOLEAN PARAMETERS, AND
           DESIGN PATTERNS

```
    public DML setRecords(List<SObject> records) {
        this.records = records;
        return this;
    }

    public DML setAllowPartialSuccess(Boolean
    allowPartialSuccess) {
        this.allowPartialSuccess = allowPartialSuccess;
        return this;
    }

    //execute() logic will be shown later
```

In the basic structure above, the operation variable will hold the type of DML operation we are executing, such as insert, update , delete, etc. The variable is of type `String`, which is **not** ideal but bear with me as I move forward with the example. We will use a much better technique later.

With this rather naive implementation, you'd be able execute DML operations like this:

```
DML dmlOperation = new DML()
    .setOperation('Insert')
    .setRecords(accounts)
    .setAllowPartialSuccess(false);

dmlOperation.execute();
```

This is already easier to read than calling the raw `Database.insert()` method with many parameters (some of them boolean ones). Given that the operation parameter is a String, you might implement the `execute()` method as follows:

78

```
public void execute() {

    if (this.operation.equals('Insert')) {
        Database.insert(this.records, this.
        allowPartialSuccess);
    }
    else if (this.operation.equals('Update')) {
        Database.update(this.records, this.
        allowPartialSuccess);
    }
    else if (this.operation.equals('Delete')) {
        Database.delete(this.records, this.
        allowPartialSuccess);
    }
    else if (this.operation.equals('Undelete')) {
        Database.undelete(
            this.records,
            this.allowPartialSuccess
        );
    }
}
```

Note Each method of the `Database` class returns a different type, such as `SaveResult`, `DeleteResult`, etc. I'm not implementing how to dynamically cast a result to its appropriate type or how to return the correct type to the caller. I'm skipping this so we can focus on the conditional logic.

CHAPTER 3   DOING ONE THING: AB STRACTION, BOOLEAN PARAMETERS, AND
             DESIGN PATTERNS

This works, but there's a lot of problems with it. First, we are checking against a very specific string, i.e., Insert. If the user passes insert, INSERT, or insertt, the if condition will never run. In other words, we rely on the user knowing exactly how to write the parameter name. We could fix this by adding logic to ignore upper and lower case, like this:

```
if (this.operation.equalsIgnoreCase('insert')) ...
```

While this certainly solves the problem of the user passing the word insert in a different case, it doesn't solve for the user passing a random value or the word insert misspelled. What's more concerning is that we are now mixing levels of abstraction. A DML operation logic shouldn't be mixed with string manipulation logic.

To get out of this situation where we find ourselves doing string manipulation, we can use a custom enum. Inside the DML class, you could define the following:

```
public without sharing class DML {

    public enum Operation {
        INSERTS,
        UPDATES,
        DELETES,
        UNDELETES,
        CONVERTS_LEAD
    }
    ...more code below
```

The Operation enum uses the plural word of the DML operation types simply because the singular words are reserved words in Apex, i.e., you cannot use the word insert as the name of a method, variable, etc.

CHAPTER 3 DOING ONE THING: ABSTRACTION, BOOLEAN PARAMETERS, AND DESIGN PATTERNS

The enum now defines that DML operations are supported, without relying on the user spelling it correctly. The operation instance variable and its setter method now needs to be updated too, as follows:

```
private Operation operation;

public DML setOperation(Operation operation) {
    this.operation = operation;
    return this;
}
```

Finally, the execute() method can be rewritten to use the enum instead of a string:

```
if (this.operation == DML.Operation.INSERTS) {
    Database.insert(this.records, this.allowPartialSuccess);
}
else if (this.operation == DML.Operation.UPDATES) {
    Database.insert(this.records, this.allowPartialSuccess);
}
...
```

And now the caller simply needs to pass the enum type to the DML class:

```
DML dmlOperation = new DML()
                .setOperation(DML.Operation.INSERTS)
                .setRecords(accounts)
                .setAllowPartialSuccess(false);

 dmlOperation.execute();
```

81

CHAPTER 3   DOING ONE THING: AB STRACTION, BOOLEAN PARAMETERS, AND
            DESIGN PATTERNS

This is a much better design. Now, the user doesn't have to worry about how to spell the DML operation type; they can simply pass the corresponding Enum. Furthermore, the enum, unlike a simple string variable, defines which values are supported.

We can now take advantage of this enum to rewrite the `execute()` method and use the switch statement, as follows:

```
switch on this.operation {

    when INSERTS {
        Database.insert(this.records, this.
        allowPartialSuccess);
    }
    when UPDATES {
        Database.update(this.records, this.
        allowPartialSuccess);
    }
    when DELETES {
        Database.delete(this.records, this.
        allowPartialSuccess);
    }
    when UNDELETES {
        Database.undelete(this.records, this.
        allowPartialSuccess);
    }
}
```

This is a big improvement. The code is now easier to read and we aren't dealing with complex string manipulation logic that is on a very different level of abstraction. This method now does one thing: it decides what method of the `Database` class to call based on the enum provided by the user. However, as we add more features to make this module feature-rich, we may add a lot more code between each when statement, like this:

CHAPTER 3   DOING ONE THING: ABSTRACTION, BOOLEAN PARAMETERS, AND DESIGN PATTERNS

```
when INSERTS {
    // a lot more code here
    Database.insert(this.records, this.allowPartialSuccess);
    // new code here over time
    // new requirements
}
when UPDATES {
    //new functionality
    //yet more functionality
    Database.update(this.records, this.allowPartialSuccess);
}
...
//many more new features
```

To prevent this switch statement from becoming even bigger, we can wrap each block of code after the when statements into their own method, like this:

```
when INSERTS {
    executeInsert(this.records, this.allowPartialSuccess);
}
when UPDATES {
    executeUpdate(this.records, this.allowPartialSuccess);
}
when DELETES {
    executeDelete(this.records, this.allowPartialSuccess);
}
when UNDELETES {
    executeUndelete(this.records, this.allowPartialSuccess);
}
```

Now, each executeX() method can have as much code as we want, without making the switch statement bigger and harder to reason about.

83

3.9 Replacing the Switch Statement with a Design Pattern

The code in the previous section was a big improvement from where we started. However, we still have a relatively large if/else statement.

Even though we are not using the `if` operator, this is still conditional logic: "If the operation is X, do X; if it's Y, do Y; and so on." There are many more DML operations than the four we implemented, such as `upsert`, `convertLead`, `merge`, `deleteAsync`, etc. If we want our DML class to support more operations, we need to modify the switch statement every time we add a new operation.

While introducing new code and making changes is inevitable, we prefer not to modify the switch statement repeatedly. This is because the entire logic of the class depends on this switch statement doing what it is supposed to do; if we make a mistake here, everything falls apart.

Another reason for not wanting to change the switch statement repeatedly is to follow the **Open/Closed Principle**, one of the SOLID principles that we will explore in detail in a future chapter. This principle *encourages* us to design modules (classes, methods, etc.) to be open for extension but closed for modification. This means that if we want to add new logic, we should be able to extend the module without changing existing code. Strict and dogmatic adherence to this principle can lead to issues in your design, but we will explore its trade-offs in a future chapter.

For now, we know that we would like to add new functionality without having to modify the switch statement every time.

What we need is a way to map the `DML.Operation` enum to its corresponding `executeX()` method. Maps are a form of `if/else` statements even if they don't appear so at first glance. Consider the following code:

CHAPTER 3   DOING ONE THING: ABSTRACTION, BOOLEAN PARAMETERS, AND DESIGN PATTERNS

```
Map<Id,Account> accountsById = new Map<Id,Account>([SELECT Id
FROM Account]);

Account parentAccount = accountsById.get(parentAccountId);
```

When we call `accountsById.get()`, we are basically saying "*if* this account Id is in the map, give me the account record, *else* give me a null object." This is basically an one-liner if/else statement that **does not change no matter how many values we add to the map**. This is exactly what we need. The ideal solution to our growing switch statement problem would be to have a map of `DML.Operation` enum values to their corresponding `executeX()` method. If this was possible, we could do something like this (the following is pseudocode, **not** real Apex code):

```
Map<DML.Operation,ExecuteMethod method> methodsByOperation =
new Map<DML.Operation,ExecuteMethod>{

//map a method to a specific enum value
    DML.Operation.INSERTS => InsertMethod,
    DML.Operation.UPDATES => UpdateMethod,
    DML.Operation.DELETES => DeleteMethod
};
```

We could then replace the entire switch statement with two lines:

```
ExecuteMethod method = methodsByOperation.get(operation);

method.execute();//execute the method that was retrieved
                 from the map
```

These two lines would *never* change no matter how many more DML operations we support. Of course, we still need to add the DML operations to the `methodsByOperation`, but at least the core logic remains unchanged. Unfortunately, this is not *natively* possible in Apex. You cannot add a method to a map, or store a method in a variable, or return a method from another method.

CHAPTER 3   DOING ONE THING: AB STRACTION, BOOLEAN PARAMETERS, AND
           DESIGN PATTERNS

This is possible in other languages like JavaScript and Java. For example, in JavaScript, functions can be passed as arguments to other functions, stored as variables, and returned by other functions, like this:

```javascript
function insertMethod() {
    return 'Insert method was executed';
}

function executeDML(operation) {
    operation();//call the function that was passed as an
                argument
}

//pass the function as an argument to another function
executeDML(insertMethod);
// prints "Insert method was executed"
```

In this example, the executeDML function takes one parameter called operation. JavaScript doesn't initially know what operation is; it could be a primitive variable, an object, or a function. In the body of the executeDML function, we execute operation by calling it with parentheses (). When we call executeDML(insertMethod), we pass the insertMethod function as the argument. Therefore, when we call operation() inside executeDML, we are *actually* executing the insertMethod function.

The code above is an example of a higher-order function, a function that can take another function as a parameter. This capability is also available in Java through Lambda expressions. The same example can be written in Java as follows:

```java
import java.util.function.Supplier;

public class Main {
```

CHAPTER 3   DOING ONE THING: AB STRACTION, BOOLEAN PARAMETERS, AND DESIGN PATTERNS

```
public static void main(String[] args) {
    Supplier<String> insertMethod = () -> "Insert method
    was executed";

    executeDML(insertMethod);
}

public static void executeDML(Supplier<String> operation) {
    operation.get();
}
}
```

This may seem completely unrelated to our switch statement problem. The point here is that in other languages, we could easily solve this problem by creating a map of methods. In Apex, we can't.

What we can do, however, is to use the **strategy design pattern**. The strategy design pattern lets you choose different actions (or strategies) at runtime by creating separate classes for each action and *switching* between them easily. Notice the emphasis on the word "switch." We still need to switch between different operations, but we'll do so without the switch statement, and we will be able to use a map.

To understand this pattern, you need to understand interfaces and polymorphism in object-oriented programming (OOP). We will do a recap of OOP in the context of Apex in a future chapter, but for the purposes of this section, I will assume you have a basic understanding of these topics (at a minimum, you should understand interfaces as they are needed to execute batch Apex).

The first step is to create an interface that describes that a class can execute DML operations. We will define this interface *inside* the DML class:

```
public Interface DMLExecutable {
```

CHAPTER 3 DOING ONE THING: AB STRACTION, BOOLEAN PARAMETERS, AND
         DESIGN PATTERNS

```
    void execute(
        List<SObject> records,
        Boolean allowPartialSuccess
    );
}
```

The methods inside an interface do not have an implementation or behavior. With this interface, we are declaring that if a class implements the `DMLExecutable` interface, it must implement the `execute()` method (again, similar to batch Apex).

Now, we need to create an *inner* class for each DML operation that we support, and each of these classes must implement the `DMLExecutable` interface. Here's what it looks like:

```
public class InsertOperation implements DMLExecutable {

    //implement the execute() method
    public void execute(
        List<SObject> records,
        Boolean allowPartialSuccess)
    {
        //specific implementation of execute() for inserts
        Database.insert(records, allowPartialSuccess);
    }
}

public class UpdateOperation implements DMLExecutable {

    //implement the execute() method
    public void execute(
        List<SObject> records,
        Boolean allowPartialSuccess
    ) {
        //specific implementation of execute() for updates
```

CHAPTER 3 DOING ONE THING: ABSTRACTION, BOOLEAN PARAMETERS, AND DESIGN PATTERNS

```
        Database.update(records, allowPartialSuccess);
    }
}
```

Now, we can create a map of `DML.Operation` values to their corresponding Apex class, like this:

```
private Map<DML.Operation, DMLExecutable> operationsByDmlAction
    = new Map<DML.Operation, DMLExecutable>();
```

```
operationsByDmlAction.put(DML.Operation.Inserts, new
InsertOperation());
```

```
operationsByDmlAction.put(DML.Operation.Updates, new
UpdateOperation());
```

```
operationsByDmlAction.put(DML.Operation.Deletes, new
DeleteOperation());
```

```
operationsByDmlAction.put(DML.Operation.Undeletes, new
UndeleteOperation());
```

This is exactly what we wanted to do all along. Now that we have this map, we can replace the entire switch statement with a few lines:

```
public void execute() {

    //get the operation based on the user-provided enum
    DMLExecutable operation = this.operationsByDmlAction.
    get(this.operation);

    operation.execute(this.records, this.allowPartialSuccess);
}
```

Now, the execute method *doesn't know* what DML operations it is executing. All it knows is that inside the map, there was an apex class that implemented the `DMLExecutable` interface, and because the interface

CHAPTER 3 DOING ONE THING: AB STRACTION, BOOLEAN PARAMETERS, AND
           DESIGN PATTERNS

forces the apex class to implement the execute method, it knows it can safely call operation.execute(). Notice that the map *definition* maps DML.Operation to DMLExecutable; but the actual *values* of the map correspond to the specific classes that implement the DMLExecutable interface; **this is polymorphism in action**.

We can now add as many DML operations as we want and the most fragile part of our logic remains unchanged. The resulting Apex class now looks like this:

```
public class DML {

    public enum Operation {
        Inserts,
        Updates,
        Deletes,
        Undeletes,
        ConvertsLead
    }

    private List<SObject> records;
    private Boolean allowPartialSuccess;
    private Operation operation;

    public DML setOperation(Operation operation) {
        this.operation = operation;
        return this;
    }

    public DML setRecords(List<SObject> records) {
        this.records = records;
        return this;
    }
```

```
    public DML setAllowPartialSuccess(Boolean allowPartial
    Success) {
        this.allowPartialSuccess = allowPartialSuccess;
        return this;
    }

    public void execute(){

        DMLExecutable operation = this.operations.get(this.
        operation);

        //we will deal with invalid or null parameters later
        if(operation != null){
            operation.execute(this.records,    this.
            allowPartialSuccess);
        }
    }

    public Interface DMLExecutable {
        void execute(List<SObject> records, Boolean
        allowPartialSuccess);
    }

public class InsertOperation implements DMLExecutable {

        public void execute(
                List<SObject> records,
                Boolean allowPartialSuccess
        ) {
            Database.insert(records, allowPartialSuccess);
        }
}
```

CHAPTER 3   DOING ONE THING: AB STRACTION, BOOLEAN PARAMETERS, AND
           DESIGN PATTERNS

```
public class UpdateOperation implements DMLExecutable {

    public void execute(
            List<SObject> records,
            Boolean allowPartialSuccess
    ) {
        Database.update(records, allowPartialSuccess);
    }
}
//more implementations of DMlExecutable

    private Map<DML.Operation, DMLExecutable> operations = new
    Map<DML.Operation, DMLExecutable> {
        DML.Operation.Inserts => new InsertOperation(),
        DML.Operation.Updates => new UpdateOperation(),
        DML.Operation.Deletes => new DeleteOperation(),
        DML.Operation.Undeletes => new UndeleteOperation()
    };
}
```

3.10 Conclusion

That was quite a journey. We started with a simple `if/else` statement with raw string manipulation, refactored it to use Enums and the switch statement, and ended up using polymorphism with the strategy design pattern. This progression shows an important principle in software design: as our requirements grow in complexity, our code structure needs to evolve as well. What is considered "clean" for a simple requirement can be inefficient code for a more complex requirement.

By adopting the strategy pattern, we achieved several benefits:

- **Reduced Fragility**: The core logic of our DML class remains stable, even as we add new DML operations. We've reduced the risk of making mistakes to a critical part of our logic.

- **Adherence to the Open/Closed Principle**: The DML class is now open for extension but closed for modification. We can add new operations without altering the existing code.

- **Single Responsibility Principle**: Each DML operation is encapsulated in its own class, making the code easier to understand and maintain. This *separation of concerns* ensures that each class has a single responsibility. We will talk a lot more about this principle in future chapters.

This doesn't mean that you should convert every `if/else` statement into the strategy pattern. Conditional logic is fundamental to programming and can often be simple and sufficient. However, as we've learned in this section, when the complexity and number of conditions grow, and we want to adhere to clean code principles, advanced design patterns like the strategy pattern can provide great benefits.

Once again, here are the takeaways:

- Always be thinking of abstractions. Make your code easy to understand at a high level, and hide unnecessary details.

- Don't go too far; too many layers of abstraction will make your code very hard to reason about.

- If you need to create methods that do the same with a few variances, consider creating a new method before introducing boolean parameters.

- Ensure your methods do one thing, but don't obsess about what one thing is; focus on testability, abstraction and reusability.

- Don't be afraid of using boolean parameters in your code, as they do have their place.

- Consider more advanced design patterns like the fluent interface or the strategy pattern when the number of boolean parameters grows.

CHAPTER 4

How Long Should Methods Be: Length, Depth, and Subtasks

The best modules are those that provide powerful functionality, yet have simple interfaces.

—John Ousterhout

The second piece of common wisdom when it comes to methods is that they should be short. In this chapter, we will go over advantages and disadvantages of short methods and why larger methods have their place, and we'll talk about when you should split a larger method into shorter ones.

4.1 Short Methods

Methods should be short because short methods

- Are easier to test in isolation
- Are easier to reason about

- Can be reused by other modules
- Isolate different levels of abstraction

Of course, the immediate question is: "But how short should they be?"

4.2 The Clean Code Philosophy

One school of thought is that methods should be as short as possible. The biggest proponent of this idea is Robert C. Martin, the author of the famous book *Clean Code*. In his book, Martin advocates for methods to be extremely small, to the point where they literally hold **one block of code and nothing else.**

Here's an example from his book:

```
private void includeSetupPages() {
  if (isSuite)
    includeSuiteSetupPage();
  includeSetupPage();
}

private void includeSuiteSetupPage() {
  include(SuiteResponder.SUITE_SETUP_NAME, "-setup");
}

private void includeSetupPage() {
  include("SetUp", "-setup");
}

private void includePageContent() {
  newPageContent.append(pageData.getContent());
}
```

CHAPTER 4   HOW LONG SHOULD METHODS BE: LENGTH, DEPTH, AND SUBTASKS

```
private void includeTeardownPages() {
  includeTeardownPage();
  if (isSuite)
    includeSuiteTeardownPage();
}

private void includeTeardownPage() {
  include("TearDown", "-teardown");
}

private void includeSuiteTeardownPage() {
  include(SuiteResponder.SUITE_TEARDOWN_NAME, "-teardown");
}
```

As you can see, most methods are indeed one line long and most of them are pass-through methods. Pass-through methods are methods that simply pass their arguments to another method. Pass-through methods do offer certain benefits, which we will explore soon, but it is my opinion that making every method in your code a pass-through method is an extreme.

If we were to follow this pattern, our simple password generator from the previous chapter would go from this:

```
public static String generatePassword() {

        String chars = '12345abcdefghijklmnopqrstuvwxyz';
        String password = '';
        while (password.length() < 8) {
            Integer i = Math.mod(
                            Math.abs(Crypto.
                            getRandomInteger()),
                            chars.length()
                        );
            password += chars.substring(i, i+1);
```

97

            }
            return password;
    }

    To this:

```
public static String generatePassword() {

    String chars = getAllPossibleChars();
    String password = initialiseEmptyPassword();
    while (isPasswordLengthLessThanEight(password)) {
        password = appendRandomChar(password, chars);
    }
    return password;
}

private static String appendRandomChar(String password, String chars) {
    Integer i = getRandomIndex(chars);
    return password += chars.substring(i, i+1);
}

private static String getAllPossibleChars() {
    return '12345abcdefghijklmnopqrstuvwxyz';
}

private static String initialiseEmptyPassword() {
    return '';
}

private static Boolean isPasswordLengthLessThanEight(String password) {
    return password.length() < 8;
}
```

CHAPTER 4   HOW LONG SHOULD METHODS BE: LENGTH, DEPTH, AND SUBTASKS

```
private static Integer getRandomIndex(String chars) {
    return Math.mod(
        Math.abs(Crypto.getRandomInteger()),
        chars.length()
    );
}

private static String appendRandomChar(String password, String chars, Integer i) {
    return password += chars.substring(i, i+1);
}
```

What used to be a simple and elegant method of 11 lines has become 36 lines long. I will agree that the main method, generatePassword, is now easier to read than the first version. For example, the string `12345abcdefghijklmnopqrstuvwxyz` was a magic number (as discussed on Section 2.12), and now, the method `getAllPossibleChars` explains what this string represents. This is good. However, now there's a lot more code to read, which means a lot more cognitive load. The "area" of this method has become so large that now we need to understand each individual method before we can really understand what's going on.

Another side effect of this philosophy is that the containing class, `Password`, becomes much larger due to the all the small methods. This makes the class appear overly busy, which may lead developers to suggest that new functionality should be added in a *separate* class, such as `PasswordMasker`. If we had kept all the logic within the generatePassword method, a new requirement for masking passwords could simply be added as a new method, such as `Password.mask()`. Don't get me wrong; there is value in classes having a single responsibility. The **Single Responsibility Principle** is something we will explore in depth in a future chapter. However, my point here is that breaking down a method into many small methods can push us to create *many* additional classes. I argue that there's *also* value in keeping related functionality within a single class. I will come back to this in Section 4.5.

Finally, the biggest problem with this technique is that it makes us focus on the wrong thing. Methods can only be short if we split larger methods into shorter methods, so the real question is not how short methods should be but, instead, **when should we split methods into shorter methods**. Does splitting a method increase its complexity, or does it decrease it? Are there situations when splitting a method into smaller ones has negative consequences? This is a much more interesting discussion than simply focusing on method length. Before we get there, I do want to explore some of the advantages of very short methods.

4.3 Very Short Methods

Here are some scenarios where you should use very short methods.

4.3.1 To Explain

Sometimes, you need to be able to explain why you made certain design decision, even if that design decision it just one line of code. Consider the following JavaScript code from my open source project HappySoup.io.

```
/**
 * Some metadata types are not fully supported by the
 * MetadataComponentDependency API
 * so we need to manually query related objects to find
   dependencies.
 * An example of this is the
 * EmailTemplate object, which is when queried, does not return
 * WorkflowAlerts that reference the template
 */
```

```
function lacksDependencyApiSupport(entryPoint){
    return [
        'Flow',
        'EmailTemplate',
        'CustomField',
        'ApexClass',
        'CustomObject']
    .includes(entryPoint.type);
}
```

This implementation is very simple. I simply check if a metadata type is part of the array. But the reason I'm doing that, and what it means to the overall flow, is not that simple. I needed to add a big comment to explain that these are the metadata types that are not supported by the `MetadataComponentDependency` tooling API. If I didn't have this method, I would have to use the array directly, and adding such a big comment **in the middle of some other code** would be highly disruptive. By moving the logic to a method, I suddenly have a lot more space to add a detailed comment.

4.3.2 To Hide Information

Another reason to create very short methods is to hide implementation details from the users of that code. This is typically known as information hiding; this is very much related to modularity, which is a topic that will be discussed at length in a future chapter.

The idea is we don't want to expose internal information regarding how something is implemented. A great example of this can be found on Mitch Spano's Trigger Actions Framework. This is one of the popular open source trigger frameworks that exist at the time of this writing. One of the functionalities this framework provides is the ability to bypass a specific trigger action at run time. In the `MetadataTriggerHandler` class, we can find the following method:

```
public static Boolean isBypassed(String actionName) {
    return MetadataTriggerHandler.
        bypassedActions.
            contains(actionName);
}
```

To determine if a trigger action should be bypassed, the action name is added to a `Set` of strings called `bypassedActions`. Imagine if your code had to call `MetadataTriggerHandler.bypassedActions.contains(actionName)` every time it needed to check if an action needed to be bypassed. This would mean that your code would have to have intimate knowledge of the internals of the `MetadataTriggerHandler` class.

By providing the `isBypassed` method (which is very short), the framework provides a simple API for callers to use. Callers don't know to be concerned about how or what determines if an action should be bypassed.

4.3.3 To Simplify the API

Another reason for using very short methods is when they help simplify the public API that you expose to your users. Here, again, we can look at an example from Mitch Spano's Trigger Actions Framework.

```
public void beforeInsert(List<SObject> newList) {
    this.executeActions(
        TriggerOperation.BEFORE_INSERT,
        newList,
        null
    );
}
```

CHAPTER 4   HOW LONG SHOULD METHODS BE: LENGTH, DEPTH, AND SUBTASKS

In the above snippet, we see that the public method is a lot simpler than the method that it actually calls. Calling `beforeInsert(newAccounts)` is a lot simpler than calling `this.executeActions(TriggerOperation.BEFORE_INSERT, newAccounts, null)`. If callers had to use the latter, they would need to know all the possible values of the `TriggerOperation` enum, and the fact that in this scenario, the last argument must be null. This is too much complexity for the callers to maintain. The public method makes all this complexity go away.

4.3.4 To Give the Action a Name

In one of my implementations, I had to concatenate two record IDs to form a single ID that was used to retrieve items from a map. The code that concatenated IDs was extremely simple:

`String uniqueKey = parent.Id+'-'+child.Id;`

I had the same line of code at least four times in the same Apex class. Because it was such a simple line of code and I was certain I wasn't going to change it any time soon, I was hesitant to create a method just for it. However, I noticed that the variable name wasn't enough to give clarity on *why* I was doing this, so I wrapped the code inside of a method:

`createUniqueKeyForRelationship(parent.Id,child.Id)`

The combination of the variable and the method gave the concept a bit more room to explain itself. However, the method name was not enough, so I ended up adding a comment on the method signature as we saw on Section 4.3.1. This is just another variation of the previous examples, but the focus here is that I wasn't trying to simplify the API, have more space for a comment, or hide internal implementation details. My goal was to give the action of concatenating two strings a name that could provide

CHAPTER 4   HOW LONG SHOULD METHODS BE: LENGTH, DEPTH, AND SUBTASKS

more context to the reader as to why I was doing that. This was a good reason to create a method even if the implementation is just one line of code.

These are all valid reasons for creating one-liner methods, and you should not be afraid to use them. This doesn't mean, however, that all methods should be this short.

4.4 Longer Methods

One good reason to have longer methods is to coordinate different internal methods into a single coherent functionality. This is a version of the facade design pattern, where multiple moving parts are hidden behind a simpler API. Consider the getDependencies JavaScript method from HappySoup.io, which retrieves metadata dependencies using several Salesforce APIs. I've highlighted the calls to the internal methods for clarity.

```
async function getUsage(){

    let query = usageQuery(entryPoint);
    await query.exec();
    let callers = query.getResults();

    if(lacksDependencyApiSupport(entryPoint)){
        let additionalReferences = await seachAdditional
        References(connection,entryPoint,cache);
        callers.push(...additionalReferences);
    }

    callers = await enhanceData(callers);

    let unsortedCallers = [];
    let sortedCallers = [];

    callers.forEach(caller => {
```

```
        if(caller.sortOrder){
            sortedCallers.push(caller);
        }
        else{
            unsortedCallers.push(caller);
        }
    })
    //sort alphabetically
    unsortedCallers.sort((a,b) => (a.name > b.name) ? 1 : -1 );

    sortedCallers.push(...unsortedCallers);
    callers = sortedCallers;

    let files = format(entryPoint,callers,'usage');

    let csv = files.csv();
    let excel = files.excel();
    let packageXml = files.xml();
    let datatable = files.datatable();

    let usageTree = createUsageTree(callers);
    let statsInfo = stats(callers);

    return{
        packageXml,
        usageTree,
        stats:statsInfo,
        entryPoint,
        csv,
        excel,
        datatable
    }
}
```

CHAPTER 4 HOW LONG SHOULD METHODS BE: LENGTH, DEPTH, AND SUBTASKS

The goal of this method is to coordinate several smaller methods to provide a coherent response to the client. One advantage of methods that coordinate smaller methods is that they act as order of execution documentation. We can see all the moving parts required to achieve a particular goal. If we were to follow a simplistic rule such as "methods shouldn't be longer than 15 lines," then I'd have to break this method down further. I encourage you to consider the consequences that would happen if I broke this down into smaller methods that then call other smaller methods.

Another advantage to long methods is they can provide *depth*.

4.5 Deep vs. Shallow Modules

> **Note** For the purposes of this discussion, a module can be either a class or a method. Also, in this discussion, an interface is the public API of a module, which is basically everything that a developer needs to understand before they can use the module.

In the book, *A Philosophy of Software Design*, author John Ousterhout introduces the idea of "deep" and "shallow" modules. Ousterhout makes the case that the best modules are those that are deep: they have a lot of functionality hidden behind a simple interface. Here, we shift the focus from method length to method *depth*.

A good example of a deep module is the `Limits` class of the standard Apex library. We can use this class to determine how much of a specific governor limit has been consumed during a transaction. For example:

```
Limits.getDMLStatements();
```

CHAPTER 4   HOW LONG SHOULD METHODS BE: LENGTH, DEPTH, AND SUBTASKS

This is a simple method. We don't know all the complex logic Salesforce must employ to track limits usage on a transaction; those details are completely hidden from us. The module is deep because it provides powerful functionality with a very simple interface.

Imagine if Salesforce had provided us with multiple methods to calculate limits usage. For example:

```
Limit dmlLimit = new Limit(LimitType.DML);
dmlLimit.setContext(ApexContext.BatchApex);

dmlLimit.startTracking();
// run your code here
dmlLimit.stopTracking();

dmlLimit.getLimit();
```

Each method is shallow because it provides very little functionality and is not useful on its own. Multiple methods need to be used together to get value from the interface.

In this case, having smaller methods that each do one thing makes the interface a lot more complex and forces the developers to understand the order in which multiple methods need to be called. In contrast, a deep module should just work.

4.6 Smaller Methods Increase Coupling

A real example of a shallow module is the `Http` class in the standard Apex library. Here's how you send an HTTP request in Apex:

```
HttpRequest req = new HttpRequest();
req.setEndpoint('http://www.yahoo.com');
req.setMethod('GET');

Http http = new Http();
HTTPResponse res = http.send(req);
```

The `HttpRequest` class cannot send a request without the `Http` class. At the same time, the `Http` class doesn't provide any functionality of its own; the only method it has is the `send()` method, which depends on an `HttpRequest` object.

So, on one hand, it's great that the classes are separate as each has its own responsibility; they do one thing. However, they are tightly coupled and don't provide any useful functionality without the other. The question then becomes: Does it make sense for the `send()` method to be separate from the `HttpRequest` class? What benefit does that separation provide **to the developer *using* this code**?

The only benefit may be for the developers who maintain this code (the Apex language team), and the separation is likely due to dependency injection (which will be covered in a future chapter).

In contrast, let's see how we can send HTTP requests in C#, using the .NET framework:

```
HttpResponseMessage res = await new HttpClient().
                         GetAsync("http://www.contoso.com/");
```

What takes five lines of code and two classes in Apex and takes one line of code and one class in .NET. As we can see, .NET offers a **deeper** module than Apex, and it's easier to use.

4.7 Not All Methods Are the Same

What we are seeing here with the comparison between deep and shallow modules is that not all methods are the same. **Public methods that are meant to be used by other developers should be deep**; they should provide as much functionality as possible behind a simple interface. Do not confuse "powerful functionality" with "multiple things." As we saw earlier, the `Limits.getDmlStatements()` method does one thing, but that one thing provides a lot of benefit to the user with a very simple interface.

CHAPTER 4   HOW LONG SHOULD METHODS BE: LENGTH, DEPTH, AND SUBTASKS

At the same time, the internal implementation of a deep method doesn't need to be all inside that method. **How the method provides its functionality to callers must be broken down into smaller methods to improve readability, reusability, and testing.**

We still haven't answered the question from the beginning of the chapter: When is the right time to extract some logic into its own method (aside from the very small methods discussion we saw earlier)?

4.8 Subtasks Should Be Separate Methods

When you can clearly identify a piece of logic as a subtask of the parent task, you should extract that to its own method. What is a subtask? A subtask makes sense on its own. It doesn't need to have intimate knowledge of the parent method; you should be able to read the method signature and understand what it does.

A good example of this is in the sample code from a previous chapter:

```
public static User createUser(
    String firstName,
    String lastName,
    String username) {

    //throws exception if any of the parameters are missing
    validateParams(firstName, lastName, username);

    List<User> existingUsers = [SELECT Id FROM User WHERE
    Username = :username];
```

I can read the name `validateParams()` and keep reading the code in the parent method without having to drill down further. The method name tells me clearly what it does. At the same time, I can read the details of that method and understand what it does without having to know anything about the parent method; it stands on its own:

109

CHAPTER 4   HOW LONG SHOULD METHODS BE: LENGTH, DEPTH, AND SUBTASKS

```
private static void validateParams(
    String firstName,
    String lastName,
    String username) {

    if (String.isBlank(firstName) ||
        String.isBlank(lastName)  ||
        String.isBlank(username))
        {
        throw new PortalException('Missing required user
        information');
    }
}
```

In a way, **the subtask is a general-purpose task**. Let's see an example of something that is not a subtask.

In the same code, I have a setUserDefaults() that initializes the user and sets default fields:

```
User newUser = setUserDefaults(firstName, lastName, username);

insert newUser;

System.setPassword(newUser.Id,Password.generatePassword());
```

Here's the implementation of setUserDefaults():

```
private static User setUserDefaults(String firstName,
            String lastName,
            String username) {

    User newUser = new User();
    newUser.Username = username;
    newUser.FirstName = firstName;
    newUser.LastName = lastName;
```

110

CHAPTER 4   HOW LONG SHOULD METHODS BE: LENGTH, DEPTH, AND SUBTASKS

```
    newUser.Email = username;
    newUser.Alias = username.substring(0, 8);
    newUser.TimeZoneSidKey = 'America/Los_Angeles';
    newUser.LocaleSidKey = 'en_US';
    newUser.EmailEncodingKey = 'UTF-8';
    newUser.ProfileId = [SELECT Id FROM Profile WHERE Name =
    'Standard User'].Id;
    newUser.LanguageLocaleKey = 'en_US';
    return newUser;
}
```

This method needs intimate knowledge of the parent method for it to work. It knows that the parent will have instantiated and verified the variables `firstName`, `lastName`, and `username`. Without the parent having verified that these variables were not `null`, this method cannot work. Also, when you look at the method itself, you really can't understand how it is meant to be used, as it instantiates a `User` variable that was never passed as an argument.

To understand this method scope, you need to flip back and forth between itself and the parent. **That is a red flag that you broke down that logic at the wrong place and time**. What I should have done is the following:

```
User newUser = new User();
newUser.Username = username;
newUser.FirstName = firstName;
newUser.LastName = LastName;
newUser.Email = username;
newUser.Alias = username.substring(0, 8);

newUser = addDefaultFieldValues(newUser);
```

111

Then, the subtask method would have a simpler interface.

```
private static User addDefaultFieldValues(User user) {
    user.TimeZoneSidKey = 'America/Los_Angeles';
    user.LocaleSidKey = 'en_US';
    user.EmailEncodingKey = 'UTF-8';
    user.ProfileId = [SELECT Id FROM Profile WHERE Name =
    'Standard User'].Id;
    user.LanguageLocaleKey = 'en_US';
    return user;
}
```

This has now made the subtask method more general-purpose. You can read it top to bottom and understand exactly what it does without having to understand how the parent method uses it. I also could have wrapped the initial user creation logic into a separate method:

```
User newUser = instantiateUser(firstName, lastName, username);
newUser = addDefaultFieldValues(newUser);
```

However, now the caller of these two methods needs to know that they need to be called in the right order. In a way, both methods are now somewhat shallow, as they provide little functionality and need each other. Perhaps, having everything in one larger method was a better idea, as it improves cohesion: it keeps all the knowledge on how to instantiate a user in the same place.

This back-and-forth between the different approaches is on purpose so that you can see that each decision comes with benefits and drawbacks.

4.9 Conclusion

So, how long should methods be? They should be short, but not because method length is a goal in and of itself. Methods should be short because we split larger methods into shorter ones so that we can

- Make the interface simpler
- Hide information that callers don't need to know about
- Explain (with comments) why you made certain design choices
- Give the action a name
- Make a clear separation between a task and its subtasks
- Test the method in isolation

Following these guidelines will naturally lead to shorter methods. However, the focus isn't on method length but on adhering to these design principles. Shorter methods are simply a beneficial side effect.

CHAPTER 5

Comments Don't Lie, Developers Do

When you find dead code, do the right thing. Give it a decent burial. Delete it from the system.

—Robert C. Martin

How to properly use comments and when to avoid them is cause for endless debate in online communities. In this chapter, I start by sharing my opinion on two popular misconceptions about comments. Then, I go over different types of comments and explain their pros and cons.

5.1 Everybody Lies

If you've been programming for a while, you may have heard developers saying that code should be self-documenting and that comments shouldn't be used because they tell lies. This idea comes from the very real fact that compilers don't check comments for validity, so you could end up with something like this:

```
// insert the account record
update opportunity;
```

CHAPTER 5   COMMENTS DON'T LIE, DEVELOPERS DO

Clearly, the comment is saying one thing but the code does another one completely different; in other words, the comment is telling lies. And to state the obvious, the code's logic is what will actually be executed, not what the comment says. Clean code purists use this argument to say comments should hardly ever be used.

In reality, **any programming construct can tell lies or be misleading**, consider the following code:

```
void deleteOpportunity(Account caseRecord) {
    insert new Contact(LastName = 'FirstName');
}
```

This may be a pedantic example, but the point is that everything about this method is a lie. The method does not delete an opportunity, it does not take a case record as its parameter and ends up actually inserting a contact. All these lies and yet there isn't a single comment here.

So, it's not the comments lie by default, it's that it's easy for programmers to not pay attention to the names they are using in their programming constructs. All the practices we explored in Chapter 2 should help you avoid misleading other developers.

Now, what can happen is that comments can often fall out of sync with the code that they once supported. When the code changes and the comments are not updated, they start telling lies and misleading. But this is also true for code; consider the example where a developer writes a method to deactivate an account:

```
public void deactivateAccount(Account account) {
    account.IsActive = false,
    update account;
}
```

Imagine that a few months later, the business requests that when an account is deactivated, contacts should be deleted too, and the developer does the following:

```
public void deactivateAccount(Account account) {
    account.IsActive = false,
    update account;

    delete [SELECT Id FROM Contact WHERE AccountId =
    :account.Id]
}
```

Now, the method does two very different things. A naive developer may reuse the `deactivateAccount` method in places where he did not intend for contacts to be deleted. So, **this method lies by omission**. It says it will deactivate an account, but it also deletes its contacts.

A better approach would have been something like this:

```
Public void deactivateAccount(Account account, Boolean deleteContacts) {
    ...
}
```

   Or

```
public void deactivateAccountWithContactDeletion(Account account) {
    ...
}
```

In Chapter 3, we spoke extensively about how to properly structure methods to do multiple things without breaking the "do one thing" principle. The point of this example is that the method, once accurate, started telling lies as soon as the business requirements changed.

So, all programming constructs can lie. The onus is on us as developers to keep them updated as our code evolves.

5.2 Self-documenting Code

The next idea that is popular in the developer community is that code should be self-documenting, i.e., that the code itself is the documentation and that comments shouldn't be needed to explain the code. I think it's not that simple.

To illustrate this, consider this method from the Nebula Logger open source Apex library, which is popular at the time of this writing for logging and exception management in Apex:

```
global void finish(Database.BatchableContext batchableContext) {
    Logger.setAsyncContext(batchableContext);
    Logger.setParentLogTransactionId(this.
    originalTransactionId);
    LoggerBatchableContext input = new LoggerBatchableContext
    (batchableContext, this.currentSObjectType);
    this.executePlugins(BatchableMethod.FINISH, input, null);

    Id nextBatchJobId;
    if (this.currentSObjectType != Schema.Log__
    c.SObjectType) {
    nextBatchJobId = Database.executeBatch(this,
    this.chainedBatchSize);
    }
...more code here

}
```

CHAPTER 5   COMMENTS DON'T LIE, DEVELOPERS DO

Spend a few seconds reading this, and think if you can decipher with 100% certainty what this code is doing, why, and what purposes it serves. If you are stuck, try again, now by adding the comment that the developer added just above the method:

```
/**
 * @description Required by the Database.Batchable interface.
 * This method runs after all batch jobs are complete.
 * This method writes a status to the Log__c object
   indicating that
 * the purge has finished.
 * @param batchableContext - The context of the batch jobs
 */
```

Was it any easier?

The point I'm trying to make here is that the names of our programming constructs can only take us so far. Most of the times, to be able to make sense of a piece of code, you need

- To really understand the context in which the code lives (is it within a method or a larger class)
- The overall purpose of the project or product
- The problem domain
- Any specific limitations or constraints that the product is working against
- The previous design or architectural decisions that influence every aspect of the code base

Now, this doesn't mean we shouldn't try to make code as self-documenting as possible. Good names (Chapter 2) and deep methods (Chapter 4) can go a long way in ensuring the code does what it says it does.

CHAPTER 5   COMMENTS DON'T LIE, DEVELOPERS DO

Having explored these two misconceptions (comments lie and code can be 100% self-documenting), let's explore different types of comments.

5.3 Version Control Comments

In Apex code bases, it's very common to see comments that aim to support some sort of version control. For example:

```
/**
 * History
 * 2021-06-30 - [BUG-452] - Rahul.Patel - Initial method for
   geocoding.
 * 2021-07-01 - [ENH-89] - Maria.Sanchez - Added state
   handling.
 * 2021-07-02 - [DEVOPS-2235] - Alex.Wu - Added postal code
   validation.
 * 2021-07-03 - [DEVOPS-2236] - Priya.Kumar - Support for
   country-specific addresses.
 * 2021-07-04 - [DEVOPS-2237] - David.Johnson - Minor refactor
   for performance.
 * 2021-07-05 - [DEVOPS-2238] - James.Lee - Fixed typo and
   updated international logic.
 */
@InvocableMethod(callout=true label='Geocode address')
public static List<Coordinates> geocodeAddresses(...)
```

This is a huge antipattern. However, I will play devil's advocate for a while as there are some nuances to why this isn't ideal. The typical argument against these type of comments is that they shouldn't be used because you should use Git instead (for version control). While that's true, saying "you should use Git for that" isn't helpful. I've dedicated the last three years of my Salesforce career to Salesforce DevOps and I can tell you

CHAPTER 5   COMMENTS DON'T LIE, DEVELOPERS DO

there are many teams that aren't yet using version control. Now, it's clear that they should, but because of different circumstances, many developers find themselves working in an environment where version control isn't yet configured. Here are some reasons that come to mind:

- Until recently, the org was very simple and they didn't have developers. There's only a newly hired developer in the team, and they don't know how to set up version control end-to-end.

- Perhaps a company hires a developer as a contractor for a few months, and because of compliance and security reasons, the developer isn't given access to version control.

- Maybe the team does use version control, but they are in a period where they are migrating to using a Salesforce DevOps product like AutoRABIT or Salto, and during that transition, they have to fallback to these type of comments.

One good thing about these comments is that they add an extra layer of business context that wouldn't normally be there. The ticket where the requirement was defined probably has ten times more context than what you could figure out by reading the code alone. Sometimes, this context can make a huge difference, especially when troubleshooting something that was written years ago.

The problem though, is that if they are used everywhere, they can really clutter the code. They can also become outdated very quickly and start "telling lies." It's also not easy to tell which ticket corresponds to which part of the code, something that you could do if you used Git instead. Finally, they may reference tickets from old systems that are no longer available, so the ticket reference isn't helpful anymore (notice in the sample above the first two entries reference a different tracking system).

121

Ultimately, using Git is the correct solution to this problem, but recognizing that that is a decision that may not be in your control, my recommendation is that you use these types of comments with care; **only use them when you think that the added business context outweighs the clutter that the comment creates and as a temporary measure while you work with your team to implement Git.**

5.4 Aha! Comments

Sometimes, you are reading a piece of code that is really hard to understand. After reading for a bit, you may go "Aha! that's what it does!" Right there and then, **add a comment explaining what you just figured out**. Think what comment would've been useful 15 minutes ago when you started to decipher the code. That's a great comment.

However, sometimes refactoring the code would be better than leaving a comment, as the comment is again prone to becoming out of sync with the code as soon as the requirements change. Whether to refactor or leave a comment depends on the complexity of the code, how much you understand it, whether there are good unit tests, etc.

5.5 Why Comments

About four years ago (at the time of this writing), I wrote the code for HappySoup.io, a popular open source library for discovering metadata dependencies in a Salesforce org. Some of the code for finding these dependencies and representing them in a treelike structure is very complex. I remember I spent a few days with a pen and paper writing down the algorithm step by step until I finally cracked it.

CHAPTER 5   COMMENTS DON'T LIE, DEVELOPERS DO

When I finally wrote the code, I had to add comments explaining some of my design decisions. Here's a snippet from the library, which is written in JavaScript:

```
/**
 * This is the the ids of the returned dependencies, for which
   we want to query dependencies one level down
 * For example ClassA > Field1
 * Field1.Id is one of the ids that we want to check
   dependencies for
 * We don't necessarily want to check dependencies for every
   returned dependency.
 *
 * This is because if a dependency has already been queried, we
   don't want to query it again and add its
 * references under yet another node in the hierarchy/tree.
   This also prevents an infinite loop when classes or fields
 * have circular references (i.e ClassA > ClassB > ClassA
   ...infinity)
 */
let nextLevelIds = [];

dependencies.forEach(dep => {

    let alreadyQueried = (idsAlreadyQueried.indexOf(dep.
    id) != -1);

    /**
     * Whether the id has already been queried or not, we still
       want to show this node
     * on the tree, this allows circular references to be
       display at max one level down
     */
```

123

```
    result.push(dep);

    if(alreadyQueried){
        /**
         * if it's been queried already, we mark is as repeated
           and we dont add it to the list of ids
         * to query one level down
         */
        dep.repeated = true;
    }
    else{
        /**
         * if it's not been queried already, then we know it's
           safe to query it for dependencies
         * but only if it's not a dynamic reference
         */
        if(!utils.isDynamicReference(dep)){
            nextLevelIds.push(dep.id);
        }
    }
}
```

Those are some big comments, I admit. But I also admit that if you asked me today **why** the code is doing what it is doing, I'd have no idea. I've been lucky that I've never encountered a bug in this part of the logic, but if I ever do, I feel reassured that these comments will help me remember why I wrote this the way I wrote it four years ago.

These types of comments, which explain the **why** behind certain design decisions—especially when influenced by nonobvious factors like performance, governor limits, or Apex-specific quirks—are some of the most valuable to have.

Likewise, there may be instances where when faced with a limitation of the Salesforce platform, you make a design decision that is outside the norm. It's not a decision that you would normally make. In that scenario,

CHAPTER 5   COMMENTS DON'T LIE, DEVELOPERS DO

a future developer may read the code and think "Why didn't they do x,y,z instead?" This is a great opportunity for a "why not" comment. **Leave a comment explaining why you didn't take the normal path.** This will help ensure future developers don't remove that decision by thinking they know better.

A valid question is whether these large comments shouldn't instead be formal documents in Notion, Confluence, Lucid Chart, or something along those lines. External documentation, like comments, will quickly fall out of sync as the requirements change. In my experience, such documentation is useful for documenting high-level architectural changes, while comments, like the ones in the example above, are better for documenting implementation details.

5.6 Dead Code

A very common (anti) pattern in Salesforce code bases is seeing Apex code that has been completely commented out. You may be reading an Apex class and suddenly you stumble upon something like this:

```
**/***
@AuraEnabled(cacheable=true)
public static Account getSingleAccount() {
    return [
        SELECT Id, Name, Phone, Type
        FROM Account
        WITH USER_MODE
        LIMIT 1
    ];
}***/**
```

125

CHAPTER 5   COMMENTS DON'T LIE, DEVELOPERS DO

This is known as dead code. This code that is never called, not referenced anywhere, never executed, etc. It just sits there for years. Nobody dares to touch it or delete it because they fear someone may need it. I admit I have felt this fear before. Now, there are multiple reasons developers create dead code.

The most common reason is the code was needed, but due to changing requirements, it is no longer needed. And so, rather than deleting the code, they comment it out just in case they need it in the future. One problem with these comments is they reinforce the idea that somehow our future selves won't be as smart as we are today. If we were able to write the code today, why do we doubt that we can figure it out again in the future?

Another reason developers may do this is that they aren't using version control, as explained in Section 5.3. If you find yourself in this circumstance, then I understand why this type of comments may be common, though they are not ideal.

Finally, developers may choose to do this because the code is still in development and not ready for production deployment. However, the code lives in a class that has other changes that *are* ready for deployment. Because they don't want the in-progress code to make it to production, they comment it out. An alternative approach to solve this scenario is to use feature flags.

Feature flags can be used to turn code off without having to modify the code itself. For example, you may use the open source Apex library called `salesforce-feature-flags` to do something like this:

```
FeatureFlags flags = new FeatureFlags();

if(flags.evaluate('enhancedQuoteEditor').isEnabled()){
    //run the new code (still in development)
}
```

```
else{
  //run the existing code
}
```

This way, all the code inside the `if` condition will only run if you enable this feature via custom metadata types or custom permissions. As long as the feature isn't enabled, you can safely deploy the code to production with the confidence that it will not be executed; this is much better than commenting out the code. You could argue that code behind a feature flag is dead code, and it is, but only for a period of time while the feature is in development. Once the feature is fully released, you can remove the feature flag and let the new code run.

Now, what if you find dead code that is indeed not needed by anyone anymore? Do the decent thing. **Bury it.**

5.7 Funny Comments

A code base I worked on years ago had a class that started with a loud comment:

```
// Oh god I hate this code!
```

While I don't recommend that you leave this type of comments, the comment was actually useful because it helped me understand that this was a painful area of the code base. This led to a conversation with my manager, and eventually, we refactored the code and made it much better and easier to follow (and he stopped hating it).

5.8 ApexDoc Comments

ApexDoc used to be an open source project by the Salesforce Foundation team that aim to replicate the functionality of JavaDocs, a standard for adding comments to methods to explain their structure. Many Salesforce code bases are riddled with these type of comments, which look like this:

```
/***************************************************************
    * @description Returns field describe data
    * @param objectName the name of the object to look up
    * @param fieldName the name of the field to look up
    * @return the describe field result for the given field
    * @example
    * Account a = new Account();
    */
    public static Schema.DescribeFieldResult
    getFieldDescribe(String objectName, String fieldName) {
```

These type of comments can be really noisy. They are especially noisy when they just state what the method signature already tells you, like this:

```
/**
* This method is used to insert an account record.
* @param acc The account record to insert.
* @return The ID of the inserted account record.
*/
public static Id insertAccount(account acc) {
  insert acc;
  return acc.Id;
}
```

This comment does not add any value as it only repeats what the code clearly does. Also, like I said earlier, once the requirement changes, if developers don't update this comment, it will be out of sync.

That said, these comments can be valuable in open source Apex libraries, where you may have multiple contributors and you want to make it easier for others to be able to contribute and use your library. This can work well because these type of comments are typically shown as a help pop-up in most modern IDEs, which makes the code a type of on-the-spot documentation.

Figure 5-1 is an example of such pop-up from a JavaScript library that interacts with the Salesforce API.

Figure 5-1. A comment displayed as a help pop-up in VSCode

This is the only redeemable quality of these comments. My recommendation is to only use them when you are indeed creating some type of Apex library that will have many different consumers.

5.9 To-Do Comments

To-do comments are used when you want to remind yourself or other developers that a design decision is temporary and that it will be refactored in the future. Here's an example from the Amoss open source Apex library:

```
for ( String thisParameterName : parameters.keySet() ) {
```

CHAPTER 5   COMMENTS DON'T LIE, DEVELOPERS DO

```
// TODO: is there a way of removing the if from
   here.  Feels uncomfortable
if ( parameterDefiner == null ) {
    parameterDefiner = withParameterNamed(
    thisParameterName ).setTo( parameters.get(
    thisParameterName ) );
} else {
    parameterDefiner = parameterDefiner.withParameterNamed(
    thisParameterName ).setTo( parameters.get(
    thisParameterName ) );
}
}
```

To-do comments are useful when you don't have time to implement the best solution or you recognize that your knowledge of the problem domain is still evolving. Of course, like any other programming construct, they can quickly become old and irrelevant.

Some argue that using to-do comments is an antipattern and suggest logging tasks in issue tracking tools like Jira or GitHub instead. However, the choice depends on the use case. In my role as a Product Manager at AutoRABIT, I don't create tickets for every small refactor my team does. While some believe all work should be tracked in tools like Kanban boards, it's not always practical for minor to-dos and refactoring tasks.

Another example if the Salesforce CLI, which is open source and uses GitHub for tracking issues. I downloaded the source code and searched for the word "todo" in my code editor and found many such comments as seen in Figure 5-2.

CHAPTER 5   COMMENTS DON'T LIE, DEVELOPERS DO

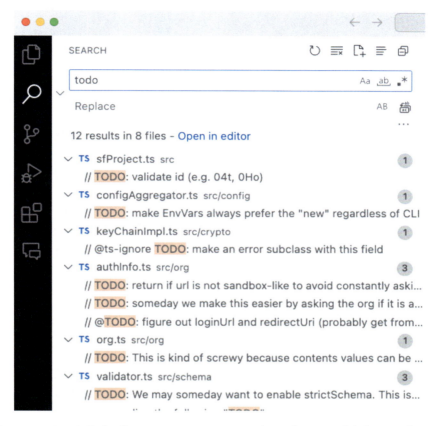

Figure 5-2. A Salesforce open source project shows a high number of "todo" comments

I'm not giving you this example to say "see, Salesforce does it, so it's ok"—but instead to show that it is common and that there's a place for them in software development.

Finally, there are many extensions for VSCode that act on to-do comments. These can be to automatically generate documentation from them or to highlight them in a different color so they stand out. See Figure 5-3.

131

CHAPTER 5   COMMENTS DON'T LIE, DEVELOPERS DO

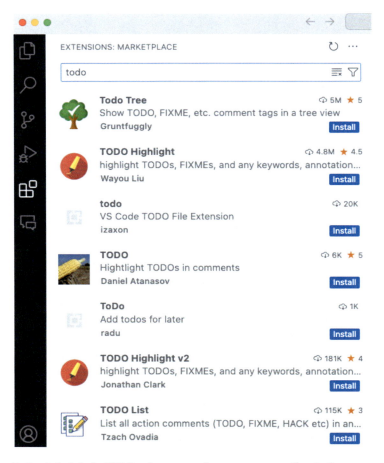

Figure 5-3. *Multiple VSCode extensions support "todo" comments*

Again, the fact that so many extensions exist and that many of them have thousands of downloads shows that this is a common practice.

5.10 Reference Comments

Sometimes, you can use comments as a way to reference external documentation that is relevant to a specific design decision. Here's another example from HappySoup.io, written in JavaScript:

async function readMetadata(type,fullNames){

> //https://developer.salesforce.com/docs/atlas.en-us.api_meta.meta/api_meta/meta_readMetadata.htm
> const MAX_READMETADATA_LIMIT = 10;
>
> let batches = splitInBatchesOf(fullNames,MAX_READMETADATA_LIMIT);

...

Here, I implemented a wrapper around the `readMetadata` API call from the Metadata API, which enforces a limit of ten metadata items that can be read at any given time. Even though MAX_READMETADATA_LIMIT is a pretty descriptive name for this limit (instead of using a "magic number," see Chapter 2), I left a comment with the link to the official API documentation that explains what this limit is.

I did this because I don't think it's obvious from the variable name that this is not a limit **I** am imposing but one that is being imposed on me by the Salesforce platform. Rather than leaving a huge comment explaining that, the small comment pointing to the docs does the job.

Of course, you could argue that if the URL to the Salesforce docs changes, then my comment becomes invalid, but at least this would make the next developer think that this limit is probably documented somewhere, and it would encourage them to do some searching to understand it more.

5.11 Implementation Comments

Sometimes, when I'm implementing something that is somewhat complex, I write some comments first just to write down the logic or algorithm in plain English. This is helpful because I can forget about the code for a moment and focus on making sure that I really understand the problem I'm solving.

You could also use a napkin or a Notion or Quip document; however, I find that those notes work best when they are in the context of the code they are supporting.

Of course, once you actually write the code, you should delete the comments (unless they fall into the categories of useful comments we've explored in the previous sections).

5.12 Conclusion

Comments can lie, but so can any other programming constructs or pieces of documentation. That doesn't mean you shouldn't use them. We've seen plenty of examples where comments can be incredibly helpful in reducing complexity from an Apex code base.

CHAPTER 6

Null, Validations, and Guard Clauses

I call it my billion-dollar mistake. It was the invention of the null reference in 1965.

—Tony Hoare

Many validations in Apex are done simply because of a misunderstanding of the differences between null and empty. If you understand the differences well, you will write cleaner code.

6.1 Null

In my experience, there's confusion among developers about the difference between null and empty. A variable is null when memory hasn't been allocated to it or when it's been explicitly initialized to null, for example:

```
String myName;//no value is assigned, therefore it's null
String city = null; //explicitly set to null
```

CHAPTER 6   NULL, VALIDATIONS, AND GUARD CLAUSES

Calling methods on a null variable or passing a null variable to an Apex standard method will throw the dreaded `NullPointerException` (NPE for short), for example:

```
List<Account> accountsToUpdate;
accountsToUpdate.size();//will throw a NPE
```

Or

```
Account acct;
Database.insert(acct);//will throw a NPE
```

The exception occurs because there's no object on which to actually call the method. Let's review different strategies for getting around null values.

6.2 Safe Navigation Operator

The ? operator in Apex can be used to avoid redundant checks for nulls. Consider the following code:

```
User user; //null by default
String providedUsername = user.username;// will throw NPE
```

Because user is null by default, we can't call the username property on it without getting an NPE. You could attempt to avoid the NPE by doing the following:

```
String providedUsername;
if(user != null){
    providedUsername = user.username;
}
```

CHAPTER 6   NULL, VALIDATIONS, AND GUARD CLAUSES

The `if` condition ensures that we only access the username property if user is not null. In contrast, with the safe navigation operator, you could do this instead:

```
User user;
String providedUsername = user?.username;
```

This code runs successfully without throwing any exceptions because the ? operator makes it so that the call to the username property is made **only** if `user` isn't null. If user isn't null, providedUsername will be initialized to user.username. The benefit here is that we don't need nested logic inside of an if condition.

However, this comes at a cost. This operator, ironically, **returns null if the object it is applied to also null**. In our example above, because `user` is null, `providedUsername` ends up being null as well as there's no way to access the `username` property. So, we have avoided an NPE, but now, we have a string variable that has a null value. I argue that we've simply moved the NPE later in our code, for example:

```
String providedUsername = user?.username;

//NPE because providedUsername is null
if(providedUsername.contains('pablogonzalez.io')){
    //do something
}
```

Read the code above a few times. We've escaped from the NPE once, but it comes back just a few lines of code later. I encourage you to pause here and think about this scenario. What did we really achieve?

To get around this, you may think the ? operator can be used again, like this:

```
//add ? operator
if(providedUsername?.contains('pablogonzalez.io')){...}
```

137

However, this still throws an NPE because it's equivalent to doing

```
Boolean check = null;
if(check){
    //throws NPE
}
```

The correct way to write this condition without getting an NPE is like this:

```
if(providedUsername?.contains('pablogonzalez.io') == true){...}
```

This works because the expression is equivalent to saying `if(null == true)`, which is a valid expression. In the end, the entire code would look like this:

```
User user;//initialised somewhere else
String providedUsername = user?.username;
```

```
if(providedUsername?.contains('pablogonzalez.io') == true){...}
```

There are a few problems with this code. First, we have this looming uncertainty that at any time, `user` or `providedUsername` may be null. The `?` operator is supposed to save us from redundant checks, but this code actually has redundant checks for null. Also, we are forced to use `== true` along with `providedUsername.contains(...)`. In my opinion, this isn't too clean.

Finally, the `?` operator can easily be misused, and as we saw above, it simply delays an inevitable NPE. In other words, **we move the problem of null down the line, but we eventually have to deal with it**. It is for these reasons that I rarely use this operator.

What I would prefer is to simply exit the method as early as possible if something is not right. For example:

```
User user;
```

```
//get out of here as fast as possible!
if(user == null) return;

//normal processing continues here
String providedUsername = user.username;
```

Notice that I've inverted the boolean logic. In the original version of this code, we had

```
if(user != null){
    //access `user` properties
}
```

And now we are saying

```
//get out of here if it's null
if(user == null) return;
```

This way, we know that any code below this line will not be dealing with null objects. We've effectively avoided redundant checks for null. This pattern is known as a guard clause, and I will come back it later.

6.3 Null Coalescing

Another way to deal with nulls in Apex is with the null coalescing operator (??). This can also be used to avoid explicit and verbose null checks. Suppose you have the following code that assigns the account `BillingCity` to a contact's `MailingCity` field:

```
Account acct = new Account(BillingCity='Dublin');
Contact cont = new Contact();

if(acct.BillingCity != null) {
    cont.MailingCity = acct.BillingCity;
}
```

```
else {
    cont.MailingCity = 'Default';
}
```

If the account `BillingCity` isn't null, we use that; otherwise, we assign a `Default` value. This `if/else` can be removed by using the null coalescing operator, like this:

```
Account acct = new Account(BillingCity='Dublin');
Contact cont = new Contact();

cont.MailingCity = acct.BillingCity ?? 'default';
```

This is one operator that I do use quite often, because unlike the safe navigation operator, it does something useful if a value is null, i.e., you can use it to assign default values. It also makes the code a lot less verbose and, therefore, clean.

Now, you can combine the safe navigation and null coalescing operators. Suppose we have another version of the original code where we check if the account variable is not null:

```
if(acct != null) {
    if(acct.BillingCity != null) {
        cont.MailingCity = acct.BillingCity;
    }
    else {
        cont.MailingCity = 'Default';
    }
}
else {
    cont.MailingCity = 'Default';
}
```

CHAPTER 6   NULL, VALIDATIONS, AND GUARD CLAUSES

This can be replaced with the following:

cont.MailingCity = acct?.BillingCity ?? 'default';

Whether this code is cleaner than the original is somewhat subject to interpretation. Some argue that the original one is very explicit; there's no room for uncertainty about what it does. On the other hand, the second one is a little weird to look at and is not obvious it its intention.

Others, like me, argue that **you should know your programming language of choice well**. If you are a Salesforce developer, you must understand Apex well and that includes being able to read, parse, and understand statements like the above.

6.4 Empty

Now that we understand null values better, we can look at empty values. An empty variable has memory allocated to it, but the value is simply empty. We can look at the same examples we saw on Section 5.1 but using empty instead of null:

List<Account> accountsToUpdate = new List<Account>();
accountsToUpdate.size();//*safe*

Account acct = new Account();
Database.insert(acct);//*safe*

Acting on empty variables will **not** throw an NPE.

Note   You will get a DML exception in the example above because you can't insert an account without a name, but the point is that the variable is not null, simply empty, and so the exception that is thrown is completely different.

6.7 Validating Maps

When using maps, you will get a null value if you pass a key that doesn't exist. Calling a method on that value will throw an NPE.

```
Map<String,String> namesByCity = new Map<String,String>();

namesByCity.get('notInTheMap').trim(); //NPE!!
```

For this reason, you should check if the key exists in the map before you retrieve it, like this:

```
Map<String,String> namesByCity = new Map<String,String>();

if(namesByCity.containsKey('notInTheMap')){
    namesByCity.get('notInTheMap').trim();//safe
}
```

The exception to this rule is if you are iterating over the keys of a map to iterate over the values, like this:

```
Map<Id, Case> newCasesById = new Map<Id, Case>(
    [SELECT Id, Subject, Status FROM Case WHERE Status = 'New']
);
// Iterate over the keys of the map
for (Id caseId : newCasesById.keySet()) {

    //safe to do because it's very unlikely that
    //the record isn't in the map
    Case caseRecord = newCasesById.get(caseId);

}
```

CHAPTER 6   NULL, VALIDATIONS, AND GUARD CLAUSES

In this scenario, because the map was created by passing the results of a SOQL query, you can be sure that the record that maps to a specific Id is not null. However, if you didn't create the map and it was passed to you from another method, then you should definitely check if the key exists before you retrieve it.

6.8 Validating If Lists Are Empty

Validating if a list is not empty before proceeding is very common in Apex programming. And the most common pattern is checking if a list is empty right before executing a DML operation, like this:

```
//DML only if the list is not empty
if(newAccounts.size() > 0){
    insert newAccounts;
}
```

There are multiple reasons developers do this check:

- Some may misunderstand the difference between empty and null, so they do the check to prevent an NPE.

- Some think that Salesforce will consume unnecessary DML calls, so by checking if the list is empty before issuing the DML call, we save precious governor limits.

- For performance.

For the first reason, we have already seen that there are no exceptions if you try to insert an **empty** list, so this check isn't needed.

For the second reason, it turns out that Apex is smart enough to do the check for you. As a result, the following code compiles and runs successfully **without affecting the number of DML calls**.

CHAPTER 6 NULL, VALIDATIONS, AND GUARD CLAUSES

```
insert new List<Account>();
update new List<Account>();
upsert new List<Account>();
delete new List<Account>();
```

I encourage you to run the above code and check the debug logs. You will see no DML calls were actually executed. Based on my research, in the distant past, Salesforce did consume DML calls when doing a DML operation on an empty list. I've gone as far as version API 22.0 (the oldest one I can use as the time of this writing; older ones have been deprecated), and I haven't been able to reproduce the scenario where DML calls are consumed. In any case, let's be clear: **executing a DML operation against an empty list will not consume governor limits.**

The only valid reason to do this check is performance. It turns out that letting Apex do the check for you natively has some performance implications. To understand this problem better, I created three methods, each of which use a different way of validating if a list is not empty/null before executing a DML operation. For all of these, I track how much CPU time is consumed.

This one checks the CPU time consumed when checking with List.size().

```
public static void withSizeCheck(){
    List<Account> accounts = new List<Account>();

    for(Integer i = 0; i < 100000; i++){

        if(accounts.size() > 0){
            update accounts;
        }
    }

    System.debug(LoggingLevel.Error,'Checking size() took '+Limits.getCpuTime()+' ms');
}
```

CHAPTER 6   NULL, VALIDATIONS, AND GUARD CLAUSES

This one checks the CPU time when using `List.isEmpty()`.

```
public static void withEmptyCheck(){
    List<Account> accounts = new List<Account>();

    for(Integer i = 0; i < 100000; i++){
        if(!accounts.isEmpty()){
            update accounts;
        }
    }

    System.debug(LoggingLevel.Error,'Checking isEmpty() took '+
    Limits.getCpuTime()+ ' ms');
}
```

And this one lets Apex do the check natively.

```
public static void withoutCheck(){
    List<Account> accounts = new List<Account>();

    for(Integer i = 0; i < 100000; i++){
        update accounts;
    }

    System.debug(LoggingLevel.Error,'Without check took '+Limits.getCpuTime()+ ' ms');

}
```

I ran this in the developer console with minimum debug levels, and the results were as follows:

DML Insert

Checking size() took 59 ms
Checking isEmpty() took 52 ms

147

CHAPTER 6   NULL, VALIDATIONS, AND GUARD CLAUSES

Without check took 700 ms

DML Update

Checking size() took 67 ms
Checking isEmpty() took 64 ms
Without check took 727 ms

As we can see, letting Apex do the check natively consumes **10 times more the CPU** than if you do the check yourself using `size()` or `isEmpty()`. Now, ten times more is a lot. For small Salesforce implementations, this will only equate to a few more milliseconds of processing time. However, once your org reaches the level where you have multiple teams working on it, dozens of managed packages, etc., CPU will become a concern.

From a purely aesthetic point of view, my personal preference would be to not do the check and let Apex do it itself. I like using native language features and not reinventing the wheel. However, I can't ignore the fact that this will become a problem over time as CPU starts adding up. For that reason, my recommendation is that **you always check if the list isn't empty before you execute a DML operation.**

Finally, when checking if a list is empty, I recommend you use `isEmpty()` over `size() > 0`. This may come down to personal preference, but to me, `isEmpty()` does what it says it does, and there's no room for error. I always need to translate the `size() > 0` expression to "is not empty" in my head, and I prefer to avoid that extra second of cognitive load.

This brings an interesting question: how do you consistently apply this pattern (checking that a list isn't empty) across all DML operations and across all developers or teams in your org? One way is to always use a DML wrapper class like the one we created in Chapter 2. Here's a reminder of what it looked like:

CHAPTER 6 NULL, VALIDATIONS, AND GUARD CLAUSES

```
DML dmlOperation = new DML()
         .setOperation(DML.Operation.Inserts)
         .setRecords(accounts)
         .setAllowPartialSuccess(false);

dmlOperation.execute();
```

If everyone on your team uses this class (or similar) for DML operations, you can then add the check for empty lists inside the execute method, as follows:

```
public void execute(){

    DMLExecutable operation = ...

    if(!records.isEmpty()){
        operation.execute(
            this.records,
            this.allowPartialSuccess
        );
    }
}
```

Because the DMLExecutable variable can represent an insert, update, delete, or any other DML operation at runtime (thanks for polymorphism), you can ensure that no matter what DML operation is being requested, it will never be executed on empty lists. This way you save precious CPU time, and your team doesn't have to worry about remembering to use this pattern.

CHAPTER 6   NULL, VALIDATIONS, AND GUARD CLAUSES

6.9 Validating If Lists Are Null

A variation of this list validation pattern is checking if the list is null, which is valid and necessary to prevent NPEs. However, this can be misused and lead to issues.

> **Note** For the following example, assume that **we** create the nonempty list, and **we** execute the DML insert; in other words, the list is not passed to us as a method parameter; all the code below happens inside the same method.

```
//could be empty if there are no accounts, but not null
List<Account> newAccounts = [SELECT Id From Account];

//some processing here

if(newAccounts != null && !newAccounts.isEmpty()){
    update newAccounts;
}
```

Here, we instantiate the list to a non-null value but later check if it's not null. Why should it be null if we just instantiated it? There are three possible answers:

- We are checking against null "just to be sure."
- We want to save CPU time by not doing DMLs on empty lists (see Section 5.5), but because we don't really understand the difference between null and empty, we are checking against null "just to be sure."
- In case the list became null somewhere in between its instantiation and the DML call.

CHAPTER 6   NULL, VALIDATIONS, AND GUARD CLAUSES

The first too reasons aren't valid reasons to do this check. If we are to write clean code, we must understand the difference between null and empty. As for the third reason, if the variable was instantiated and later became null, that could be a bug. Think about it, you started with a non-null variable, and then, some code, either yours or someone else's, made it null. Is that expected behavior? Or is it a bug?

So what I recommend is that if **you** instantiate a list (it wasn't passed to you as method parameter) and later you do a DML on it, **don't check if it's not null**. Consider the scenario where you just have a simple if statement with no else counterpart, like this:

```
if(newAccounts != null && !newAccounts.isEmpty()){
    update newAccounts;
}
// no "else" statement
```

In this scenario, because there's no else block, you don't have a place to run alternative logic if the list is indeed null. This means, you will never know that the list is null. This DML operation will simply be skipped, and you will not know why. On the other hand, if you let the NPE happen, then you know something is wrong, and you can figure out how and why the list became null. This may be a controversial recommendation, but worst case, you will get an NPE in production one day and this gives you the opportunity to find out how and why the list became null before the DML call. With this information, you can fix the root cause rather than letting the code silently fail.

Note   The above recommendation may only be feasible if you work for an in-house development team where you can quickly respond to the error. If you are developing a managed package for customers to use in their org, you must avoid NPEs.

151

CHAPTER 6   NULL, VALIDATIONS, AND GUARD CLAUSES

This doesn't mean you should never check against null. If you have a method that takes a list, **you should validate that it isn't null as soon as possible**, for example:

```
public void notifyOwners(List<Account> accounts) {

    //15 lines of code here

    // if this list is null, you executed
    // 15 lines of code for no reason
    update accounts;

}
```

Instead, you should do the following:

```
public void notifyOwners(List<Account> accounts) {

    if(accounts == null){
        throw new IllegalArgumentException('Accounts list
        cannot be null');
    }

    //15 lines of code here

    update accounts;
}
```

This is again a guard clause as we saw earlier, and in this particular example, it's also a manifestation of the "fail fast" design pattern. The code throws an error and exits immediately, rather than delaying the error further down the stack trace.

6.10 Guard Clauses and Multiple Returns

We've seen two examples of guard classes in previous sections, so it's time to give them a proper definition. A guard clause is a piece of code at the beginning of a method that checks if a condition is **not** met. If the condition isn't met, the guard clause causes the method to exit early, preventing the main logic from being executed. Consider the following example that does not implement a guard clause:

```
public void validateAccounts(List<Account> accounts){

    if(accounts?.isEmpty() == false){
        //main logic starts here
        //now that we know the list is not empty or null.
    }

}
```

In this code, you proceed with the main logic only when you know the it's safe to do something with the accounts variable. However, now the main logic is nested inside of an `if` statement. If we assume that the main logic will have its own set of `if` statements, then this means we'll end up with deeply nested logic. One way to get rid of this additional nesting is to **invert the if condition** and turn it into a guard clause, like this:

```
public void validateAccounts(List<Account> accounts){

        if(accounts?.isEmpty() == true) return;
        //main logic starts here without nesting
}
```

153

CHAPTER 6   NULL, VALIDATIONS, AND GUARD CLAUSES

This basically says that if the list is null or empty, we should simply exit the method as soon as possible to avoid further processing. Now, the main logic that follows is not nested. An interesting question that arises is whether this should throw an exception instead of simply returning, like this:

```
public void validateAccounts(List<Account> accounts){

    if(accounts?.isEmpty() == true){
        throw new IllegalArgumentException('Accounts list is
        empty');
    }

}
```

Both versions serve the same purpose: exit the method as soon as a condition isn't met. For now, I encourage you to pause and think which version is more appropriate. I will come back to this example and give concrete guidelines on when to throw exceptions in a future chapter.

Like all things in this book, guard clauses can be misused. One valid question you may have is whether you should always return early if a condition isn't met. Consider the following example (don't pay too much attention to whether this makes sense from a business logic point of view):

```
public static Boolean isAccountValid(Account account){

    if(String.isBlank(account.Industry)){
        return false;
    }

    if(account.AnnualRevenue < 100){
        return false;
    }
```

154

```
    if(account.NumberOfEmployees < 1){
        return false;
    }

    return true;
}
```

In this example, we return early as soon as one of the invalid conditions isn't met. If none of the conditions are met, we return true as we assume the account is valid. This results in multiple return statements. If we were to apply this pattern to a very complex piece of business logic, we could easily end up with ten or more return statements scattered around the logic. **This would make it very difficult to understand when a method stops executing.**

We could refactor this so that it only returns at a single place, like this:

```
public static Boolean isAccountValid(Account account){

    Boolean isValid = true;

    if(String.isBlank(account.Industry)){
        isValid = false;
    }

    if(account.AnnualRevenue < 100){
        isValid = false;
    }

    if(account.NumberOfEmployees < 1){
        isValid = false;
    }

    return isValid;
}
```

CHAPTER 6   NULL, VALIDATIONS, AND GUARD CLAUSES

We start by assuming that the account is valid and store that in the `isValid` variable. The `if` conditions can turn that variable to `false` if necessary. At the end, we simply return the `isValid` variable, without caring whether it's `true` or `false`. This is easier to read because you don't need to think that at any random point, the method will stop executing.

However, multiple returns can indeed be very useful in making code easier to read and getting rid of deeply nested logic. Consider the following example:

```
public static void syncAccount(Account account) {
    if (account != null) {
        if (String.isNotBlank(account.Industry)) {
            if (account.AnnualRevenue > 100) {
                if (account.NumberOfEmployees > 0) {
                    // Main logic for processing
                       the account
                    if (account.AccountType ==
                    'Customer') {
                        NetSuiteAPI.syncAccount(account);
                    }
                    account.Processed__c = true;
                    update account;
                }
            }
        }
    }
}
```

Here, the main logic (syncing with NetSuite) happens five levels deep. If you've been developing in Apex for a while, this pattern surely brings a lot of memories. We could refactor this to exit early if any of the conditions aren't met, like this:

156

CHAPTER 6   NULL, VALIDATIONS, AND GUARD CLAUSES

```
public static void syncAccount(Account account) {

    //You could group all these booleans into one.
    //Seeing them 1 by 1 helps you see the pattern
    if (account == null) return;
    if (String.isBlank(account.Industry)) return;
    if (account.AnnualRevenue <= 100) return;
    if (account.NumberOfEmployees <= 0) return;

    // no longer buried 5 levels deep!
    if (account.AccountType == 'Customer') {
        NetSuiteAPI.syncAccount(account);
    }

    account.Processed__c = true;
    update account;
}
```

This is basically multiple guard clauses stack on top of each other, which, by definition, results in multiple return statements. This is a perfectly valid use case. Where you should be careful is if the multiple return statements are **scattered** all over the place, like this (this is pseudocode):

```
if(someLogic){

    someOtherLogic();

    if(someCondition) return;

    otherLogicHere();

    moreLogic();

    if(someOtherCondition) return;

    if(ifTrue){
```

157

```
        if(isTrueAsWell){
            if(badCondition) return;
            keepGoing();
        }
    }
}
```

In this example, you may find return statements in places you wouldn't expect them to be, which means the method can exit at almost any point. This makes it harder to understand the end-to-end flow of the logic.

You probably have noticed that I'm mixing multiple topics here:

- Returning early when a condition isn't met
- Whether we should have multiple returns

It's impossible to separate these two topics because, by definition, the guard clause introduces an additional return statement that wouldn't normally be there. I've also mixed the pros and cons of each approach because that's most likely the kind of back-and-forth you will experience (in your head) when you write code that could be refactored to use guard clauses.

Let's finish by looking at some concrete guidelines:

- Use guard clauses (early returns) at the beginning of a method if certain conditions aren't met.
- It's acceptable to use multiple guard clauses at the beginning of the method.
- If possible, refactor your code to minimize **unnecessary** return statements, but don't avoid multiple returns if they make the code clearer and easier to follow and if they can help getting rid of deeply nested logic.

CHAPTER 6   NULL, VALIDATIONS, AND GUARD CLAUSES

6.11 Should You Return Null

A common source of debate is whether you should ever return null; let's look at this simple method as an example:

```
public User findUser(String username) {

    //some logic here to find the user

    return foundUser;

}
```

What should this method return if the user is **not** found? I encourage you to pause and think about it for a while before you keep reading.

If we return null, the caller will have to check if the return value is not null before doing something with that value; otherwise, an NPE will be thrown, for example:

```
User existingUser = findUser('testuser@company.com');
```
```
if(existingUser != null){
    //do something with the user
}
```

Another option would be return an empty User object, like this (note the below is pseudocode):

```
public User findUser(String username) {

    User foundUser = new User();

    if(weFoundTheUser){
        foundUser = theUser;
    }
```

CHAPTER 6   NULL, VALIDATIONS, AND GUARD CLAUSES

```
    //this may be empty
    return foundUser;
}
```

If the `if` condition is not true, we will return `foundUser` as it was first instantiated, which is a non-null but empty object. In this case, the caller still needs to check if the User isn't empty, for example:

```
User existingUser = findUser('testuser@company.com');

if(existingUser?.getPopulatedFieldsAsMap().isEmpty() == false){
    //do something with the user
}
```

Here, we use the `getPopulatedFieldsAsMap()` method from the `sObject` class to get a map of all the fields that have been populated in memory for this object. If the map is not empty, then the user was found. This is not a good pattern though as it forces the caller to mix different levels of abstraction and to know internal details about the logic inside of `findUser()`. It's also not guaranteed to work because default field values can be present in the `sObject` if you create it with the `newSObject` method of the `sObjectType` class instead of the `new` operator. For example:

```
Boolean loadDefaultValues = true;

User existingUser = (User)User.sObjectType.newSObject(null,
**loadDefaultValues**);

if(existingUser?.getPopulatedFieldsAsMap().isEmpty() == false){
    System.debug('user is NOT empty');
}
else{
    System.debug('user is empty');
}
```

CHAPTER 6   NULL, VALIDATIONS, AND GUARD CLAUSES

In the above example, `user is NOT empty` is printed to the debug log because default values are loaded into memory.

The last option would be to throw an exception, like this:

```
public User findUser(String username) {
    if(weDidntFindTheUser){
        throw new NoDataFoundException('User not found');
    }
}
```

In this case, the caller would have to wrap the call to `findUser()` inside a `try/catch` block, like this:

```
try {
    User existingUser = findUser('testuser@company.com');
} catch (NoDataFoundException e) {
    // log the exception or rethrow it
}
```

We can see that no matter what approach we take, **the caller will always have to check if the returned value is what it actually expected**. There is no way around this.

For this particular example, I think returning null makes sense because you asked for a value that isn't there. This would follow convention used in maps, where using the `Map.get(key)` method returns null if the key doesn't exist in the map.

On the other hand, if the method is meant to return multiple records, then returning an empty list would be more appropriate because it follows the convention used in SOQL queries, for example:

```
// if there are no accounts, the list will be empty
// not null
List<Account> accounts = [SELECT Id FROM Account];
```

161

Therefore, the following code would make sense; we return a list that may be empty.

```
public List<User> findUsers(Set<String> usernames) {
    List<User> users = [SELECT Id, Name FROM User WHERE
    Username IN :usernames];
    //this returns an empty list if no users are found
    return users;
}
```

What is the conclusion then? Should we return null? I recommend you follow these guidelines:

- Return null if a method is supposed to find something and that object does not exist.

- Throw an exception if an exceptional condition occurs—not finding an object is usually not exceptional.

- If a method is meant to return a list, return an empty list of the records that cannot be populated for whatever reason; this follows the SOQL convention.

6.12 Clean Validations

When validating parameters, it is better to do so in a separate method as validation is a lower level of abstraction than the method acting on those parameters. We saw an example of this in previous chapters:

```
...createUser(String firstName, String lastName, String
    username) {
    //throws exception if any of the parameters are missing
```

CHAPTER 6   NULL, VALIDATIONS, AND GUARD CLAUSES

```
    validateParams(firstName, lastName, username);
...
```

Here's what the `validateParams()` method looks like:

```
private static void validateParams(...) {
    if (String.isBlank(firstName) ||
        String.isBlank(lastName) ||
        String.isBlank(username)) {
        throw new IllegalArgumentException('Missing required
        user information');
    }
}
```

This keeps the parent method clean and operating at a single level of abstraction.

6.13 Conclusion

You should always validate that a list is not empty before executing a DML operation; it will save you precious CPU time. Consider using `!isEmpty()` over `size() > 0`. If you check against null, make sure you know what to do if the variable is indeed null. In most scenarios, throwing an exception and failing fast is appropriate. Validate parameters in a separate method to keep levels of abstraction separate and to benefit from shorter methods.

CHAPTER 7

Cascading Failures in Trigger Boundaries

At the end of the day, it's important that your requirements drive the architecture rather than the other way around.

—Dan Appleman

In the previous chapter, we discussed several techniques for validating parameters and variables. The whole reason for doing these type of validations is to prevent errors or exceptions in our code. However, there are some types of errors and exceptions that are much harder to reason about, especially because they require a deep understanding of Apex's transaction model. In this chapter, we explore how to prevent cascading failures in Apex triggers.

7.1 The Exception Dilemma

Note Throughout this chapter, I will refer to Apex transactions using terms like **processes**, **subprocesses**, **parent processes**, and **threads**. These terms help provide additional context about the structure and behavior of Apex transactions. While they may

CHAPTER 7　CASCADING FAILURES IN TRIGGER BOUNDARIES

not be Salesforce-specific, they are common in broader software engineering, and using them will help you better understand both Apex and general software development concepts.

All the code you've seen so far in this book omits exception handling. This is on purpose because as we'll see shortly, how and **where** you handle exceptions is a complex topic that deserves a whole chapter.

To illustrate the complexity that exceptions bring to an Apex code base, consider the scenario where over a period of one year, the business requested to implement the following three requirements:

- When an account owner is changed, the opportunities are reassigned to the new owner.
- When an opportunity is assigned to a user, a task is created for them.
- When a task is created, we increase the open task count field on the owner's user record

Consider as well that **not all requirements were requested at the same time,** and each of them was implemented by a different developer.

To avoid showing too much code, I will only show the stack trace of each operation. The methods are being executed from top to bottom:

```
(when)                  (do this)
Account owner change > reassign opportunities
Trigger.AccountTrigger
Class.AccountTriggerHandler.afterUpdate
Class.AccountTriggerHandler.onOwnerChange
Class.AccountOwnership.reassignRelatedRecords
Class.AccountOwnership.reassignOpptys (executes a DML on Opportunity)
```

CHAPTER 7   CASCADING FAILURES IN TRIGGER BOUNDARIES

(when)   (do this)
Opportunity assigned > create task
Trigger.OpportunityTrigger
Class.OpportunityTriggerHandler.afterUpdate
Class.OpportunityTriggerHandler.notifyNewOwners (executes a DML on Task)

(when)   (do this)
Task created > increment task count
Trigger.TaskTrigger
Class.TaskTriggerHandler.afterInsert
Class.TaskTriggerHandler.increaseOpenTaskCount (executes a DML on User)

You may have noticed that even though each requirement is independent, **they will all run in sequence when the first one is triggered**. For example, if an account's owner is updated:

- The opportunities will be reassigned to the new owner.
- This triggers the creation of a task for the new owner.
- This triggers the update on the user record to reflect the count of open tasks.

In other words, when an account owner's is updated, the path of the code is as follows:

Trigger.AccountTrigger
Class.AccountTriggerHandler.afterUpdate
Class.AccountTriggerHandler.onOwnerChange
Class.AccountOwnership.reassignRelatedRecords
Class.AccountOwnership.reassignOpptys (executes a DML on Opportunity)

167

CHAPTER 7   CASCADING FAILURES IN TRIGGER BOUNDARIES

Trigger.OpportunityTrigger
Class.OpportunityTriggerHandler.afterUpdate
Class.OpportunityTriggerHandler.notifyNewOwners (executes a DML on Task)

Trigger.TaskTrigger
Class.TaskTriggerHandler.afterInsert
Class.TaskTriggerHandler.increaseOpenTaskCount (executes a DML on User)

Again, even though all three requirements are independent, when the first one is triggered, the rest of them will follow.

Now, let's say that the business now wants to make sure that each user has a fair workload, and so, the number of open tasks assigned to one user should not exceed four open tasks. This requirement was then implemented as a simple validation rule on the user object. With this validation rule in place, the last action on this stack trace *can* throw a DML exception, like this:

Trigger.AccountTrigger
Class.AccountTriggerHandler.afterUpdate
Class.AccountTriggerHandler.onOwnerChange
Class.AccountOwnership.reassignRelatedRecords
Class.AccountOwnership.reassignOpptys (executes a DML on Opportunity)

Trigger.OpportunityTrigger
Class.OpportunityTriggerHandler.afterUpdate
Class.OpportunityTriggerHandler.notifyNewOwners (executes a DML on Task)

Trigger.TaskTrigger
Class.TaskTriggerHandler.afterInsert

Class.TaskTriggerHandler.increaseOpenTaskCount (executes a DML on User)

**System.DmlException: Update failed. FIELD_CUSTOM_VALIDATION_ EXCEPTION
You have too many open tasks!**

If we don't have any exception handling anywhere, the exception will **bubble up** all the way to the `Trigger.AccountTrigger` execution. For example, if I add a simple try/catch block on the code that changes the account owner, we can see that the DML exception on the user object arrives all the way here:

try{

   //fire the first requirement
   account.OwnerId = newOwnerId;
   update account;*//this will fire Trigger.AccountTrigger*

} catch (Exception e){
   *// This happened 4 levels deep yet it found its way to the
       very top of the stacktrace*
 FIELD_CUSTOM_VALIDATION_EXCEPTION
   You have too many open tasks!
}

This is standard behavior in Apex: **exceptions propagate up the call stack, traveling through each layer of execution until they are caught by a try/catch block.** I call this a cascading failure.

CHAPTER 7   CASCADING FAILURES IN TRIGGER BOUNDARIES

And here's where things get complicated. An exception four levels deep from a different business process has bubbled up to the account trigger, which fired for unrelated reasons. Here, I encourage you to pause and ponder the following questions:

- Who should have caught this exception?
- Should it have been caught at the source (`TaskTriggerHandler.increaseOpenTaskCount`), somewhere in the middle, or by the parent process (`Trigger.AccountTrigger`)?
- Which code has the necessary context and knowledge to understand what to do with this exception and how to recover from it?
- How does Apex distinguish where one business process ends and another begins?

Let's address some of these questions while keeping this scenario in mind.

7.2 Business Process Boundaries and Atomic Operations

In the example above, Apex is executing three different business processes in the same transaction due to how triggers work. But how do we determine if all three business processes combined are meant to be considered a single atomic operation? **An operation is atomic when every step must succeed, or none should.** This is important when we don't want partial updates that leave the system in an inconsistent state.

To illustrate this, let's pivot to a simpler example. Here, I've created a validation rule that will make any task insert to fail. Here's an example of a nonatomic operation:

CHAPTER 7   CASCADING FAILURES IN TRIGGER BOUNDARIES

```
try {
    insert new Account(Name='Non Atomic Account');
    insert new Contact(LastName='Non Atomic Contact');
```
   //This will fail due to a validation rule
```
    insert new Task(Subject='Non Atomic
Task',          ActivityDate=Date.today());
}
catch(Exception e){

    Account a = [SELECT Id FROM Account WHERE Name = 'Non
    Atomic Account'];
    Contact c = [SELECT Id FROM Contact WHERE LastName = 'Non
    Atomic Contact'];
```
   Assert.istrue(a != null);
   Assert.istrue(c != null);
```
}
```

In this example, the account and contact are inserted successfully, even though an error is thrown when inserting the task. Interestingly, the first two inserts succeed **only because we are catching the exception.** If we don't catch the exception, the entire operation is rolled back, for example:

```
public static void defaultBehaviour(){

    insert new Account(Name='Default Account');
    insert new Contact(LastName='Default Contact');

    //This will fail due to a validation rule
    insert new Task(Subject='Atomic Task', ActivityDate=Date.
    today());
}
```

171

In the above example, the account and contact are not committed to the database; everything is rolled back. This is expected behavior as far as Apex is concerned, but it might not be what you expect. To be clear:

- If you catch an exception, only that specific DML operation is rolled back. Any other DML operation that occurred before it will be committed to the database.

- If you do not catch an exception, all DML operations that came before it will be rolled back.

Now, if the set of operations is meant to be atomic, we can explicitly ensure that no partial updates are made by using a database save point. This means that if any step fails, everything is rolled back, preventing partial success that could leave the system in an inconsistent state.

```
Savepoint sp = Database.setSavepoint();
try{
    insert new Account(Name='Test Account');
    insert new Contact(LastName='Test Contact');
    insert new Task(Subject='Test Task', ActivityDate=Date.today());
}
catch(Exception e){
    Database.rollback(sp);
}
```

In the above example, when the exception is caught, we rollback the database to the point just before the first DML operation. This effectively means that if any error occurs on any of the DML calls, all three are rolled back. All three steps act as **a single unit of work**. This is the exact same behavior we would've seen if we hadn't caught the exception; the difference here is we are being **intentional** about the atomicity of the operations; we aren't letting Apex decide for us.

So, how is this related to the main example we explored in Section 7.1? We need to determine if the three steps are meant to be atomic or not. In pseudocode:

```
User updates account owner
    1. Account trigger reassigns opportunities
    2. Opportunity trigger creates tasks
    3. Task trigger updates count on user record
```

In other words, should a failure in step 3 cause everything that occurred in steps 1 and 2 to be rolled back? If all three steps are meant to act as one, then yes. However, if they are completely separate, a failure in step 3 should not prevent steps 1 and 2 from completing successfully.

So, how do we tell if these three steps are part of the same business process? When I introduced this example, I mentioned that the three requirements were requested separately over a period of one year and that each requirement was implemented by different developers. Hypothetically, we could assume that when requirement 2 was requested, the business wasn't thinking it as an extension of requirement 1.

We could try asking the business, but they are unlikely to even know all three steps exist. Perhaps one business unit requested steps 1 and 2 and another one requested step 3. The reality is that unless you were there when all three requirements were requested and you yourself implemented them, it's nearly impossible to tell if they are meant to act as an atomic operation.

How can we ensure others know if our code is meant to be atomic?

CHAPTER 7   CASCADING FAILURES IN TRIGGER BOUNDARIES

7.3 Avoid Using Triggers for Cross-Object Operations

One way to avoid the atomic vs. nonatomic dilemma we explored in the previous section is to **avoid using triggers for business processes that span multiple objects**. Let's assume that the example in 7.1 (the three main requirements we've been working with so far) was indeed meant to be a single atomic operation. In that case, I argue that all the DML operations and the business logic should have been part of a single **deep module** (see Chapter 4).

For example, we could do something like this in the `AccountOwnership` class:

```
public static void reassignRelatedRecords(Map<Id,Id> ownerIdsByAccountId){

    Database.Savepoint sp = Database.setSavepoint();

    try{
        reassignOpptys(ownerIdsByAccountId);
        createTasksForNewOwners(ownerIdsByAccountId);
        increaseOpenTaskCount(ownerIdsByAccountId);
    }
    catch(Exception e){

        ExceptionLogger.log(e,'AccountOwnership.reassignRelatedRecords');

        Database.rollback(sp);
    }
}
```

First, all the functionality related to account reassignment is inside the `reassignRelatedRecords` method. This makes it a deep module; it does everything it needs to do and provides a simple interface.

Second, we wrap everything inside a database save point, which allows us to handle failures gracefully while leaving the database in a consistent state.

Finally, when other developers see this code, it will be immediately obvious that all these three operations combined are meant to be atomic. This is better than spreading out the business requirement across different triggers, as it's nearly impossible to tell if one trigger is meant to be the continuation of another process somewhere else.

Furthermore, if you split a single business process across multiple triggers, this means that by design, the operation isn't atomic. In our example, the opportunity trigger could fire whether or not the account owner was changed, or the task trigger could fire even if the account doesn't have opportunities. In other words, each step of the process can start independently, which means all three steps are not a unit of work. The best thing to do is to **not** use multiple triggers to design an atomic process that spans multiple objects. Instead, **consolidate the logic in a deep module where you have full control on the atomicity of the operation.**

Now, what if the business did not intend for these operations to act as one? In that case, spreading them out across different triggers makes sense. However, if there's no exception handling anywhere, Apex's default behavior for bubbling exceptions will make all three operations act as one, even if that wasn't the business' intention.

This brings some interesting questions:

- What if you don't want these three operations to act as one?
- What if you wanted to allow for exceptions in the task trigger handler while still allowing the account ownership change to succeed?
- How should you model your Apex code to accomplish this?

7.4 Decoupling in Trigger Frameworks

Traditional literature on trigger frameworks covers about two types of decoupling:

- **Deployment-time decoupling**: This is about decoupling the trigger handlers from the trigger themselves so that they don't reference each other directly. Most trigger frameworks achieve this by using custom metadata types and dynamically instantiating handler Apex classes.
- **Governor-limit decoupling**: This is about spinning of a separate asynchronous transaction or thread to enjoy higher governor limits that are independent of the original thread.

We are missing two types of decoupling: decoupling triggers so that **failures in one trigger don't cause a cascading failure** and **decoupling triggers to avoid mixing different business processes in the same thread.** In many cases, these are just two sides of the same coin.

There are two ways to achieve this level of decoupling:

- Use some form of asynchronous process.
- Triggers should not let exceptions bubble up, unless certain conditions are met.

Let's explore these patterns.

7.5 Async Processing to Avoid Cascading Failures

> **Note** The following section explains **thinking patterns** that will help us determine how cascading failures could be avoided. These are not meant to be production-ready recipes that you can simply copy/paste. Nor do they cover all possible scenarios and edge cases. The focus is on how we **think** about these problems, not their specific implementation.

As we saw earlier, an exception in a trigger handler that is several levels deep in the stack can cause all preceding processes to fail. To avoid this, our goal is to allow a subprocess to fail without impacting the parent process.

A good example of when to decouple subprocesses is in `after` triggers. By definition, `after` triggers are used primary to fire subprocesses on records **other than the record that caused the trigger to fire**. Here's where you should think if such processes are really part of the same business process or if they are simply coupled together because of how Apex works. In the context of cascading failures, we should consider whether DML failures on related records that occur in an `after` trigger should cause the original process to fail as well.

Let's assume you determine that the `after` logic should be decoupled as it's a completely different business process. How can asynchronous processing help us achieve this decoupling?

7.5.1 Using Queueable Apex to Isolate Failures

One possible way is to use Queueable apex. You could wrap all `after` operations in a class that implements the `Queueable` interface, like this:

```
switch on Trigger.operationType {

    when BEFORE_INSERT {
        //call some classes
    }

    when AFTER_INSERT, AFTER_UPDATE {

        // this is a custom type
        TriggerEvent event = new TriggerEvent()
        .setNewRecords(Trigger.newMap)
        .setOldRecords(Trigger.oldMap)
        .setOperationType(Trigger.operationType);

        System.enqueueJob(new TaskAfterTriggerHandler(event));
    }

}
```

In this example, all the after logic is encapsulated in the `TaskAfterTriggerHandler` class. The class takes a `TriggerEvent` class, which is simply a wrapper for the `Trigger` context variables. This lets the handler work with the trigger context even if the operation happens in a different thread. Going back to our goal, the benefit is that any failures that occur in this class will not affect the `before` trigger handlers, so **creating or updating a task will succeed no matter what happens in the after** handler. Assuming that the `after` handler has a lot of side effects on other objects as part of different business processes, we've effectively avoided cascading failures if any errors occur.

Now, there are some serious drawbacks to this approach. A few come to mind.

By definition, the async handler will run on a separate thread and only when resources are available (there's no SLA for async processing). Because of this, the handler could try to execute some logic that is no longer valid because the original records have changed since the async process was queued. You could solve this by requerying the context records in the handler and evaluate if the original criteria is still met.

Another problem is there are serious limits to how many Queueable processes you can spin off, especially if you are **already** in an async context (see the Apex documentation for specific details). You could quickly max out your daily allocation of Queueable apex, which is arguably worse than cascading failures, especially considering you can't `try/catch` governor limit exceptions.

Finally, it's great that we've isolated failures from the parent process, but if failures do occur, how do we get notified and how do we debug them? In order for this pattern to work well, you must use a good logging framework such as Nebula Logger or Pharos Triton, and you must have a process to review errors and exceptions.

Let's explore another alternative.

7.5.2 Using Change Data Capture to Isolate Failures

Change Data Capture (CDC) is a feature that fires a specific type of platform event in response to changes in Salesforce records. The official use case for it is to sync Salesforce data with external systems in near-real time. However, buried somewhere deep in in the documentation, we can find the following statement:

CHAPTER 7 CASCADING FAILURES IN TRIGGER BOUNDARIES

> With Apex triggers, you can capture and process change events on the Lightning Platform. Change event triggers run **asynchronously** after the database transaction is completed. Perform resource-intensive **business logic asynchronously in the change event trigger, and implement transaction-based logic in the Apex object trigger**. By **decoupling** the processing of changes, change event triggers can help reduce transaction processing time.

I find it interesting that the documentation itself mentions decoupling as a benefit of using CDC. However, it only mentions decoupling in the context of processing time, not business process or failure decoupling (cascading failures). That doesn't mean it cannot be used for that purpose. Let's see how.

Having configured CDC, you can create a trigger that catches updates on an object. Here's what such a trigger would look like for the Account object:

Note You shouldn't write logic in a trigger. I'm only doing it here to keep the example simple and focused on decoupling business logic. Also, there's a query inside a for loop, but each CDC is bulkified by default, so each iteration contains multiple records in the `recordIds` variable.

```
trigger ChangeEventAccountTrigger on AccountChangeEvent (after insert) {
    for (AccountChangeEvent event : Trigger.New) {
        EventBus.ChangeEventHeader header = event.ChangeEventHeader;
```

CHAPTER 7 CASCADING FAILURES IN TRIGGER BOUNDARIES

```
    if (header.changeType == 'UPDATE') {

        List<String> accountIds = header.recordIds;

        List<Account> accounts = [SELECT Id, Industry FROM
        Account WHERE Id IN :accountIds];

        for (String field : header.changedFields) {
            if (field == 'Industry') {
                for (Account acc : accounts) {
                    // do something
                }
            }
        }
    }
}
```

Here, we respond to a change in the account object, and we can determine what fields have changed via the changedFields variable, just like we can do in a traditional trigger. From here on, we can execute other logic that should be independent of the original parent process (whichever process changed an account record). Again, going back to our goal, any failures that occur here will not affect the parent process, which is good if those failures are on a completely different business process. However, like in the case of Queueable, there are several drawbacks.

The first one is you need licenses to enable CDC in more than five objects, which makes this pattern very expensive to implement. Also, unlike with Queueable, the CDC trigger runs under the Automated Process user, which means capturing debug logs via the developer console is not possible. You have to configure specific debug logs for this special user.

Finally, we also need very strong logging mechanisms to be able to react to any failures that occur here.

CHAPTER 7 CASCADING FAILURES IN TRIGGER BOUNDARIES

Still, even with these drawbacks, the core idea here is that in certain scenarios you *could* use CDC to isolate business processes that would otherwise run in the same thread. Isolating those processes prevents cascading failures, which simplifies exception handling.

7.5.3 Using Platform Events to Isolate Failures

Platform events can be used to isolate failures by triggering events in response to specific actions, allowing the subsequent processing to run asynchronously in a separate thread through a platform event trigger.

For example, suppose you create a platform event called `New sObject` that is meant to fire every time new records are created, as seen in Figure 7-1.

Figure 7-1. *A platform event definition for capturing new records*

This is a generic platform event that notifies subscribers when new records are created. The `recordIds__c` field allows us to include all new record IDs, so we only need to fire one event per bulk transaction. Another approach is to flag the new records with a field like `processing_required__c`, which the platform event trigger would then query. Both patterns are simply ways to signal changes in data, and which one you use is somewhat irrelevant to our discussion on decoupling business processes.

CHAPTER 7   CASCADING FAILURES IN TRIGGER BOUNDARIES

The sObjectType__c field can then be used to determine what type of object this is. With this configuration, you can fire an event every time new records are created, like this:

```
New_SObject__e event = new New_SObject__e(
    recordIds__c = taskIds,
    SObjectType__c = 'Task'
);

Database.SaveResult result = EventBus.publish(event);
```

Then, you can write a trigger on the New_SObject__e platform event that will catch the event and execute some business logic. Again, the idea is that this business logic is **separate** from the original logic that created the task records, thus preventing cascading failures.

Such a trigger could look something like this:

```
trigger NewSObjectTrigger on New_SObject__e (after insert) {

    for (New_SObject__e event : Trigger.New) {

        Set<Id> recordIds = new Set<Id>();

        for (String recordId : event.recordIds__c.split(',')) {
            recordIds.add(recordId);
        }

        switch on event.SObjectType__c {

            when 'Task' {

                Map<Id,Task> newTasksById = new Map<Id,Task>([
                    SELECT Id, OwnerId, CompletedDateTime,
                    Subject
                    FROM Task
                    WHERE Id IN :recordIds]);
```

183

```
                TaskCounter.increaseOpenTaskCount(newT
                asksById);
            }
        }
    }
}
```

One concern with both platform events and CDC is that, ironically, the process and its subprocesses can become *too* decoupled. Your main process creates some records and optionally fires an event, and that's it; there's no clear indication of what happens next. It may not be obvious to other developers that *other* business processes will fire in response to those events.

All in all, it's clear that no pattern is perfect. As I mentioned at the start of this section, these are intended as thinking patterns, not "ready-to-go" implementations. When considering exception handling, **we should first determine whether we are dealing with an exception that's part of the main process or one that's entirely unrelated.** If it's the latter, we should then ask whether the subprocess can or should run on a separate thread. In many cases, this can simplify exception handling by allowing us to focus on managing direct exceptions rather than unrelated ones.

7.6 Triggers Should Be Able to Stop All Exceptions

In the previous section, we explored how asynchronous processing can help prevent cascading failures. However, each method comes with its own drawbacks that, depending on the situation, can create new challenges. In this section, we'll explore alternative ways to prevent cascading failures without relying on async processing.

CHAPTER 7   CASCADING FAILURES IN TRIGGER BOUNDARIES

Another reason I excluded exception handling from all the examples in this book up until now is because what you actually do with an exception depends on the context. Let's revisit the example we used in the preceding sections. We have a task trigger that increases a counter on the user record each time a task is created:

```
public static void afterInsert(Map<Id, Task> newTasksById){
    increaseOpenTaskCount(newTasksById);
}
```

If this method is called four levels deep in a transaction, as we saw earlier, any exceptions that occur here can bubble up all the way to the parent process, reverting all DML operations along the way. And so, let's say that we want to add exception handling logic to this bit of code by adding a try/catch block, like this:

```
try {
    increaseOpenTaskCount(newTasksById);
} catch (Exception e) {
    // TBD
}
```

Now, what should happen if an exception happens here? If an exception occurs **when** this method is four levels deep in the stack, we could argue that we don't want to let it bubble up all the way to the parent process so that it doesn't undo all previous DML operations. We could do something like this:

```
try {
    increaseOpenTaskCount(newTasksById);
  } catch (Exception e) {
      //log it to a custom object so it doesn't
      //disrupt all the processes before it
```

185

CHAPTER 7   CASCADING FAILURES IN TRIGGER BOUNDARIES

```
    Logger.error(e.getMessage());
    Logger.saveLog();
}
```

However, what if the exception happens when `increaseOpenTaskCount` is the **first** method on the stack? What if the user manually created a task? In that case, I argue that we should let the exception bubble up to the parent process, which is the Salesforce UI. This way, the user would see the exception in the Salesforce UI itself as seen in Figure 7-2.

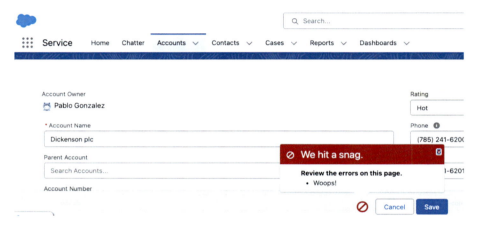

Figure 7-2. *An error message in the Salesforce UI*

So, what's apparent here is that **how we handle exceptions depends on the runtime context of the code.** If the code is the main logic being executed, letting the exception go all the way may be a good idea. But if the same code is running multiple levels deep, perhaps logging the exception is a better idea so that the parent process can continue.

We can dynamically let triggers decide what to do with exceptions by implementing a simple stack data structure to keep track of how many triggers have been called during a single transaction. Such stack could look like this:

CHAPTER 7   CASCADING FAILURES IN TRIGGER BOUNDARIES

```
public class TriggerStack {

    static private Map<String,Integer> countByTriggerName
    = new ...
    static private List<String> orderedTriggerNames = new ...

    public static void push(String triggerName){
        ...// add to map and list
    }

    public static Integer size(){
        //return size of map
    }
}
```

Then, at the beginning of each trigger, we can register the trigger in the stack. In our example, we need to register for the account, opportunity, and task triggers, like this:

```
trigger AccountTrigger on Account (...) {

    TriggerStack.push('AccountTrigger');
```

then

```
trigger OpportunityTrigger on Opportunity (...) {

    TriggerStack.push('OpportunityTrigger');
```

and

```
trigger TaskTrigger on Task (...) {

    TriggerStack.push('TaskTrigger');
```

Then, in the task trigger, we can catch exceptions and decide what to do with them depending on whether this is the first trigger in the stack or whether it was called by other processes:

CHAPTER 7   CASCADING FAILURES IN TRIGGER BOUNDARIES

```
switch on Trigger.operationType {
    when AFTER_INSERT, AFTER_UPDATE {
        try {
            TaskTriggerHandler.afterInsert(Trigger.newMap);
        } catch (Exception e) {
            // let the caller know that something
               went wrong
            // by throwing the exception again
            if(TriggerStack.size() == 1) {
                throw e;
            }
            // if this is not the first trigger in
               the stack
            // log the error to prevent cascading failures
            else {
                System.debug(TriggerStack.toString());
                Logger.error(e.getMessage());
                Logger.saveLog();
            }
        }
    }
}
```

Now, this may not work in all scenarios, but as with everything else in this chapter, these are **thinking patterns**, not recipes. The idea that Apex triggers can "know" the context in which they are being executed and act accordingly is something that can be explored more deeply, and I hope that at least I inspired you to think more about this.

7.7 Conclusion

The core idea of this chapter is that we should understand the exception handling is not just about logging errors or recovering from them, it's also about understanding how our code interacts with the rest of the code base at runtime and what appropriate action we should take given the circumstances.

[1] Swallowing an exception means catching it but doing nothing meaningful with it, such as failing to log, rethrow, or handle it properly.

CHAPTER 8

Object-Oriented Programming in Apex

I made up the term "object-oriented", and I can tell you I didn't have C++ in mind.

—Alan Kay

The subject of object-oriented programming (OOP from now on) has caused endless debates in the software community. Alan Kay, who coined the term, has often said that what we think of OOP today is not at all what he intended. This is to say that it is a complex topic, and it would be impossible for me to explain everything about this design paradigm in a single chapter. However, for better or worse, Apex is an OOP language, and we **must** understand advanced OOP techniques if we want to move forward in our journey to practicing clean code.

To be clear, advanced knowledge of OOP is **not optional** if you want to understand the rest of the chapters in this book. Even if you already know OOP, I highly recommend you don't skip this chapter. All future chapters assume you thoroughly understand the concepts laid out here. That said, this is a very broad topic so I also recommend you take your time with it.

CHAPTER 8   OBJECT-ORIENTED PROGRAMMING IN APEX

8.1 A Bit of History

> **Note** You may be tempted to skip this section. You may think that knowing the history of OOP won't help you write cleaner Apex code. I encourage you to read the section and see if you still feel that way afterward. You may be surprised.

OOP is a paradigm for solving problems in software systems. A paradigm is a set of ideas, beliefs, and points of view about how something should be addressed. It's important to be clear about this because OOP is **not** the only paradigm for software design; other paradigms include **functional programming** and **procedural programming.** Along the same lines, we must understand that OOP is not inherently better than the others. There are some requirements or domains where OOP might be a better choice than other paradigms, and the reverse is also true.

Let's go back to the origins of OOP. The term "object-oriented programming" was coined by Alan Kay in the 1970s while he was working on the development of the Smalltalk programming language. Smalltalk was one of the first programming languages designed to fully embody the principles of OOP. Interestingly, Kay later admitted that the term "object-oriented" might have been a poor choice. He coined it while envisioning a new way to architect software systems, inspired by his background in biology. In his words:

> *I thought of objects being like biological cells and/or **individual** computers on a network, only able to communicate with messages.*

Years later, he said:

> A good example of a large system I consider "object-oriented" is the Internet. It has billions of completely **encapsulated** objects (the computers themselves) and uses a pure messaging system of "requests not commands", etc.
>
> By contrast, I have never considered that most systems which call themselves "object-oriented" are even close to my meaning when I originally coined the term.
>
> So part of the problem here is a kind of "colonization" of an idea — which got popular because it worked so well in the ARPA/PARC community — by many people who didn't take the trouble to understand why it worked so well.

What I draw from this bit of history is two things:

- The version of OOP we know today is not the original vision from Kay, for better or worse.
- At the heart of Kay's vision lies the concept of **individuality**. Objects are **individual**, **modular**, and **encapsulated**.

Whether today's OOP aligns with Kay's original vision is somewhat irrelevant. What matters for us is honoring these three principles: **individuality**, **modularity**, and **encapsulation**. I will cover these three terms in this chapter (and future ones will expand on them as well).

CHAPTER 8   OBJECT-ORIENTED PROGRAMMING IN APEX

8.2 What Is an Object?

The first idea behind OOP is that we think of software design in terms of real-life objects. The typical example is that of a banking application: If you were developing such a system under the OOP paradigm, we'd expect our code to be modelled around the concepts of the banking domain.

Each object has different **responsibilities** and **attributes**. For example:

- **BankAccount**:
    - **Attributes**: `accountNumber`, `accountType` (e.g., savings, checking), `balance`, `currency`, and `status` (e.g., active, dormant).
    - **Responsibilities**:
        - Deposit or withdraw funds.
        - Check the current balance.
        - Apply interest or fees.
- **Customer**:
    - **Attributes**: `name`, `address`, `email`, `phoneNumber`, and `customerID`.
    - **Responsibilities**:
        - Update personal information.
        - Link to accounts they own or are authorized to access.
- **Transaction**:
    - **Attributes**: `transactionID`, `amount`, `date`, `type` (e.g., debit, credit), `sourceAccount`, and `destinationAccount`.

- **Responsibilities**:
    - Record transaction details.
    - Validate transaction rules (e.g., sufficient funds).

The second main idea is that these objects are meant to communicate with each other by **sending messages**. In essence, this means that objects don't care about the internals of other objects; they just care that they respond to messages, for example:

```
BankAccount savings = new BankAccount('12345', 'Savings', 5000.00);
BankAccount checking = new BankAccount('67890', 'Checking', 2000.00);

// send a message to the savings object to transfer funds
Transaction transaction = savings.transferFunds(1000.00, checking);
```

The concept of "sending a message" is not so popular these days, even though it's in Kay's original definition. For now, we can think of sending messages as calling methods on an object: methods that trigger some action or behavior.

8.3 Challenges with the Object Model

One of my personal frustrations with OOP is that it forces everything to be an object. The typical example of a banking application is convenient because we can easily model those concepts as objects, but this isn't true for all domains. Consider the example of a Math class in Apex, which contains the max method to return the largest of two integers:

```
Integer max = Math.max(1,4);
System.debug(max);
```

CHAPTER 8   OBJECT-ORIENTED PROGRAMMING IN APEX

Is `Math` a real-life object? Is `Math` something I can see and touch or interact with? How about the `LeadConvert` class?

```
Lead myLead = new Lead(LastName = 'Fry', Company='Fry
And Sons');
insert myLead;

Database.LeadConvert lc = new Database.LeadConvert();
lc.setLeadId(myLead.id);

Database.LeadConvertResult lcr = Database.convertLead(lc);
```

Can you tell me what a `LeadConvert` looks like?

In my opinion, this paradigm would've better been called "concept-oriented programming," because the term "concept" is a lot more flexible and frees us from the idea that objects must model real-world entities. `Math` is a concept, and so is `LeadConvert`.

Another problem with the object model dogma is that it leads to unnatural constructs. For example, if everything must be an object, then `Math` becomes an antipattern because it isn't a real-world object. This leads to a philosophy where every operation needs to be tied to an actual object, for example:

```
Integer one = 1;
Integer whoIsMax = one.max(4);
```

In the example above, the `max` method belongs to the `Integer` class, a "real-life" object. To me, this feels unnatural; I wouldn't expect `Integer` to be able to tell me if another `Integer` is greater than itself.

Finally, sometimes, you don't really need an object or even a concept. Sometimes you just need a function that takes some input and returns some output. For example, imagine you need to validate if a string is 18 characters long; you may create a method like this:

```
public Boolean is18Char(String input){
    return input?.length() == 18;
}
```

In what class should you place this method? I encourage you to pause and think about it for a few minutes.

If we were dealing with a programming language that is more on the functional side, like JavaScript, we'd simply create this function and call it a day. However, in OOP, we are forced to think which object should hold this responsibility. I know I've agonized for hours thinking if I placed a method under the correct class. In this example, we might end up putting this in a `LeadUtils` class, which makes sense to me. However, OOP purists will call this an antipattern because `LeadUtils` isn't a real-life entity.

> **Note** To be clear: I'm not saying "utils" classes are a good pattern. There are definitely antipatterns when these classes become huge "catch-all" placeholders for unrelated methods. However, I'd say anyone who's programmed for a few years has ended up creating a "utils" class of some sort, which further proves that not everything can be forced into an object model.

Long story short, I argue that we can make better use of OOP by thinking of objects as concepts. While this diverges from Kay's original vision, it matches with the realities of software design. Concepts can still honor individuality, modularity, and encapsulation—without forcing every idea into a "real-life" object. This is, of course, just my personal opinion, and you are welcome to think differently about objects.

That said, throughout this chapter, I'll use the term "object" for simplicity, but keep in mind that we're really working with concepts: flexible, modular ideas that don't always need to mirror the real world.

8.4 Class vs. Instance

The concepts of **class** and **instance** are central to OOP. Before I can explain how objects work in Apex, we must ensure these two concepts are clear.

A class is typically defined as a blueprint of what an object looks like. For example, I can have a class that defines a bank transaction:

```
public class BankTransaction {

    private Decimal amount;
    private String type;

    public BankTransaction(Decimal amount, String type) {
        this.amount = amount;
        this.type = type;
    }

    public void validateType() {
        //this should be an Enum...I'm focused on the
        //definition of class vs instance :)
        if (type != 'debit' && type != 'credit') {
            throw new TransactionException('Invalid transaction
            type: ' + type);
        }
    }

    public class TransactionException extends Exception {}
}
```

The class defines the properties of the transaction (`amount` and `type`) and the actions the object can perform (`validateType()`). But this class doesn't do anything on its own. It's only useful if I create an instance and do something with it:

CHAPTER 8   OBJECT-ORIENTED PROGRAMMING IN APEX

```
// create a transaction instance (actual object based on the
class blueprint)
BankTransaction transaction = new BankTransaction(200.00,
'debit');

// interact with the instance by calling a method
transaction.validateType();
```

I like to think about classes as the **abstract concept** and instances as the **actual thing** that I can interact with. This abstract vs. actual distinction is easier to understand with an analogy.

Imagine I tell you I will bring cookies tomorrow and describe them like this:

- They'll be big.
- They'll have chocolate chips.
- They'll go great with a glass of oat milk.

Now, imagine I show up to your house with a piece of paper listing these three bullet points instead of the actual cookies. Aside from the fact that this would be very upsetting, the piece of paper is useless; it only describes what the cookies will look like.

If I did bring the cookies, you'd be able to eat them, interact with them, and see the properties I described earlier. The cookies are the **actual** thing that the paper only conceptualized.

Just like this analogy, the class is the blueprint (the cookie description), while the instance is the real object (the cookies you can enjoy).

Like all things in software, there are exceptions. A class can be useful without instances if it has static methods. Static methods belong to the class itself and can be called without creating an instance. For example, the `Database` class in Apex allows you to call methods directly:

```
Database.insert(myAccount);
```

CHAPTER 8   OBJECT-ORIENTED PROGRAMMING IN APEX

It would be a little strange if every time you wanted to use the class you'd have to create an instance of it:

```
Database db = new Database();
db.insert(myAccount)
```

In this case, the `Database` class acts as a container for grouping related database operations logically. Some might argue that the database should be an object with instances, but in Apex, there's only one database. There's no way to have two databases working together, so static methods make sense here.

That said, **there are scenarios where forcing a concept to be an object is necessary**. For example, nonstatic objects allow for dependency injection and mocking, which we'll explore in later chapters.

8.5 Objects in Apex

If the concept of objects wasn't confusing enough, the term "object" in Salesforce means something entirely different from "object" in OOP. And to make it even trickier, Salesforce objects are also OOP objects by design. Let's separate the two concepts, and see how they work together.

In Salesforce, an object is really just a database table where you can store any type of information. Typical objects are the standard `Account` and `Lead` object and custom objects like `Attendance__c`. For the remainder of this section, I'm going to refer to Salesforce objects as "database tables" so that it's clear which "object" type I'm talking about.

Salesforce's database tables are also a special type of OOP objects. For example, if you create a custom database table called `Attendance__c`, you can use it in Apex as an OOP object, like this:

```
Attendance__c attendance = new Attendance__c();
attendance.location__c = 'Dublin';
```

```
insert attendance;
```

200

CHAPTER 8   OBJECT-ORIENTED PROGRAMMING IN APEX

We typically only use database tables in Apex to add field values and manipulate them through DML statements, but these types of OOP objects also support several methods like any other OOP object would, for example:

```
Attendance__c attendance = new Attendance__c();
attendance.put('Status__c', 'Completed');
attendance.getPopulatedFieldsAsMap();
if (attendance.isSet('Date__c')) attendance.get('Date__c'
attendance.addError('Test error on record');
attendance.hasErrors();
attendance.getErrors();
attendance.getSObjectType();
Attendance__c clonedAttendance = attendance.clone(false, true, false, false);
attendance.clear();
```

These type of objects also support inheritance; they all inherit from the SObject class. In fact, all the methods from the above example are defined in the SObject class; you can call them on the specific database table instances because they inherit from it (I will cover inheritance in detail later).

These types of objects also support polymorphism, which allows you to write code that can operate on different types of database table instances (e.g., Account, Attendance__c, or Lead) as if they were of the same type. For example, I could create a generic method that checks if a field is set on a record and, if so, it updates it:

```
public static void checkAndUpdate(SObject record, String field) {
    if(record.isSet(field)) {
        update record;
    }
}
```

201

I can then call this method with an `Account` instance as the first parameter. This is only possible because the Account class inherits from the `SObject` class.

```
Account account = [SELECT Id, Name FROM Account LIMIT 1];
ObjectsApex.checkAndUpdate(account,'Name');
```

I'd like to point out how spoiled we are as Salesforce developers: in all other programming languages, database tables are **not** natively accessible as OOP objects. In traditional software development, you would need to use an Object Relational Mapping (ORM) tool.

An ORM allows you to model database tables as simple OOP objects so that you can easily do CRUD operations on them without having to manipulate database tables directly via SQL. For example, in Java, you could use Hibernate to map a database table to a class like this:

```
@Entity
public class Attendance {
    @Id
    private Long id;
    private String location;
}
```

With Apex, **standard and custom database tables magically appear as OOP objects**. This is an amazing capability that we can only appreciate when we explore other programming languages and realize how much extra effort is required to do the same.

8.6 Encapsulation

The concept of encapsulation is so important in OOP that many argue that without good support for encapsulation, a programming language cannot be considered an OOP-language. Encapsulation is very similar to the definition of **abstraction** we discussed in Chapter 3: it's a way for us to simplify complex concepts, so that **we don't need to understand their inner workings**; we just need to know enough to make them useful.

Specifically, encapsulation is about hiding the inner state and methods of an object and only exposing the variables or methods that we want users to interact with. This is typically done with modifiers such as `private`, `public`, and `protected`, for example:

```
public with sharing class AccountOwnership {

    //this method is exposed to others
    public static void reassignRelatedRecords(Map<Id,Id> ownerIdsByAccountId){

        //these 2 are private as they are internal
        //implementation details
        reassignOpptys(ownerIdsByAccountId);
        reassignCases(ownerIdsByAccountId);

    }
}
```

Encapsulation is also a variation of **deep modules**, a concept we explored in Chapter 4. To recap, deep modules hide unnecessary complexity while providing a clean, simple interface. We can revisit an earlier example: the `Limits` class. You can use this class to tell how many DML operations have been consumed in an Apex transaction, for example:

```
Limits.getDMLStatements();
```

This is a deep module because it does everything we expect it to do. In contrast, a shallow module would force us to understand the inner workings of tracking governor limits in Apex transactions, for example:

```
Limit dmlLimit = new Limit(LimitType.DML);
dmlLimit.setContext(ApexContext.BatchApex);
```

CHAPTER 8   OBJECT-ORIENTED PROGRAMMING IN APEX

```
dmlLimit.startTracking();
// run your code here
dmlLimit.stopTracking();

dmlLimit.getLimit();
```

So in a way, **a shallow module is a module that is not well encapsulated**. This is what we call a **leaking abstraction**: when a module's internal workings are exposed, the abstraction is no longer useful because it requires unnecessary understanding (like having to understand the inner workings of a car engine to be able to drive it).

It's not a coincidence that deep modules, abstraction, and encapsulation all share similar characteristics. They are all about **information hiding**, which is a design principle that encourages us not to expose too much of the inner workings of a module and to provide an interface that is easy to work with.

Some proponents of the OOP paradigm argue that encapsulation is one of the advantages of using objects. I partially agree, because encapsulation can be applied at the micro and macro levels, and it's not exclusive to objects. For example, I can have a JavaScript function that gets all Salesforce active users:

```
const activeUsers = getActiveUsers(sfConnection);
```

How `getActiveUsers` gets the list of active users is completely irrelevant to me. All I know as that if I call it, I'll get the list of users. Internally, it may use a combination of SOQL queries, the SOAP or REST API, and other logic. None of this is exposed to me. The function is well encapsulated; it's also a deep module and a good abstraction.

At the macro level, it applies to larger systems, such as microservices or APIs. For example, imagine integrating Salesforce with SAP via Mulesoft. Mulesoft will provide a simple connector that allows information to pass between both systems. How Mulesoft achieves that and what specific API it uses behind the scenes is irrelevant. The entire API is encapsulated.

8.6.1 Encapsulation in Apex

One way Apex supports encapsulation is through the private, protected, public, and global access modifiers when defining methods and variables, as well as "getters" and "setters." Salesforce has extensive documentation on how and when to use the access modifiers, so I would do you a disservice if I simply regurgitated that information here.

For the purposes of this discussion, I want to focus on getters and setters, which are often considered an antipattern. Getters and setters are methods used to expose private variables in a more controlled way. For example:

```
public class BankTransaction {

    private Integer amount;

}
```

If we made amount a public variable, we'd break encapsulation, as we are exposing the inner workings of this class. The traditional way to "fix" this is by making the variable private and creating a getter and a setter method for it, like this:

```
public class BankTransaction {

    private Integer amount;

    public void setAmount(Integer newAmount){
        this.amount = newAmount;
    }

    public Integer getAmount() {
        return this.amount;
    }
}
```

CHAPTER 8　OBJECT-ORIENTED PROGRAMMING IN APEX

This pattern creates **artificial encapsulation**. We can still get and set the private property of the class through these new methods. Also, you are signaling to other modules that somewhere inside there's a variable called amount. Our abstraction is leaking.

Of course, the getter and setter methods can still be useful if you want to define what should happen when the value is set or returned, but you are still exposing the fact that there's an instance variable called amount.

A better approach to encapsulation is to **expose behavior rather than raw data**. Instead of directly setting or retrieving amount, you could design the class to expose meaningful operations. For example:

```
public class BankTransaction {

    private Integer amount;

    public void increaseAmount(Integer increment) {
        this.amount += increment;
    }

    public String getFormattedAmount() {
        return '$' + String.valueOf(this.amount);
    }

}
```

Of course, one could argue that these methods *still* reveal the presence of an amount property somewhere in the BankTransaction class; that may be unavoidable in the domain of bank transactions, but the point here is that now we are focused on exposing behavior through a clean interface and not giving direct access to the specific variables through getters and setters.

8.7 About Polymorphism

The next three sections will cover **inheritance**, **interfaces**, and **abstract** classes. All these three constructs enable polymorphism. If you don't know what polymorphism is, then it's not obvious why these three constructs exist or why they are needed. On the other hand, without understanding these three constructs deeply, you will not be able to understand polymorphism. It's really a chicken–egg situation.

So, to ensure you are not lost for the next three sections, let me provide a **quick and naive** definition of polymorphism. Don't worry if it doesn't make much sense yet. It will later.

Polymorphism is the ability to **treat different classes as if they were of the same type**. This is achieved by having those classes extend another class or by implementing an interface. Then, your code can work with the high-level base type or interface, not with the specific classes that inherit or implement it.

A common example is being able to pass a variable of type `Lead` to a method that accepts a parameter of type `SObject`, like `Database.insert()`, for example:

```
//the signature of insert accepts an SObject, not a lead
Database.insert(myLead);
```

This is possible because behind the scenes, the `Lead` class inherits from the standard `SObject` class. The `insert` method doesn't care whether the object is a `Lead`, `Account`, or `Opportunity`. It treats all these classes as `SObject`, **enabling a single method to handle multiple types as if they were the same**. Imagine how strange it would be if there was a method for each type of `SObject` you could insert, i.e.:

```
Database.insertLead(...)
Database.insertOpportunity(...)
Database.insertAccount(...)
Database.insertCase(...)
```

CHAPTER 8   OBJECT-ORIENTED PROGRAMMING IN APEX

By having all the specific SObjects inherit from the `SObject` class, you can write one method that can act on all of them.

We saw another example of polymorphism in Chapter 3, where we saw how to create a DML wrapper class, and in doing so, we created an interface called `DMLExecutable`:

```
public void execute() {

    //get the operation based on the user-provided enum
    DMLExecutable operation = this.operationsByDmlAction.
    get(this.operation);
    //execute the operation
    operation.execute(this.records, this.allowPartialSuccess);
}
```

In the above example, the `execute` method doesn't know the specific class behind `DMLExecutable` is; all it knows and cares about is that it will respond to the `execute()` method. The actual implementation is provided by specific classes handling different DML operations.

Polymorphic methods are then highly reusable because they can act on many different classes as long as those classes inherit a class or implement an interface. Again, this may not be the greatest explanation, but keep it in mind as you go over the next three concepts. As we go through them, you will slowly start to see how they enable polymorphism.

Finally, the last section of this chapter explains **why** you should use polymorphism.

8.8 Inheritance

Inheritance is another pillar in OOP. The original purpose of inheritance is to **promote code reuse and provide specialized behavior**. We do this by defining that a class is a special kind of another class.

208

> **Note** Inheritance is always explained with silly examples such as animals or pizzas. While I personally dislike this due to its poor applicability to real-world programming, it is indeed the best way to explain it. In this section, I will explain inheritance using one of such examples, but I will do my best to tie it back to real-world Apex programming.

Before we look at the specifics, it's worth noting that inheritance is a concept we use in our everyday lives. Think of a bug (the animal, not the programming mistake). What does a bug look like? You may have an image in your head, but really, it isn't possible to define what a bug looks like, as there are many kinds of bugs. Some bugs fly, others crawl, and others jump. Some are green and some are almost transparent. They can be completely different from one another yet in our minds, we think of them as one concept: a bug.

Thinking of the higher-level concept (the bug) is a form of abstraction. It allows us to think about bugs without specifying all the details of a particular bug. But why do we group them into a single category? Because they share common traits, such as having six legs, compound eyes, and an exoskeleton.

How does this relate to knowledge reuse? Imagine you have a friend who has never seen a beetle. If you told them that a beetle is a bug, they would immediately understand certain things: it's small, it might be able to fly, it lays eggs, and so on. **Their existing knowledge about bugs can be reused to understand something new.**

We do this with many concepts in our everyday lives. For example, when we think of higher-level categories like cars, airplanes, burgers, pizzas, humans, or computers, we apply our general understanding of those types without needing to know the specifics. Each of these is a "base type," and the specific instances (a Tesla, a cheeseburger, a MacBook) are specialized variations.

CHAPTER 8 OBJECT-ORIENTED PROGRAMMING IN APEX

And so, going back to our example, I could define a Bug class like this:

> **Note** In apex, you have to use the virtual keyword if you want a class to be base type that can be extended with specialized behavior.

```
public virtual class Bug {

    public virtual void fly() {
        System.debug('The bug is flying!');
    }

    public virtual void move() {
        System.debug('The bug is moving!');
    }

    public virtual void eat() {
        System.debug('The bug is eating!');
    }
}
```

The class provides the general behavior. If I want to create a Grasshoper class, I can simply extend the Bug class and **automatically inherit all its behavior**.

```
public class Grasshoper extends Bug {

    public void sayName() {
        System.debug('patience, grasshoper');
    }
}
```

CHAPTER 8   OBJECT-ORIENTED PROGRAMMING IN APEX

Just by extending the Bug class, the Grasshoper class has access to the fly, move, and eat methods. For example, I can do the following:

Grasshoper jiminy = new **Grasshoper**();

jiminy.**fly**();
jiminy.**eat**();

Notice that I never defined the fly and eat methods in the Grasshoper class. By extending the Bug class, **I can automatically reuse that behavior.**

The second part of inheritance is being able to reuse behavior while at the same time being able to provide specialized behavior. Imagine I'm not satisfied with what the fly method does given that grasshoppers don't really fly (they fly for only a few seconds). In that case, I can override that method and provide my own behavior:

```
public class Grasshoper extends Bug {

    public override void fly() {
        System.debug('Fly for only a few seconds');
    }

}
```

Now, when I call fly on the Grasshoper, I get the specialized behavior defined in this subclass and not the generalized behavior of the base class.

The common way to think about inheritance is that the subclass **is a** special kind of type of the base class. I highlight "is a" because that's how you know that a class is a candidate for inheriting from a base class. If in your mind you can say "this thing is a special kind of that thing," then you could model that relationship between the classes using an inheritance hierarchy.

8.8.1 Inheritance in Apex Programming

Now, unless you are a Salesforce developer at a university's biology department, it's very unlikely that you are creating bug classes. In Apex, we are mostly dealing with CRUD operations, moving data from an object to another and reacting to trigger events. It is then not obvious when you could use inheritance in Apex.

First of all, let me remind you that all Salesforce database table objects inherit automatically from the SObject class. So even if we don't create our own inheritance hierarchies, we use inheritance every day. If you look at the method signature of the methods of the Database class that deal with database tables, you'll see they take an SObject parameter, which is the base class of all database table objects.

```
public static Database.SaveResult[] insert(SObject[]
recordsToInsert, Boolean allOrNone)
```

Furthermore, **all objects in Apex inherit from the Object class**. This is the class that sits at the top of the hierarchy. Every single class implicitly inherits from this class. One of the methods of this class is toString(), which returns a string that represents the object. Let's try it:

```
Grasshoper jiminy = new Grasshoper();

System.debug(jiminy.toString());
System.debug(new Lead(LastName='me').toString());
```

When I run this, I get the following in the debug log:

```
15:20:45:008 USER_DEBUG [3]|DEBUG|Grasshoper:[]
15:20:45:008 USER_DEBUG [5]|DEBUG|Lead:{LastName=me}
```

Notice that I never defined the toString method in Grasshoper or Bug, yet it is available for me to use it. It's also there in the Lead class.

I could also override this method:

CHAPTER 8   OBJECT-ORIENTED PROGRAMMING IN APEX

```
public class Grasshoper extends Bug {

    public override void fly() {
        System.debug('Fly for only a few seconds');
    }

    public override String toString() {
        return 'Grasshoper is such a weird bug';
    }
}
```

Now the debug log shows the following:

```
15:20:45:008 USER_DEBUG [3]|DEBUG|Grasshoper is such a weird bug
15:20:45:008 USER_DEBUG [5]|DEBUG|Lead:{LastName=me}
```

So, this shows that inheritance, code reuse, and specialized behavior is fully supported in Apex and we can use it every day without knowing. Still, this does not answer the question of how or when we should use this in everyday Apex programming.

The answer is that it depends on what you are doing. I once worked at a company where we had a custom lead conversion process. Leads could be converted to either an opportunity or a custom object. Because the business logic was so specific, we couldn't use the standard lead conversion process. However, both types of conversion (lead to opportunity or lead to custom object) had a lot of common behavior, such as how fields were mapped, etc. But they also had specialized behavior.

In this case, I ended up creating a base class called `LeadToObjectConversion`
    and two subclasses

`LeadToOpportunityConversion`
`LeadToAttendanceConversion`

CHAPTER 8 OBJECT-ORIENTED PROGRAMMING IN APEX

Like this:

```
public virtual class LeadToObjectConversion {...}

public class LeadToOpportunityConversion extends
LeadToObjectConversion {...}

public class LeadToAttendanceConversion extends
LeadToObjectConversion {...}
```

Whenever I had to change behavior that would apply to both types of conversion, I only had to make the change in the `LeadToObjectConversion` class. The two subclasses would immediately inherit the change.

More importantly, I was able to trigger either type of conversions in bulk **without knowing which specific conversion type was being executed**. If this sounds familiar, it is because this is a classic example of polymorphism. My code looked something like this (this is pseudocode):

```
//list is instantiated using the base class
List<LeadToObjectConversion> conversions = new List<LeadToObjec
tConversion>();

for (Lead lead : someLeads){

    if(//some condition){
        //specific implementation
        conversions.add(new LeadToOpportunityConversion(lead));
    }
    else{
        //specific implementation
        conversions.add(new LeadToAttendanceConversion(lead));
    }
}
```

```
for(LeadToObjectConversion cv : conversions){
    //convertLead is defined in the base class
    cv.convertLead();
    //it doesn't matter what type of conversion it is!
}
```

In the above example, the last `for` loop doesn't care what specific type of conversion it is dealing with; it just knows that it has a `convertLead()` method that will do something specific.

This is a real-life example of one of the few times I've used inheritance. The example also highlights that as a side effect of using inheritance, I was able to create a polymorphic method. This shows how inheritance's purpose is to **encourage code reuse through inheriting behavior and enabling polymorphism.**

8.8.2 When to Use Inheritance in Apex

I recommend that you use inheritance only when you have a strong reason to do so. A common mistake when people learn OOP is they go around the code base trying to find places to use their new knowledge. I still have bad dreams of Apex code bases where everything was forced into an object and every class inherited from another one. Don't do that.

Use inheritance when you find yourself with a business process that has variations and commonalities. If the entire business process is implemented in Apex, consider whether centralizing shared logic in a base class and specializing behaviors in subclasses would add value. If you never come across such scenario, that's ok. Not everything in OOP is solved through inheritance.

Finally, **it's generally recommended to favor composition over inheritance**. Rather than sharing behavior by means of extending other classes, simply model that behavior in a separate class that can be used alongside other classes.

CHAPTER 8　OBJECT-ORIENTED PROGRAMMING IN APEX

Here's an example of when composition is better than inheritance. Imagine you have a `Logger` class that defines methods for logging errors, messages, etc.

```
public virtual with sharing class MyLogger {
    public void log(String message) {
        System.debug(message);
    }
}
```

Now, my `MassLeadConversion` class can do logging by extending `MyLogger` and reusing the `log` method:

```
public with sharing class MassLeadConversion extends MyLogger {
    public MassLeadConversion() {
        //super.log() refers to the log method in MyLogger
        super.log('Starting MassLeadConversion');
    }
}
```

While this allows for behavior reuse, it forces the `MassLeadConversion` class to have all the methods of `MyLogger`. Also, using the keyword `super` to call the methods of the extended class is optional. You could simply use `log()` directly in the subclass, but that might confuse readers of the code, as the method isn't defined in the subclass, making it less obvious where the behavior is coming from.

A better approach is to let `MassLeadConversion` take `MyLogger` as a constructor parameter, like this:

```
public with sharing class MassLeadConversion {
    private MyLogger logger;

    public MassLeadConversion(MyLogger logger) {
```

```
        this.logger = logger;
        logger.log('Starting MassLeadConversion');
    }
}
```

This is composition. The class **has an** instance of MyLogger it can use for logging; it is no longer a subclass of it. I emphasize "has an" because that's how we think of this relationship:

MassLeadConversion has a logger.

Instead of the previous relationship type:

MassLeadConversion is a kind of logger.

This is better because the dependency is more obvious, and in the future, we can swap MyLogger for a mock object to make testing easier (we'll explore this in detail in a future chapter).

8.9 Interfaces

> **Note** Remember that throughout this book, the term "interface" has two meanings. The first refers to the external behavior or controls of a module, such as its methods, variables, or documentation. When we talk about deep modules having a clean interface, we mean they are easy to use and understand.
>
> In OOP, however, an interface is a specific construct that enables polymorphism and programming-by-contract. In this section, we're discussing the OOP construct, not the user-facing module interface.

CHAPTER 8 OBJECT-ORIENTED PROGRAMMING IN APEX

Unlike base classes, interfaces cannot be used to reuse code or behavior; they are mostly a tool to enable polymorphism and advanced design patterns such as dependency injection and mocking (we'll explore those two in detail later in future chapters).

You use an interface when you want to define that a class must adhere to a contract. That contract specifies what behaviors the class must implement, but the interface does not specify how they should be implemented.

Let's go back to the example in Chapter 3. We wanted to create a DML wrapper to simplify DML operations and provide a cleaner interface.

```
DML dmlOperation = new DML()
        .setOperation(DML.Operation.INSERTS)
        .setRecords(accounts)
        .setAllowPartialSuccess(false);

dmlOperation.execute();
```

Initially, the execute method had a long and fragile `switch` statement that would call a different method depending on the `operation` parameter passed to the `setOperation` method.

```
public void execute() {
        switch on this.operation {
        when INSERTS {
            executeInsert(this.records, this.
            allowPartialSuccess);
        }
        when UPDATES {
            executeUpdate(this.records, this.
            allowPartialSuccess);
        }
        when DELETES {
```

CHAPTER 8 OBJECT-ORIENTED PROGRAMMING IN APEX

```
            executeDelete(this.records, this.
            allowPartialSuccess);
        }
        when UNDELETES {
            executeUndelete(this.records, this.
            allowPartialSuccess);
        }
    }
}
```

Our goal was to simplify this code and ensure it **does not change when new DML operations are added**. Think about that for a moment: if the method should not change when a new DML operation is added, then **the method must treat all DML operations the same way**. In other words, the method shouldn't care what DML operation it's executing. I hope that by this point this sounds all too familiar. To support this, the method must be polymorphic.

Our solution was to create an interface that defines a contract: whoever implements the interface must provide an implementation of the execute method:

```
public Interface DMLExecutable {
    void execute(List<SObject> records, Boolean allowPartial
    Success);
}
```

Notice that the interface is very small. It doesn't contain any logic. Then, we created an inner class for each DML operation we want to support, and we ensured each inner class implemented the interface

```
public class InsertOperation implements DMLExecutable {
    ...
}
```

219

CHAPTER 8 OBJECT-ORIENTED PROGRAMMING IN APEX

```
public class UpdateOperation implements DMLExecutable {
    ...
}
...//repeat for delete and undelete
```

Each class can decide how to implement the execute method. The interface doesn't care. The contract simply states that

- The class must implement a method called execute.
- The method must take an SObject list and a Boolean parameter.
- It must return void.

Finally, we created a map of strategies. Each DML operation is mapped to a specific implementation of the DMLExecutable interface:

```
private Map<DML.Operation, DMLExecutable> operationsByDmlAction
= new Map<DML.Operation, DMLExecutable> {
        //map the specific class to its corresponding
        enum value
        DML.Operation.Inserts => new InsertOperation(),
        DML.Operation.Updates => new UpdateOperation(),
        DML.Operation.Deletes => new DeleteOperation(),
        DML.Operation.Undeletes => new UndeleteOperation()
};
```

Finally, the execute method becomes two lines:

```
public void execute() {
    DMLExecutable operation = this.operationsByDmlAction.
    get(this.operation);
    operation.execute(this.records, this.allowPartialSuccess);
}
```

CHAPTER 8   OBJECT-ORIENTED PROGRAMMING IN APEX

This works because the `operation` variable is declared with the type `DMLExecutable`. As long as variables are declared with the type of the interface or base class, methods can act on them without knowing their specific implementation.

As I said earlier, interfaces also allow you to swap out the implementation of a class at runtime. For example, imagine something like this:

```
LeadConversionLogic conversionLogic;

if(Test.isRunningTest()) {
    conversionLogic = new MockConversionLogic(record);
} else {
    conversionLogic = new StandardLeadConversionLogic(record);
}
conversionLogic.convert();
```

In the above example, both `MockConversionLogic` and `StandardLeadConversionLogic` implement the `LeadConversionLogic` interface. Then, at runtime, the implementation will be different depending on whether we are executing a test.

I will come back to this pattern in much more detail in future chapters.

8.9.1 Interfaces in Apex

Other than custom interfaces, Apex also supports standard interfaces like `Queueable` or `Batchable`. For example, when you want to create a class that can run asynchronously, you implement the `Queueable` interface:

```
public class BankTransaction implements Queueable
```

CHAPTER 8 OBJECT-ORIENTED PROGRAMMING IN APEX

The moment you make a class implement Queuable, you will get this warning in your IDE:

```
Class BankTransaction must implement the method:
void System.Queueable.execute(System.QueueableContext)
```

This is because Queuable is an interface like any other. It defines a contract that specifies you must provide an implementation for the execute method. What actually happens inside of this method is irrelevant.

You may wonder why the developers of the Apex language used this mechanism to create asynchronous Apex classes. The reason is probably because behind the scenes, there's Apex code that we don't see that calls all Queueable classes in the queue and runs them, like this:

```
public InternalQueueableProcessor {

    public void processQueue(){

        List<Queuable> queue = [SELECT... FROM JOB_QUEUE__c
        WHERE status = 'Pending'];

        for(Queuable q : queue){
            q.execute();
        }
    }
}
```

Again, the processQueue method doesn't care about each individual class that implements Queuable or what it does. It just cares that it can respond to the execute method.

To summarize, interfaces are very useful when you want to define a contract that other classes must implement. The code using those interfaces becomes very flexible because it only cares that those classes adhere to the contract, not what they do. This, in turn, enables polymorphism.

CHAPTER 8   OBJECT-ORIENTED PROGRAMMING IN APEX

8.10 Abstract Classes

Abstract classes are somewhat of a combination of base classes and interfaces. An abstract class can define behavior that can be reused (just like a base class) while also defining specific methods that must be implemented by subclasses (just like an interface). It's the best of both worlds.

Given that we've already gone through inheritance reuse and interface implementations, I'm going to skip the theory and jump straight to an example, and you'll see for yourself the value of abstract classes.

I want to use an example inspired from James Simone's blog: *Joys of Apex*. Let's say we have a `Queueable` class that processes some account records:

```
public class AccountProcessor implements Queueable {
    public void execute(QueueableContext context) {
        List<Account> accounts = [SELECT Id, Name FROM Account
        WHERE Processed__c = false];

        for(Account acc : accounts) {
            acc.Processed__c = true;
        }

        update accounts;
    }
}
```

This is a dummy implementation. We process accounts that are not processed, and we marked `Processed__c` as `true` and update the accounts.

223

CHAPTER 8 OBJECT-ORIENTED PROGRAMMING IN APEX

Now, it is possible that some new accounts are created while the job is executing, which means some accounts will not be picked up. To address this, I'm going to add a method called shouldRunAgain as follows:

```
private Boolean shouldRunAgain() {
  return [SELECT COUNT() FROM Account WHERE Processed__
  c = false] > 0;
}
```

Then, I can update the execute method to call shouldRunAgain and queue itself:

```
public void execute(QueueableContext context) {
        List<Account> accounts = [SELECT Id, Name FROM Account
        WHERE Processed__c = false];
        for(Account acc : accounts) {
            acc.Processed__c = true;
        }
        update accounts;

        if(shouldRunAgain()) {
            System.enqueueJob(new AccountProcessor());
        }
    }
```

Let's say that this worked pretty well, and so, I decided to use **similar** mechanisms across other queueable classes. Of course, every class would have **different** logic on how to determine if it should queue itself again (I highlighted those two words on purpose; think about it for a bit).

Here's an example of another class

CHAPTER 8   OBJECT-ORIENTED PROGRAMMING IN APEX

```
public class LeadProcessor implements Queueable {

    public void execute(QueueableContext context) {
        //define some leads to process

        if(shouldRunAgain()) {
            System.enqueueJob(new LeadProcessor());
        }
    }

    private Boolean shouldRunAgain() {
        Integer openLeads = [SELECT COUNT() FROM Lead
        WHERE ... ];
        Integer availableReps = [SELECT COUNT() FROM User
        WHERE ... ];
        return openLeads > 0 && availableReps > 0;
    }
}
```

Here, the implementation of shouldRunAgain is completely different as this is a very different use case.

Now, let's say that my org grew in size and complexity, and now, Queueable jobs are failing because I'm hitting the governor limit of Queueable jobs that can be queued in a single transaction. To fix this, I can modify shouldRunAgain and check if I haven't hit the limit:

```
public class AccountProcessor implements Queueable ...

private Boolean shouldRunAgain() {

  Integer queuedJobsThisTransaction = Limits.
  getQueueableJobs();
  Integer maxQueueableJobs = Limits.getLimitQueueableJobs();
```

```
Boolean isThereSpace = queuedJobsThisTransaction <
maxQueueableJobs;
Boolean areThereUnprocessedAccounts = [SELECT COUNT() FROM
Account WHERE Processed__c = false] > 0;

return isThereSpace && areThereUnprocessedAccounts;

}
```

With this new implementation, the job is only queued again if there are accounts yet to be processed and if I haven't hit the governor limit.

But now I have a big problem. I was so happy with this design pattern that I have 27 different Apex classes all with their own implementation of `shouldRunAgain`. Now, I will have to go to each of those and copy/paste the bit of logic that checks the governor limit. Also, if Salesforce introduces a new governor limit related to `Queueable` Apex, then I need to go an update 27 classes again.

Before I jump to the solution, think about this for a moment. All Queueable classes should have a way to queue themselves again. What logic they use to decide that is up to each class. But every class must check the governor limit first.

If I were to generalize the idea: I need a way to force each class to do something (like an interface would), and every class should reuse the logic for governor limit checks (like a base class would allow), yet each class should be allowed to specify exactly when they should queue themselves again.

This is what an abstract class is for. **An abstract class allows me to define a partial implementation**. Some core logic is implemented and reused across multiple classes, but other logic must be implemented by each subclass.

For our example, I can create a new abstract class that implements the `Queueable` interface:

CHAPTER 8 OBJECT-ORIENTED PROGRAMMING IN APEX

```
public abstract class AutoQueueable implements Queueable{

    public void execute(QueueableContext context) {

        doExecute(context);

        if(limitNotHit() && shouldRunAgain()){
            System.enqueueJob(this);
        }
    }

    public abstract void doExecute(QueueableContext context);
    public abstract Boolean shouldRunAgain();

    public Boolean limitNotHit(){
        Integer queuedJobsThisTransaction = Limits.
        getQueueableJobs();
        Integer maxQueueableJobs = Limits.
        getLimitQueueableJobs();
        return queuedJobsThisTransaction < maxQueueableJobs;
    }
}
```

Let's break it down.

The abstract class implements the Queueable interface and implements the generalized behavior of the execute method. The generalized behavior is that it should do whatever it's supposed to do (process accounts, etc.) and queue itself if the governor limit hasn't been hit and if the business logic demands for the job to be queued again (there are remaining accounts, etc.)

However, what the job should actually do is up to each subclass, so we define that in the abstract method doExecute. Each subclass must define what doExecute does. Also, what determines if the job should be queued again is also defined in an abstract method, shouldRunAgain. Each class subclass must define this.

227

CHAPTER 8   OBJECT-ORIENTED PROGRAMMING IN APEX

With this abstract class in place, I can modify `AccountProcessor` like this:

```
public class AccountProcessor extends AutoQueueable {
    protected override void doExecute(QueueableContext context) {
        List<Account> accounts = [SELECT Id, Name FROM Account WHERE Processed__c = false];
        for(Account acc : accounts) {
            acc.Processed__c = true;
        }
        update accounts;
    }
    protected override Boolean shouldRunAgain() {
        return [SELECT COUNT() FROM Account WHERE Processed__c = false] > 0;
    }
}
```

Now, the class only needs to care about defining what to execute and whether it should run again. This is the pure business logic. The mechanism of how the job can queue itself again is defined in `AutoQueueable`. This design ensures that as new `Queueable` classes are added, developers can focus solely on the unique business logic without worrying about boilerplate for limits or queueing. Now, I can queue the job as follows:

```
System.enqueueJob(new AccountProcessor());
```

This may be a little strange to look at because `AccountProcessor` doesn't directly implement the `Queueable` class. Instead, it inherits from `AutoQueueable`, which does implement `Queueable` and defines the generalized logic for execute.

When Salesforce processes `AccountProcessor`, it first looks for the `execute` method in the class. Since it doesn't find it there, it checks the base class, where `execute` is defined, and calls it. The `execute` method then delegates **back to the specific implementation** of `doExecute` in the subclass to perform the actual job.

This shows how an algorithm can move up the inheritance hierarchy to a base class for general behavior and then back down to a subclass for specialized behavior. This pattern is so common that it's recognized as a formal design pattern called the **Template Method Pattern**. The Template Method Pattern is where a base class defines the overall algorithm while allowing subclasses to provide specialized behavior for specific steps.

And so, abstract classes can be useful when you need to **provide generalized functionality to other classes while letting them define the specifics**. As I said earlier, resist the temptation to go around the code base trying to find areas where to add abstract classes. If you understood the above pattern, you would eventually find some requirements that can benefit from it.

8.11 Why We Need Polymorphism

By now, you've seen multiple examples of polymorphism in action. The original definition I provided above stated that polymorphism is the ability to treat different classes as if they were of the same type. What isn't clear is *why* we need this.

At its core, polymorphism is just a mechanism to remove complex `if/else` statements. This is achieved by allowing the program to execute an action without knowing who is actually executing the action.

The argument is that if the program must know who's executing the action, then it must have an `if/else` statement, and it must be coupled to those specific classes.

CHAPTER 8 OBJECT-ORIENTED PROGRAMMING IN APEX

We can go back to our classic example. Imagine if the DML class had one `insert` method per each `SObject` type:

```
if(record.getSObjectType() == Account.SObjectType){
    Database.insertAccount(record);
}
else if(record.getSObjectType() == Contact.SObjectType){
    Database.insertContact(record);
}
else if(record.getSObjectType() == Opportunity.SObjectType){
    Database.insertOpportunity(record);
}
```

This is complex boolean logic, and it will only get more complex as more `SObject` types are added. Also, the method is coupled to each individual method of the `Database` class. In other words, this method depends way too much on the `Database` class.

A polymorphic design would reduce the `if/else` statement and make the method depend only on one method of the `Database` class.

```
// accepts any SObject type
Database.insert(record);
```

And really that's it. There are some more complicated and academic descriptions of polymorphism, but in the real world, they are usually used to replace complex conditional logic with a design that can scale without having to modify the code frequently.

When you find yourself with very complex `if/else` logic and each branch of logic is a variation of a specific process, that's a strong indication that you could refactor the code to use an interface or abstract class and a subclass per conditional branch.

Finally, polymorphism is needed to support dependency injection and mocking, which we will explore in future chapters.

8.12 Conclusion

As I said at the beginning of this chapter, OOP is a big topic, and entire books have been written about it. My hope is that this chapter provided you either a refresher or just enough detail to get you to think more about how you could use OOP designs in your everyday Apex programming.

I insist that we must remember that OOP is only one specific paradigm for solving software problems. Throughout my career, I've seen many examples where OOP design patterns are irrelevant in languages like JavaScript or TypeScript, simply because the patterns exist to solve limitations imposed by the language or the ideology. That is to say that OOP is simply a tool. A tool that is incredibly useful in some contexts and not so much in others.

CHAPTER 9

Software Design Principles

Every piece of knowledge must have a single, unambiguous, authoritative representation within a system.

—Andy Hunt and Dave Thomas

We've gone through enough material throughout the book that now we are ready to talk about design principles. Many of these principles have appeared already in the book with different names, and some may already be familiar to you. The goal of this chapter is to provide a short overview of each principle. We will go over SOLID, DRY, and a few others. For each principle, I will give a bit of background, explain what it is, and give some guidelines on when and when not to follow it.

9.1 What Are Design Principles?

In software, principles are usually a set of rules or highly recommended patterns and thought processes that can help us manage complexity in software design. I personally dislike the term "principle" because it often leads to sentences such as "**this violates the [insert principle name]**." "Violation" is a strong word for something as complex as software design. Software is rarely binary or black and white. Also, there isn't a single rule that should always be followed no matter what; instead, all principles should be seen as **recommendations and properties that software should aspire to have**.

We must also remember that all principles were created by humans; humans who have their own biases, agendas, and particular experiences. The same humans, under different circumstances, would have come up with completely different principles. That is to say that not all principles are equally useful in all circumstances.

That said, I recognize the term is a useful shorthand for ideas that helps us manage software complexity, so I will continue to use the term "principle" throughout this chapter. Just remember to think of them as properties, recommendations, and things to think about.

Finally, my critique is on how we use the term principle and not the intentions or cleverness of these principles. Many of them have passed the test of time because they consistently address common challenges in software design. **For that, we owe their creators our gratitude.**

9.2 SOLID

SOLID stands for the following principles:

- **S**: Single Responsibility Principle
- **O**: Open/Closed Principle
- **L**: Liskov Substitution Principle
- **I**: Interface Segregation Principle
- **D**: Dependency Inversion Principle

The SOLID principles were popularized by Robert C. Martin, famous for his work on the *Clean Code* book. These are just a set of principles heavily oriented toward OOP, and there's no specific reason why they go together, other than the fact that the word "SOLID" is easy to pronounce and remember. As we'll see shortly, there are other principles that are arguably more important yet they didn't fit into a nice marketable name.

9.2.1 Single Responsibility Principle

The Single Responsibility Principle (SRP) has its roots in the work of multiple computer scientists, but it was eventually coined and popularized by Robert C. Martin. The principle states that a **module should only have one reason to change.**

> **Note** In Martin's original works, he states that "a **class** should only have one reason to change." In later publications, he changed this to "a **module**," likely to address the fact that not all languages are class-based or OOP. This is one example of how principles derive from their creators' subjective experiences at a particular point in time.

This is like saying that a module should not mix concerns or that it should do one thing as we explored extensively in Chapter 3. The immediate natural question is "what is a reason?"; not too different from the "what is one thing?" question.

By now, you probably know I'm a big fan of the `Database` class in Apex. Consider if this class has a single responsibility, or whether it does one thing, or whether it has a single reason to change? I can think of multiple reasons why this class (internally and externally) could change:

- Salesforce introduces or updates the governor limits.
- Salesforce introduces new `sharing` switches for each operation type.

- Salesforce adds Data Cloud objects support in this class.
- New capabilities that we can't even think of that might emerge in years to come.

So, does that mean that the `Database` class does not follow the SRP? Well, according to Martin's original definition, yes, the class does not follow the SRP.

However, in his later works, Martin changed the way the principle should be interpreted, and he said it is about **people and business users who benefit from our software**. Let's see an example of this.

Imagine I have a class that encapsulates all business logic related to the `Case` object. If you are using the `fflib` library (a.k.a. as Apex Enterprise Patterns), you may be following a pattern like this (this is pseudocode):

```
public with sharing class Cases extends ApplicationSObjectDomain{

    public void getSupportCaseSLA();
    public void getCaseAge();
    public void createMarketingCase();
}
```

This looks like a reasonable class. All the logic related to dealing with `Cases` is nicely tied together. However, notice that the three methods **may serve different business users or personas.**

- getSupportCaseSLA:
    - Likely used indirectly by **support agents** to determine when a case response is due

- `getCaseAge`:
  - Used to create a custom report in a custom object to support quarterly business reviews conducted by **support managers**
- `createMarketingCase`:
  - Used within a marketing application to enable **the marketing team** to request feature updates and documentation from the product team

Now, what do you think would happen if the marketing team asks for changes in this logic, and you inadvertently break how SLAs are calculated? The support team will naturally be upset that something broke due to a change they didn't even ask for.

So, the SRP states that a responsibility or a reason to change is **a group of users to whom the module responds to.** If changes to the marketing case logic can affect the SLA logic, it's better to separate these modules so that they are only responsible for one group of users.

In even later works, Martin again provided another way to think of the SRP:

> *Gather together the things that change for the same reasons. Separate those things that change for different reasons.*

You might feel like this sentence is completely different from the original description I gave above, and the notion of personas or business users is not here. This is another example of how the creators of these principles often change their mind as they get more experience, which is why we should hold the principles lightly and not consider them gospel.

Still, I believe this particular sentence is profound, and I recommend you read it out loud a few times.

CHAPTER 9   SOFTWARE DESIGN PRINCIPLES

I started by posing the question on whether the `Database` class does not follow the SRP? Well, it depends on which version of the principle we are following. I'd argue that this class somewhat follows the principle because the only reason for it to change is to change how Salesforce developers interact with the database. Given that we are a distinct group of people, this class follows the SRP.

To put this principle in practice, you should consider whether a module is serving different business units or completely different contexts. If this is true and if this module is likely to change constantly, you should think deeply about separating them. In the next chapter, I will give more concrete guidelines on when to keep modules together or apart.

Finally, I want to acknowledge that I gave three different descriptions of the principle and that all of them are somewhat saying the same but also saying something completely different. I could have simplified this and simply say "do one thing," but that would be a disservice. My goal was to show you that a principle that is often treated as the holy grail of software design is nuanced, messy, and sometimes confusing. That is the reality of software design.

9.2.2 The Open/Closed Principle

The Open/Closed Principle (OCP) states that a module should be **open for extension, but closed for modification.** What this means is we should be able to extend the functionality of a module without modifying the existing code; instead, we write new code.

> **Note**   In general, this principle is more useful for those creating reusable Apex libraries that other developers will consume, such as Nebula Logger, Trigger Actions Framework, etc. For everyday development, you should consider if the principle is applicable to your specific circumstances.

CHAPTER 9   SOFTWARE DESIGN PRINCIPLES

The idea here is that if we can add behavior to a module without modifying its core logic, less bugs are likely to occur on clients that depend on that core logic. Our classic example of the DML wrapper class is an example of the OCP.

```
public void execute() {

    DMLExecutable operation = this.operationsByDmlAction.
    get(this.operation);
    operation.execute(this.records, this.allowPartialSuccess);
}
```

We can add more DML operations simply by adding a new implementation of the `DMLExecutable` class. The execute method **can be extended to support new logic without it being modified at all.** So, in a way, polymorphism is a manifestation of the OCP. In this example, this was an implementation of the strategy pattern.

We also saw in the previous chapters how we can add new behaviors of the `shouldRunAgain` method for all `Queueable` classes using the Template Method Pattern.

```
public abstract class AutoQueueable implements Queueable{

    public void execute(QueueableContext context) {

        doExecute(context);

        if(limitNotHit() && shouldRunAgain()){
            System.enqueueJob(this);
        }
    }

    public abstract void doExecute(QueueableContext context);
    public abstract Boolean shouldRunAgain();
```

239

CHAPTER 9   SOFTWARE DESIGN PRINCIPLES

Every time we want to add a new variation of what determines if a `Queueable` class should run again, we simply create a **new** class that implements `AutoQueueable`. In other words, the behavior of `AutoQueueable` is open for extension without needing changes in its code (it's closed for modification).

Another example is the Trigger Actions Framework open source library by Mitch Spano. To add new behavior to a trigger handler, you simply create a new class and add it to the custom metadata type that the handler reads to determine what actions should be executed. The handler class never changes. In the GitHub repo itself, Spano mentions how this framework follows the OCP and the SRP:

> *The Trigger Actions Framework conforms strongly to the Open-closed principle and the Single-responsibility principle. To add or modify trigger logic in our Salesforce org, we won't need to keep modifying the body of a TriggerHandler class; we can create a class or a flow with responsibility scoped to the automation we are trying to build and configure these actions to run in a specified order within a given trigger context.*
>
> *The work is performed in the* `MetadataTriggerHandler` *class which implements the Strategy Pattern by fetching all Trigger Action metadata that is configured in the org for the given trigger context.*

Now, we should only follow this principle when we know (either by evidence or experience in the domain) that the behavior is very likely to change or have variations. For example, if Salesforce only supported two DML operations for the past ten years, the following method would be completely acceptable:

```
public void execute() {

    switch on this.operation {

        when INSERTS {
            executeInsert(this.records, this.
            allowPartialSuccess);
        }
        when UPDATES {
            executeUpdate(this.records, this.
            allowPartialSuccess);
        }
...
```

I would be wasteful to use the strategy pattern just to hide such simple boolean logic. However, we know there are multiple DML operations, and we know Salesforce has added new variations in recent years (with sharing, async, etc.), so in this case, it makes sense for the execute method to allow extension without modification.

9.2.3 The Liskov Substitution Principle

The Liskov Substitution Principle (LSP), introduced by Barbara Liskov in 1988, states that objects of a derived class must be able to replace objects of their base class without changing the expected behavior of the program. In other words, **if a program works as intended with a base class or an interface, it should also work as intended with any subclass or implementation of that base class or interface.**

Consider this example. As you know by now, the `Database` methods (`insert`, `update`, etc.) act on the `SObject` type and not the specific type, and so, the following works:

```
Contact record = [SELECT Id FROM Contact LIMIT 1];
Database.update(record, true);
```

CHAPTER 9 SOFTWARE DESIGN PRINCIPLES

The update method would behave the same way if record was an Opportunity:

```
Opportunity record = [SELECT Id FROM Opportunity LIMIT 1];
Database.update(record, true);
```

As we've seen already, this works because all specific object types inherit from the SObject class. So far, this logic follows the LSP. You can use a specific type of record anywhere where an SObject type is expected.

However, the logic breaks when you pass a converted lead:

```
Lead record = [SELECT LastName FROM Lead WHERE IsConverted = TRUE LIMIT 1];
Database.update(record, true);
```

This fails with the following error:

```
CANNOT_UPDATE_CONVERTED_LEAD, cannot reference converted lead: []
```

The issue here is that converted leads cannot be updated. This restriction is specific to Lead records, **diverging from the general behavior** of SObject. To handle this, you are forced to introduce type-specific logic:

```
if (record instanceof Lead) {
    Boolean isConverted = [SELECT IsConverted FROM Lead
                           WHERE Id = :record.Id].IsConverted;

    if(isConverted){
        //do nothing, cannot update
    }
    else{
        Database.update(record, true);
    }
```

```
}
else{
    Database.update(record, true);
}
```

Checking for the specific type of a type (i.e., `record instanceof Lead`) is known as "type-narrowing." You are trying to narrow down the specific type because you know that it does not conform to the contract specified in the base class (`SObject` in this case).

This diverges from the LSP because you should be able to use `Lead` every time you have a reference to an `SObject`, but it turns out, you can't when it comes to DML updates. What was a clean and short method is now polluted with logic specific to a particular type.

This also diverges from the Open/Closed Principle because if there are more types that need special handling, the method needs to be updated every time we find such special case. In other words, it's not closed for modification.

In this particular case, it's the `Lead` class who diverges from the principle.

To summarize: If a subclass needs special behavior that breaks the parent class's contract, you might want to reconsider whether

- Inheritance is the correct design choice.
- The parent class's design needs to be rethought.

9.2.4 The Interface Segregation Principle

The Interface Segregation Principle (ISP) states we should **keep interfaces small and specific so that modules don't depend on things they don't need.**

CHAPTER 9 SOFTWARE DESIGN PRINCIPLES

> **Note** Here, "interface" refers to the specific programming construct of OOP, not the external behavior of a module.

Basically, this means that **interfaces should enforce one thing**. We already know from the previous chapter that interfaces are used to force classes to adhere to a contract so that we can create polymorphic methods that can act on the interface and not the specific implementations. The ISP encourages us to **keep our contracts small** and to not force classes to implement behavior they don't need.

A good example of this is batch Apex. To create a batch class, you have to implement the Database.Batchable interface, like this:

```
public class SummarizeAccountTotal implements
    Database.Batchable<sObject> {

    ...
```

However, batch Apex also offers two additional, optional interfaces:

- Database.RaisesPlatformEvents: Allows the class to fire platform events

- Database.Stateful: Allows the class to maintain state across transactions

```
public class SummarizeAccountTotal
    implements Database.Batchable<sObject>,
    Database.RaisesPlatformEvents,
    Database.Stateful {

    ...
```

Salesforce split these behaviors into separate interfaces because not all batch classes need to raise platform events or remember the state of previous transactions. If these two behaviors were baked into the

`Database.Batchable` class, our classes would likely need some logic to bypass that behavior or to make exceptions. Those exceptions would also contradict the LSP as we saw in the previous section.

In short, the ISP encourages us to keep our interfaces **focused**, **specific**, and where possible **optional**.

9.2.5 The Dependency Inversion Principle

The Dependency Inversion Principle (DIP) is probably the most misunderstood of the SOLID principles, and it's also the hardest to explain. Let me start by saying that the DIP is **not** the same as dependency injection (DI). I will explain DI in detail in a later chapter.

The understand this principle, we must understand two concepts first. Classes or modules can be divided in two categories:

- Policy: A class or module defines a high-level policy or business requirement.

- Detail: A lower-level module defines the details that support the policy.

Let's imagine that I have a very complex `Lead` conversion process. The high-level policy or requirement is in the `CustomLeadConversion` class (this is pseudocode):

```
public class CustomLeadConversion {

    public void convertLead(Lead lead);
    public void convertLeads(List<Lead> leads);
    public List<Lead> getConvertedLeads();
    public Boolean isEligibleForConversion(Lead lead);

}
```

CHAPTER 9　SOFTWARE DESIGN PRINCIPLES

Now, imagine this class became so complex that you decided to place lower-level methods into a separate class, called `LeadConversionUtils` (we already spoke about whether utility classes are an antipattern or not). This class deals with the details that are not so important from a business point of view, such as querying the database, logging error messages, etc.

```
public class LeadConversionUtil {

    public List<String> getFieldsToMap();
    public Boolean isFieldMappable(String fieldName);
    public Boolean isFieldMappable(Schema.SObjectField field);
    public List<Lead_Conversion_Field_Mapping__mdt> getLeadConversionFieldMappings();

}
```

With this new class in place, `CustomLeadConversion` will make calls to `LeadConversionUtil` in different places.

```
public class CustomLeadConversion {

    //the policy uses the detail for lower level operations
    //we'll make this better with dependency injection later
    private LeadConversionUtil utils = new LeadConversionUtil();

    public void convertLead(Lead lead);
    public void convertLeads(List<Lead> leads);
    public List<Lead> getConvertedLeads();
    public Boolean isEligibleForConversion(Lead lead);

}
```

The DIP states that at this point, the high-level policy depends on the details. If we make changes to `LeadConversionUtil`, the policy will be impacted. Such dependency is undesirable. **The detail exists to serve**

CHAPTER 9   SOFTWARE DESIGN PRINCIPLES

the policy, so it makes sense for the detail to depend on the policy's requirements, not the other way around.

Imagine for a moment that I impersonate the policy class `CustomLeadConversion`. Here's what my thought process would be:

> *To satisfy this complex lead conversion process, I need to interact with the database, get custom settings, etc. Currently, I depend on you,* `LeadConversionUtil`. *I don't like that. I'm the policy. Why should you define what operations I can call on you?*
>
> **I should be the one to tell you what I need!** *So, I'm going to give you a contract that defines what operations I need, and you will implement it. I'm not too interested in how you do that as long as you satisfy my contract. If I ever add some new functionality, I'll amend the contract and let you know.*

To satisfy the DIP, `CustomLeadConversion` must define a contract that defines what lower-level operations it needs, and then, **both classes will depend on that contract**. Here's what it would look like:

```
public class CustomLeadConversion {
    public interface ILeadConversionUtil {
        public List<String> getFieldsToMap();
        public Boolean isFieldMappable(String fieldName);
        public Boolean isFieldMappable(Schema.
        SObjectField field);
        public List<Lead_Conversion_Field_Mapping__mdt>
        getLeadConversionFieldMappings();
    }
```

247

CHAPTER 9   SOFTWARE DESIGN PRINCIPLES

```
    private ILeadConversionUtil utils;
    public void convertLead(Lead lead);
    public void convertLeads(List<Lead> leads);
    public List<Lead> getConvertedLeads();
    public Boolean isEligibleForConversion(Lead lead);
}
```

Now, `CustomLeadConversion` has defined what it needs through the `ILeadConversionUtil` interface, created directly in the class itself. Notice that the reference to `utils` has changed to the interface too.

Now, we just have to make `LeadConversionUtil` implement the `IleadConversionUtil` interface. I will also rename it to `LeadConversionUtilImpl` so that it's clear which is which.

Note   It's a common pattern to append interfaces with the letter `I` and to suffix their implementations with the word `Impl`. Whether that's a good practice is a whole different discussion.

```
public class LeadConversionUtilImpl implements
CustomLeadConversion.ILeadConversionUtil {

    ...

}
```

With this design, `CustomLeadConversion` no longer depends on `LeadConversionUtilImpl` from a purely technical point of view. `CustomLeadConversion` doesn't have a reference to `LeadConversionUtilImpl` anywhere. It only has a reference to its interface `ILeadConversionUtil`.

Also, `LeadConversionUtilImpl` depends on `IleadConversionUtil` as it is required to implement its contract.

The policy and detail class both depend on the same interface.

From a philosophical point of view, it's now `CustomLeadConversion` who determines what the detail should be. The detail class now must implement the interface defined by the policy. The detail depends on what the policy defines in the contract, which means **the dependency has been inverted.**

I recommend reading the above a few times before you continue.

Now, I argue that on its own, the DIP achieves nothing. All we've done here is added an additional module that creates an artificial separation between the policy and the detail. Even if the policy defines what the detail should do, **the detail class still defines how it actually does it, and that can still break the policy.** So, the idea that the policy no longer depends on the detail is somewhat artificial.

However, the DIP is powerful when you couple it with dependency injection (DI), and both combined are the entire foundation for advanced mocking and testing. DI is a large topic, so for now, I will provide a naive explanation just so that we can understand how the DIP is useful.

Dependency injection is simply two things:

- Pass dependencies via a constructor
- Hide those dependencies behind an interface

In our example, we can now modify the constructor of `CustomLeadConversion` to take an implementation of `ILeadConversionUtil`, like this:

```
public class CustomLeadConversion {

    public CustomLeadConversion(ILeadConversionUtil
    leadConversionUtil) {
        this.leadConversionUtil = leadConversionUtil;
    }
    ...
```

CHAPTER 9   SOFTWARE DESIGN PRINCIPLES

Now, `CustomLeadConversion` really doesn't know about the specific implementation (`LeadConverstionUtilImpl`). This class will be passed to it via the constructor, and thanks to polymorphism, we can refer to it with its base type.

That's really dependency injection. With this in place, you can do very interesting things. For example, when testing, you can pass a mock implementation of `ILeadConverstionUtil`, for example:

```
public class LeadConversionUtilMock implements ILeadConversionUtil{
        //mock implementation of all the methods
    }
```

And then

```
@IsTest
public static void testConvertLead(){

    //define the variable as the base type
    //but instantiate the mock implementation (polymorphism!!)
    CustomLeadConversion.ILeadConversionUtil leadConversionUtil
    = new CustomLeadConversion.LeadConversionUtilMock();

    //inject the mock implementation via the constructor
    CustomLeadConversion customLeadConversion = new CustomLead
    Conversion(leadConversionUtil);
}
```

Now, `CustomLeadConversion` has been instantiated with a fake implementation of the detail class. That means that now, we can focus on testing `CustomLeadConversion` assuming that the detail does what it needs to do. This helps us make our tests more focused on a specific behavior we want to test, without relying on the dependencies of that behavior. If this isn't clear, don't worry, I'll spend a lot more time on this in a future chapter.

And so, here's where the DIP really comes in. If we want to hide dependencies behind an interface, do we model the interface as a mirror of the methods in the module we are injecting, or **do we model it based on the caller's needs?**

In other words, rather than creating a generic utility class and creating an interface that defines the methods on the class, **we define the interface based on the needs of the high-level policies**. That's what the DIP is all about.

Let's try to summarize this section:

- The Dependency Inversion Principle states that high-level policies should define the rules, while low-level details follow them.

- When combined with dependency injection, DIP becomes a foundation of decoupled architecture and testable modules.

- In practice, always consider the needs of the high-level policies when designing abstractions.

- Bonus: Be careful not to overuse the DIP. There is still value in generic modules that satisfy multiple clients via utility methods. Forcing every utility to serve a specific client reduces our chances of reusing that utility.

Those are the SOLID principles. As I've said in other sections, resist the temptation to go around your code base looking for places to implement the SOLID principles. Let the business requirements and the complexity of the code determine which design principles can help.

CHAPTER 9   SOFTWARE DESIGN PRINCIPLES

9.3 DRY

DRY stands for **Do Not Repeat Yourself**. It's a very simple principle that encourages us to avoid duplication of code. We've seen many examples of this throughout the book.

For example, we saw how the `AutoQueueable` Apex class allowed any number of Apex classes to reuse the `shouldRunAgain` logic based on governor limits availability. If we had implemented this logic in every single `Queueable` class, then any change to that logic would need to be replicated across all those classes.

DRY also applies to even the simplest of operations. For example, if I find myself concatenating two record IDs to create the ID for a map multiple times in an Apex class, I can deduplicate the logic by creating a new abstraction that captures the essence:

```
public String createMapId(Id sourceRecord,Id targetRecord)
```

That said, the biggest challenge with the DRY principle is **developers tend to apply it prematurely**. I've always thought this principle should've been called DRYTM (don't repeat yourself too much), but of course, that's not a marketable name.

I will tell you about my personal experience in writing code: I consciously duplicate a bit of logic in several places throughout a module. I am okay with this because when I'm writing the code I'm in a different headspace. I am thinking about the high-level logic and not about making the code as clean as possible yet. Sometimes, it takes me two or three instances of seeing duplicated code to uncover the underlying abstraction behind it. And if I'm not confident that I understand the abstraction, I may create **the wrong abstraction**.

CHAPTER 9   SOFTWARE DESIGN PRINCIPLES

Think for a moment which is worse:

- A bit of duplicated logic in a couple of places?
- The wrong abstraction, which forces all clients to adhere to a contract they may not need?

Another problem with applying DRY everywhere is that it creates coupling. Imagine that you realize a lot of your time as a Salesforce developer is spent dealing with collections, creating them as maps, filtering them. You may think this is wasteful and you may realize that you could abstract a lot of this logic into a `Collection` class.

```
opportunityByAccountId = (Map<Id, Opportunity>) Collection.of
(opportunities).mapBy(Opportunity.AccountId);
```

This is a valid use case for DRY. However, given that collections are so prominent in almost every Apex class, the new `Collection` class is going to be coupled to every other class in your code base.

Imagine then you realize that there's an edge case that your original abstraction did not account for. At this point, you are presented with two choices.

- Write the duplicated logic specific to that edge case (i.e., write a few for loops), and move on.
- Modify the abstraction to fit the new requirement and risk breaking all other clients that rely on that abstraction.

Which is better?

You could reduce the coupling by placing `Collection` behind an interface or letting the policy-making classes determine what their requirements for a collection should be (the Dependency Inversion Principle). That way, clients will not depend on a specific instance of `Collection`, and you can define a special type of collection that satisfies

253

the edge case. But now, what used to be a few lines of code and maybe two for loops has become a complex hierarchy of classes, inheritance, polymorphism, and possible factory patterns to decide which collection type you need at runtime.

You may be okay dealing with that complexity but what about new employees who join your team? What will happen when you leave? Will they be able to support the complex abstraction?

I'm not saying any of this to encourage you to duplicate code. My goal is to warn you about the very strong consequences of premature deduplication, which are coupling and wrong abstractions.

Again, I recommend you let yourself duplicate logic at least twice before you consider what abstractions hide underneath. If after two times of writing the same logic you are still unclear, then let it be. Eventually you may realize what the correct abstraction is, and you can always go back and refactor the code.

9.4 YAGNI

YAGNI stands for "You aren't gonna need it," and it originated from the Extreme Programming movement in the late 1990s. I placed YAGNI immediately after DRY because, in some ways, it is its counterpart.

The idea of YAGNI is to resist the temptation to create features or abstractions "just in case." As I said in the DRY section, less experienced developers are prone to creating the wrong abstractions too early because they think they may need it. They do it "just in case" they need more variations of a piece of logic.

The YAGNI principle encourages us to **let the real requirements and concrete evidence to define our designs**. If we have concrete evidence that a bit of logic will be needed in multiple places and we understand the abstraction properly, then deduplicating it makes sense. If aren't sure, better not do it yet because you aren't gonna need it.

9.5 Design Errors Out of Existence

The last design principle comes from the work of John Ousterhout and its about error handling. I like this principle because very few principles deal with errors and exceptions.

This principle doesn't have a formal name, but it's known as "designing errors out of existence." The core idea here is that dealing with errors and exceptions makes our code harder to reason about. Whenever you read a `catch` block or a guard clause, you're dealing with an **exception to the "happy path"** of the code, the main logic that fulfils the requirement. Each of these exceptions interrupts your flow, forcing you to think, *"If this happens, the code handles it like this."* These interruptions add complexity and cost us time.

Most would argue that this is inevitable as dealing with errors and exceptions is part and parcel of programming, and this is exactly where Ousterhout's principle comes in: **What if we design our code so that there are no errors at all?**

If there are no errors, there's no need for exception handling or secondary logic paths. We can achieve this by **changing the semantics of the code** to eliminate edge cases entirely.

The best example of this is something we explored in Section 6.8, where we saw how calling a DML operation on an empty list does **not** throw an exception:

```
//no exception occurs
insert new List<Account>();
```

Now, what if Salesforce had decided calling a DML operation on an empty list **should** cause an exception? **Then, our code base would be filled with secondary paths of logic**, like this:

```
//DML only if the list is not empty
if(newAccounts.size() > 0){
```

```
    insert newAccounts;
}
```

or

```
try {
    insert accounts;
} catch(EmptyListException e) {//not a real exception type
   ...
}
```

However, Salesforce **redefined the semantics of the operation** so that when you call a DML operation on an empty list, nothing happens. By doing this, Salesforce eliminated the edge case entirely, along with the need for error handling or guard clauses.

Now, this isn't applicable to all errors or edge cases, but it's a powerful design principle in my opinion: can we design our code so that edge don't feel like edge cases? I encourage you to think about that for a while.

9.6 Conclusion

These are some of the most common design principles you should know about, but remember they are not the holy grail of software design. Instead, they are useful guidelines that we should keep in mind. In fact, a good software engineer knows when to break the rules and do something that is specific to their needs.

CHAPTER 10

Modularity, Coupling, and Cohesion

> *One of the most important elements of software design is determining who needs to know what, and when.*
>
> —John Ousterhout

In the preceding chapter, we spoke about several software design principles. The one which I didn't cover is modularity because as you are about to see, it's a complex and nuanced topic that deserves a whole chapter.

10.1 Modularity

Note Throughout this chapter, I will use the word "module" to refer to a unit of logic that satisfies a particular requirement. This can be a method, a class, a library, an sfdx folder, or even a package.

CHAPTER 10 MODULARITY, COUPLING, AND COHESION

Modularity can be defined as the degree to which a system's components **may be separated and recombined**. It's closely tied to concepts we've explored throughout this book:

- Do one thing
- Abstraction
- The Single Responsibility Principle
- Information hiding and encapsulation
- Deep modules

Modularity is also an important technique to reduce the complexity of our code base. If our code base is modular, developers only need to face a small fraction of the overall complexity at a given time. In theory, the expected benefits of modularity include the following:

- Development time is shortened because separate teams can work on different modules without needing constant communication.
- It should be possible to make big changes to one module without having to change others.
- It should be possible to learn and understand the overall system one module at a time.

In short, **modularity exists to reduce complexity**.

We could also say that modularity is like building with Lego blocks: each piece has a specific purpose and can be **combined with others** to form something larger. The more reusable and self-contained the blocks, the easier it is to build, replace, or modify parts of the system. Consider the following pseudocode:

```
order.Status__c = 'Processed';
order.Processed_Date__c = Date.today();

Database.update(order);

System.debug('Order processed: ' + order.Id);
```

This simple example shows modular design in action. I can use the individual "blocks" (`Date`, `Database`, and `System`) to build something larger. Also, I don't need to understand how they work behind the scenes; if I had to, the overall complexity of the code would be overwhelming.

These blocks are modular by means of information hiding. They hide the details from me and only expose whatever is important. This is not so different from Alan Kay's original definition of object-oriented programming.

10.2 Properties of Modular Software

If you've read this book in order, none of what I said above is new to you. Now, what do you think about this version of the same code?

```
order.Status__c = 'Processed';
Date.setFieldToToday(order.Processed_Date__c);

Database.update(order);

System.debug('Order processed: ' + order.Id);
```

Here, the `Date` module has a strange method, `setFieldToToday`. I'm sure this feels wrong to you, but it may not be immediately clear *why* it feels wrong. I encourage you to pause here and try to articulate to yourself exactly why this design feels off before reading the next section.

We can go back to all the principles we've explored in this book, and none of them answer why this feels wrong. For example, one could argue that

- The method does one thing.

- It has only has one reason to change if we consider "reason to change" a group of users or a persona, as Robert C. Martin described in his original description of the SRP.

- It's a deep module, it provides useful functionality behind a simple interface.

- It has a good and intuitive name.

SOLID, DRY, and general OOP concepts are often considered the holy grail of software design. Yet they cannot answer such a simple question: why is this wrong?

The real reason this feels wrong is because this method **knows too much about its surroundings.** Should the `Date` class know that there are date fields in custom objects and that those fields can be set during an Apex transaction? Should this class know how to validate field types and check for field-level security and whatever else is needed to write into a field?

If information hiding is key to modularity, then modules should not know too much about other modules. If they do, it means **there's information leakage in other parts of the system**. In particular, this method knows that users may create date fields and that they want to populate them with a `today` value. Why is this problematic?

The challenge is we haven't defined what are the properties of modular software; i.e., what properties should a class have for it be modular? One of those properties is that modules **should be somewhat general-purpose**.

CHAPTER 10   MODULARITY, COUPLING, AND COHESION

A general-purpose module is one that provides functionality that is applicable to a wide range of use cases. The module **makes very few assumptions about how it will be used** by other modules or for what purpose. For example:

`Date.today();`

The `today` method doesn't know or care how it will be used. Similarly, the `Date` class makes a very safe assumption: users will need a way to get today's date. But it stops right there; it doesn't make any more assumptions as to why users need today's date or how they plan to use it.

In contrast, a special-purpose module serves a very specific use case. That module can only be reused by specific clients with the exact same need.

`Date.setFieldToToday(String fieldName)`

And here's where things get interesting: **general-purpose modules are deeper**, and deep modules are key to modularity. On the other hand, **special-purpose modules are shallow**.

Because the `Date` class provides general-purpose methods for interacting with dates, it provides a simple interface. It also satisfies an almost infinite number of use cases. Remember:

simple interface + powerful functionality = deep module

However, if the `Date` class had special-purpose methods, such as `setFieldToToday`, you would expect to see *even more* special-purpose methods, like

```
setFieldToYesterday(String fieldName)
setFieldToSpecifiedDate(Date target)
isFieldDateFuture(Date target)
isFieldDatePast(Date target)
```

CHAPTER 10   MODULARITY, COUPLING, AND COHESION

The number of methods in the class would grow considerably, and each method provides very little overall value. Remember:

complex interface + little functionality = shallow module

So, if we want our code to be modular and reusable, we should aim to make it somewhat general-purpose.

> **Note** The use of the word "somewhat" is on purpose and subject to your interpretation. If a module is too generic, it may become cumbersome to use because it requires a lot of additional code to adapt it for specific purposes. On the other hand, a module that is too specialized locks you into a narrow use case.

10.3 Modularity in Our Daily Work

Now, at this point, this conversation may feel too philosophical. You may think this knowledge only applies to developers creating Apex libraries. For everyday development, most of us don't work this way.

But what if we did? What if our Apex code base was architected in a way such that there are general-purpose modules that we can simply reuse to represent business logic? Figure 10-1 shows the Apex reference guide, where we can see that it contains a lot of general-purpose classes that we use in our everyday development.

Chapter 10   Modularity, Coupling, and Cohesion

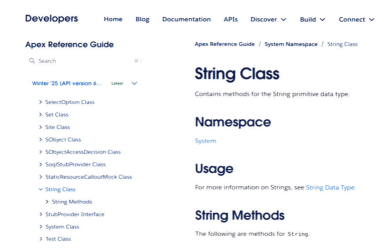

Figure 10-1. *The apex library contains many general-purpose classes that we can use*

So, why couldn't our internal code base be the same? Imagine if we took our users' business requirements and tried to "somewhat" generalize them to create internal APIs that other developers could reuse when similar requirements emerge.

I encourage you to put the book down for a while and think about this:

- What classes, modules, or APIs would exist in your org if you were to have general-purpose code as a foundation?

- How would other developers reuse them?

- Can you imagine how different your everyday work would be?

- Would deployments be easier?

- Would it be easier to onboard new developers and simply point them to the internal API library documentation?

263

CHAPTER 10   MODULARITY, COUPLING, AND COHESION

Here's an example of what a modular, general-purpose approach might look like (in pseudocode):

```
public class TA_Opportunity_StageUpdateRules
             implements TriggerAction.BeforeUpdate {

    private final FeatureFlags flags = new FeatureFlags();

    public void beforeUpdate(...) {

        Logger.info('Validating opportunity updates');
        if(flags.evaluate('enhancedOpportunityRules').
        isEnabled()) {

          List<Opportunity> closedWonOpps =
          (List<Opportunity>)

             Collection.of(newList)
                       .filter(Opportunity.StageName)
.equals('Closed Won')
                       .getList();

          for (Opportunity opp : closedWonOpps) {

                if(OpportunityValue.isHigh(opp)){
                opp.addError(...');
            }
          }
        }

        Logger.saveLog();
    }
}
```

264

CHAPTER 10   MODULARITY, COUPLING, AND COHESION

This simple example shows how to add new logic to the `Opportunity` trigger by creating a new class that plugs into the Trigger Actions Framework. For logging, developers use the `Logger` class provided by Nebula Logger. The new logic is hidden behind a feature flag using the `FeatureFlags` library, which allows us to deploy the change to production today but enable it later. List manipulation is handled via the `Collection` class, another internal library. Finally, the `OpportunityValue` module contains several functions that determine that business value of an opportunity; this is logic that is reused in many different places.

What would normally require a lot of boilerplate logic is **hidden away in deep modules that act as building blocks**. These modules can eventually evolve into an internal API library for all developers to consume.

Now, obviously, these examples are easy to imagine as modules because they represent cross-cutting concerns such as logging or triggers. But notice we do have the `OpportunityValue` module that provides several general-purpose methods related to how valuable an opportunity is. We can imagine another module simply called `Opportunities` which has other general-purpose functionality that is common across all opportunity-related business logic.

With some extra planning and attention, it should be possible to simplify business logic by composing it from reusable, general-purpose modules. To do this, we must try to

- Collect and deeply understand business requirements
- Identify the right abstractions
- Represent these abstractions as general-purpose modules
- Build business logic by combining reusable modules

265

That said, we should be careful not to take this idea to its logical extreme. Sometimes it's best to write simple and concise business logic with as little effort as possible. If a simple requirement can be expressed in a couple of functions, then we should just do it and move on; not everything should be generalized as a module. As I said earlier, if everything is too generic, irony strikes, and we end up creating a shallow module.

This brings an interesting question. How do you know if a piece of functionality belongs to an existing module or whether it should be its own? How do we know when two behaviors should be kept together or apart?

10.4 Better Together or Apart

As we said earlier, modularity exists to reduce complexity. Therefore, we can argue that the best way to determine if two behaviors should stay together or apart is whether the split reduces the overall complexity of our system.

At a high level, modularity comes into being by splitting larger modules into smaller ones, where each module is typically responsible for "one thing." However, splitting a module into smaller ones can have several negative consequences:

- The more modules, the higher the complexity. If you have a large API library, it can become difficult to find modules, know who's responsible for what, and which one has the behavior you are looking for.

- Over-dividing modules can require extra code to make them work together; code that wasn't needed when the behaviors were in a single module.

- Splitting modules creates separation. The new modules may be farther apart from each other than before, which can make it difficult to know that they are indeed related.

- Splitting modules can result in duplication. Code that only existed in a single module may now exist in several modules. You can counter this by extracting that logic into a third module, but now, all three modules are coupled together. This coupling didn't exist when all the logic was in a single module.

On the other hand, here are some guidelines that can help us determine if two behaviors should stay together:

- They share information and are always used together. We saw an example of this in Chapter 4 where we saw that the `HttpRequest` and `HttpResponse` classes are always used together, and neither works without the other one. We can argue they should've been a single module.

- They serve a similar purpose. `deleteWhitespace` and `endsWith` do completely different things, but both of them are related to string manipulation, so it makes sense that they both belong to the `String` module.

- It's hard to understand one without the other one. We also saw an example of this in Chapter 4. If you have to flip back and forth between two methods to understand either of them, then they probably should've been a single method.

Ultimately, you should ask yourself: **does this split reduce the complexity of my system?** If the answer is no, then splitting the logic into multiple modules might be counterproductive.

CHAPTER 10   MODULARITY, COUPLING, AND COHESION

10.5 Coupling

Coupling is the **degree** of dependence between modules. In other words, how much do modules depend on each other to work. Notice the emphasis on the word "degree." Coupling is normal, and even independent modules are eventually used together, which creates some level of dependency. The degree of coupling is what can make it a problem.

When modules are very dependent on other modules or are directly related to them via method calls, we call this **tight coupling.** For example, the HttpRequest and HttpResponse classes are tightly coupled because they cannot work without the other one:

```
HttpRequest req = new HttpRequest();
req.setEndpoint('<http://www.yahoo.com>');
req.setMethod('GET');

Http http = new Http();
HTTPResponse res = http.send(req);
```

We saw another example of tight coupling in the previous chapter:

```
public class CustomLeadConversion {

    private LeadConversionUtil utils = new LeadConversionUtil();

    public void convertLead(Lead lead);
    public void convertLeads(List<Lead> leads);
    public List<Lead> getConvertedLeads();
    public Boolean isEligibleForConversion(Lead lead);

}
```

CHAPTER 10   MODULARITY, COUPLING, AND COHESION

Here, `CustomLeadConversion` is directly connected to `LeadConversionUtil`. It isn't possible to delete `LeadConversionUtil` without removing its reference from `CustomLeadConversion` first. It's also not possible to deploy `CustomLeadConversion` to a new org if `LeadConversionUtil` isn't deployed first or in the same deployment package.

When modules are somewhat independent and don't know too much about other modules, we call this **loose coupling.** In our famous example of the DML wrapper class, the execute method was loosely coupled to the specific implementations of `DMLExecutable` thanks to polymorphism:

```
public void execute() {

//loose coupling because we don't know
//which specific class this is

    DMLExecutable operation = this.operationsByDmlAction.get
    (this.operation);

    //execute the operation
    operation.execute(this.records, this.allowPartialSuccess);
}
```

Some coupling will always exist. Even in our example of modularity at its prime in Section 10.3, coupling exists. The class is tightly coupled to `Logger`, `FeatureFlags`, `Collection`, and `OpportunityValue`. It cannot be deployed to another org if those classes aren't deployed as well.

And so, coupling is inevitable. The degree of coupling (lose coupling vs. tight coupling) is what can reduce or increase complexity. In general, tightly coupled code increases complexity.

Tightly coupled code increases complexity because **changes in one module require changes in others**. Here's a simple example: imagine you need to change the `Opportunity Stage` value from `Closed/Won` to `Closed/Yeah!` tomorrow. Are you confident you could make the change within five minutes? What else would have to change in your org to support this new requirement? How many validation rules would break? How many flows would stop working? What about reports, dashboards, or Apex code?

This is an example of how tight coupling can increase complexity. What seems like a simple requirement (*"Can we change the name of this thing?"*) turns into a multiday project requiring extensive regression testing (and nightmares for years to come).

In contrast, imagine you have to rename `getOpptyId()` to `getOpportunityId()`. Even if the method is used in hundreds of places, a simple "Find and replace" operation in your IDE can take care of it in seconds. Somehow, this tight coupling isn't as impactful as the first one.

Why is that? The key is the tight vs. loose coupling cannot be understood by only looking at metadata references but also **the rate of change, how likely the change is to happen, and how impactful that change is**.

If somehow we knew that `Closed/Won` will never be renamed, then the tight coupling is not problematic at all. It's just normal coupling. If we operate in an environment where for some reason this name is likely to change frequently, then the same coupling becomes problematic.

Kent Beck summarized coupling beautifully in his book *Tidy First?*:

> *Two elements are coupled* **with respect to a particular change** *if changing one element requires changing the other element.*

Coupling can also be invisible. Imagine a business requirement changes and you have to change two classes that are **not** related to each other via metadata references. This means that the classes are **coupled to the same idea or underlying abstraction**, even if that abstraction is not represented in the code.

Finally, coupling can get in the way of flexible code. As we saw in previous chapters, polymorphism allows a class to work with other classes by treating them as if they were the same. This is possible because the class is only coupled to the interface or contract of the other classes, but not to the classes themselves. If the code is coupled to each implementation of the contract, then the code needs to change every time we add a new implementation. This is exactly what the Open/Closed Principle encourages us to avoid.

What does coupling have to do with modularity? In our previous example, we said that the `setFieldToToday` method knew too much about other modules in the system.

`Date.setFieldToToday(String fieldName)`

Another way of saying this is that the method is too tightly coupled to the concept of custom fields. This means the method needs to change every time Salesforce makes changes to the underlying implementation of custom fields.

So, to make modules somewhat general purpose, **we must try to limit the degree of coupling they have with respect to changes in other modules**.

10.6 Cohesion

A discussion around coupling wouldn't be complete with its counterpart, cohesion. In a way, coupling and cohesion are opposite forces that balance each other out, like the famous yin and yang in Chinese philosophy depicted in Figure 10-2.

CHAPTER 10   MODULARITY, COUPLING, AND COHESION

Figure 10-2. *The yin and yang represents opposite forces balancing each other*

Like coupling, cohesion is not a "thing" but rather a measure. While a high degree of coupling is generally considered a bad thing, **a high degree of cohesion is considered a good thing**. Specifically, cohesion is a measure to how closely related the items of a module are: how well they are connected. That is one definition. Throughout history, different interpretations have emerged. There are three definitions that I think are cohesive (pun intended):

- Cohesion is about how well the elements within a module work together toward a single purpose.

- Cohesion is a measure to how closely related the items of a module are.

- A module is cohesive if its subelements (variables, methods, etc.) are coupled.

The first two definitions are almost the same: the elements of a module should all work together to achieve the same purpose. Let's again look at the example of the `Date` class in Apex. These are some of the methods that are available to us:

```
addDays(additionalDays)
addMonths(additionalMonths)
addYears(additionalYears)
day()
dayOfYear()
daysBetween(secondDate)
daysInMonth(year, month)
format()
isLeapYear(year)
```

While all these methods do different things, they all serve a unifying purpose: allow developers to easily work with dates. If the `Date` class suddenly contained a method called `isDateField()` to determine if a field is a date field, this would break the cohesion of the class because this method's goal is unrelated to the high-level goal.

Another way to think about it is that a module that is cohesive should be hard to break apart. Is there a logical way for us to split `Date` into multiple modules? I personally don't think so. That split would cause more complexity as we'd have to look for which module to use to satisfy our date-related needs. This is a red flag that the behaviors should've been kept together (see Section 10.4 on "Better Together or Apart").

Another example would be a generic `Utils` class. If all the methods there serve different purposes and are not connected to a higher-level goal, the class is not cohesive. This sounds suspiciously similar to the definition of a shallow module.

I find the last definition to be the most interesting one: **A module is cohesive if its subelements (variables, methods, etc.) are coupled.** Why would it be good for the subelements of a module to be coupled, if coupling is considered bad?

To answer is in the definition itself. If items are coupled **across different modules**, that's bad coupling (and low cohesion).

CHAPTER 10   MODULARITY, COUPLING, AND COHESION

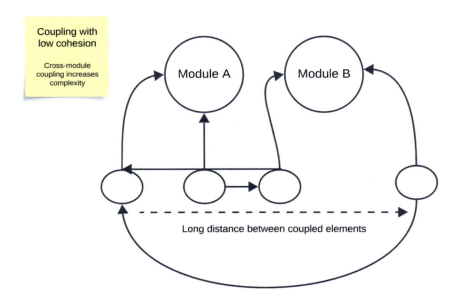

Figure 10-3. Low cohesion because dependent modules are too far apart

In Figure 10-3, the subelements of modules A and B are coupled to each other even though they belong to different modules. Changes to a subelement may cause failures or cause cascading changes in another module.

In contrast, Figure 10-4 shows that if items are coupled **within a single module**, the coupling is still there, but now, only that one module needs to change. That's better coupling (and high cohesion).

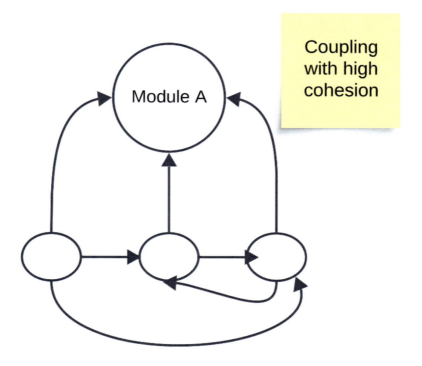

Figure 10-4. *High cohesion because dependent modules are close to each other*

We can say then that cohesion helps us limit the impact of coupling. With cohesion, **we can keep the distance between coupled elements short**; this makes the dependency obvious and easier to manage, which reduces complexity.

10.7 Cohesion in Salesforce Development

Let's see an example of cohesion in everyday Salesforce development. For this scenario, we can consider an sfdx folder a type of module as shown in Figure 10-5.

CHAPTER 10 MODULARITY, COUPLING, AND COHESION

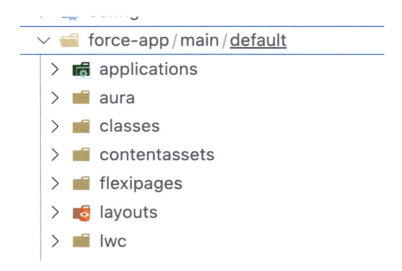

Figure 10-5. *sfdx folders can be considered modules*

After all, it is possible to create custom folders that represent a logical grouping of business logic. For example, in Figure 10-6, I've defined a folder called opportunity_calculations where I can group different metadata types that related to a single feature.

CHAPTER 10 MODULARITY, COUPLING, AND COHESION

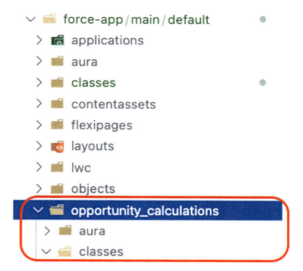

Figure 10-6. *A custom sfdx folder groups metadata related to a specific feature*

Now, consider the scenario where you have a feature that allows sales reps to specify the discount an opportunity should have based on how long the customer has been doing business with the organization. To support this feature, you have the following metadata:

- A custom field
- An apex class that does the calculation
- A validation rule that prevents stops certain values from being saved
- An LWC that users can interact with

If we change any of these elements, all the others are impacted, and the feature as a whole could break. **All these elements are coupled by the underlying idea, concept, or abstraction**, even if they are not related at a metadata level. This coupling is inevitable, but here's where cohesion comes in.

CHAPTER 10 MODULARITY, COUPLING, AND COHESION

If these elements exist in **different** `sfdx` folders, that coupling is bad. For example:

- The Apex class is in the `classes` folder.
- The custom field is inside `objects/opportunity/fields`.
- The LWC is under the `lwc` folder.
- etc.

This coupling is bad because **it spans different modules and it isn't immediately obvious that the coupling exists**. You would only know when you change an element, and all the others break.

In contrast, Figure 10-7 shows that if all the elements live inside the **same** `sfdx` folder, the coupling becomes obvious.

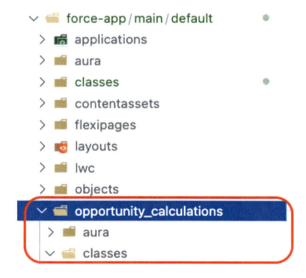

Figure 10-7. *Coupling becomes obvious when related metadata exists in a single sfdx folder*

CHAPTER 10   MODULARITY, COUPLING, AND COHESION

In the above image, all the elements related to the feature (named `opportunity_calculations`) are inside the same `sfdx` folder. The coupling is still there, and it's still highly impactful, **but at least now it's obvious**.

In short, if all your metadata lives in the default `sfdx` folders for each metadata type, your entire Salesforce org is one big module with high coupling and low cohesion. If you split your `sfdx` project into folders based on business processes or features, then these act as highly cohesive modules.

Finally, I'd like to point out and interesting dilemma. It is generally considered best practice to use all out-of-the-box and low-code Salesforce features before you resort to using Apex code. If you follow this recommendation, you end up with modules (the features) with high coupling and low cohesion.

That's because the implementation of a single business requirement is **spread out across unrelated metadata types**, such as fields, validation rules, Apex code, layouts, etc. It isn't possible to know that these are related until something breaks.

If on the other hand, you develop the whole requirement in Apex in a single class, you have high cohesion. Changes to the business requirement should only be made in one place. This greatly reduces complexity, at the cost of potentially reinventing the wheel.

And so, I leave you with something to think about: How do you strike the right balance between using Salesforce's standard features, which can lead to high coupling and low cohesion, and writing Apex code, which increases cohesion but may reduce flexibility for admins?

279

CHAPTER 10 MODULARITY, COUPLING, AND COHESION

10.8 Conclusion

We saw how modularity is a tool to reduce complexity in our code base. I highly recommend you spend time thinking about this with your team as a modular code base can unlock opportunities for reusability, dependency injection, and more reliable testing via mocks. This is what makes your org flexible and scalable.

CHAPTER 11

Dependency Injection and Boundaries

One of the undecided problems of software development is deciding what the boundaries of a piece of software is.

—Martin Fowler

Dependency injection (DI) is one of those topics that are widely misunderstood and prone to over-engineering, which adds complexity. In this chapter, I'll attempt to explain what DI is in the simplest of terms and provide guidance of when and when not to use it.

Also, DI is often confused with Inversion of Control (covered in Chapter 9) and late binding. We'll see later that these two concepts are usually used with DI, but they are completely independent, and it's important that we understand them on their own.

Finally, I want to point out that throughout this chapter I will have different examples running in parallel. I understand that for some this may be a little confusing, but my aim is to show how DI works in different contexts. Do not rush to read this chapter.

CHAPTER 11   DEPENDENCY INJECTION AND BOUNDARIES

11.1 What Is Dependency Injection (DI)?

DI is a very simple concept. What's difficult about it is understanding why you would use it, when, and when not to. Also, DI builds on the following concepts:

- OOP
- Interfaces
- Polymorphism
- The Inversion of Control Principle

If you are rusty in any of those, then DI will be hard to understand. I recommend you don't rush into understanding DI. If at any point any of those concepts isn't clear, consider going back a few chapters, study the concept well, and come back.

That said, assuming your understanding of those topics is solid (no pun intended), DI itself is very simple. In this section, I'll show a basic example of DI without too much explanation and expand on it as we go.

DI helps us decouple classes by taking away the responsibility of creating other objects they depend on. In a previous chapter, we saw how the `CustomLeadConversion` class worked together with `LeadConversionUtil` to support the necessary business logic to convert leads.

```
public class CustomLeadConversion {

    //the policy uses the detail for lower level operations
    private LeadConversionUtil utils = new
    LeadConversionUtil();

    public void convertLead(Lead lead);
    public void convertLeads(List<Lead> leads);
```

CHAPTER 11   DEPENDENCY INJECTION AND BOUNDARIES

```
    public List<Lead> getConvertedLeads();
    public Boolean isEligibleForConversion(Lead lead);
}
```

Here, `CustomLeadConversion` completely depends on `LeadConversionUtil`, to the point where they need to be deployed together, and you can't delete `LeadConversionUtil` without affecting `CustomLeadConversion`. This means that the classes are coupled at the metadata level. From now on, I will refer to this type of coupling as **metadata-based coupling**.

Also, `CustomLeadConversion` is responsible for creating an instance of `LeadConversionUtil`. In this case, `LeadConversionUtil` is easy to instantiate as it doesn't take any constructor parameters, but if it did, one could argue that how to get those parameters, the order in which they need to be passed, etc. is not a responsibility of `CustomLeadConversion`. In other words, `CustomLeadConversion` shouldn't have to know all that. This is **knowledge-based coupling.**

To remove the knowledge-based coupling, we just have to inject an instance of `LeadConversionUtil` via `CustomLeadConversion`'s constructor.

```
public class CustomLeadConversion {

    private LeadConversionUtil utils;

    // we inject the dependency (i.e dependency injection)
    public CustomLeadConversion(LeadConversionUtil utils) {
        this.utils = utils;
    }
}
```

CHAPTER 11   DEPENDENCY INJECTION AND BOUNDARIES

This frees `CustomLeadConversion` from having to know where the object comes from, how to instantiate it, etc., thereby removing knowledge-level coupling and ensuring the class can focus on its primary responsibility. Now, clearly, we've moved that responsibility to some other code, but who? We'll explore that in Section 11.8.

To remove the metadata-based coupling, we hide the instance of `LeadConversionUtil` behind an interface. This ensures `CustomLeadConversion` only depends on the contract, which allows us to swap or replace the implementation without breaking the class.

```
public class CustomLeadConversion {

    //now LeadConversionUtil is hidden behind this interface
    private ILeadConversionUtil utils;

    public CustomLeadConversion(ILeadConversionUtil utils) {
        this.utils = utils;
    }
```

Now, `CustomLeadConversion` simply takes a class that implements the `ILeadConversionUtil` interface, without knowing which implementation it is (thanks to polymorphism) and without caring how it was created (thanks to the constructor injection). The classes are now decoupled at both the metadata and knowledge levels.

That's it. That's DI. The end.

So why would we do that? With this simple change, you could

- Deploy `CustomLeadConversion` to an org where `LeadConversionUtil` does not exist, or deploy them in different `sfdx` packages.

- Delete `LeadConversionUtil` without impacting `CustomLeadConversion`.

- During tests, supply a dummy implementation of `ILeadConversionUtil`, to help you test `CustomLeadConversion` in isolation, without worrying about whether the utilities work correctly.

You might read the above bullet points and still wonder, "so what?"

- Why should we care if we can delete one class without impacting another? Isn't untangling them just a few hours of work?
- Why bother deploying two classes separately? Wouldn't it be easier to deploy them together and move on?
- Why would we want to test something in isolation if it fully depends on another class to achieve its goal? We'll have to test them together at some point anyway.

And that's the second challenge with DI. On top of relying on preexisting advanced knowledge of polymorphism and OOP, the benefits are not universal and immediately clear. It takes time and real-life experience to see the benefits.

With that said, let's unpack a few things. Again, don't worry if things don't make sense immediately; we'll slowly get there.

11.2 Not All Coupling Is Eliminated by DI

The premise of DI is that it helps us remove coupling. In our example above, `CustomLeadConversion` is no longer directly coupled to `LeadConversionUtil`; in fact, it doesn't even know it exists. However, as we discussed in earlier chapters, **not all coupling is based on metadata relationships**.

These classes are still conceptually coupled by the underlying business process or abstraction. For example, if a new business requirement changes the way leads are converted (e.g., adding a validation step for certain leads), it's likely that both `CustomLeadConversion` and `LeadConversionUtil` would need to change. Even though DI removes the metadata-based dependency, the classes are still coupled by their shared purpose (and one could argue they should just be one class, to increase cohesion).

Also, while `CustomLeadConversion` doesn't know about `LeadConversionUtil`, **it still depends on the actual implementation of the contract**. If `LeadConversionUtil` provides the wrong implementation of the interface or an implementation that doesn't fully satisfy `CustomLeadConversion`, the feature as a whole will not work correctly. DI can't magically enforce compatibility or correctness between abstractions and implementations.

This means DI doesn't eliminate dependency on correctness or quality. It ensures that `CustomLeadConversion` can work with any implementation of `ILeadConversionUtil`, but it can't guarantee that the provided implementation will behave as expected.

I mention this because often people oversimplify DI by saying "DI helps us write loosely coupled code" without considering that **loose and tight coupling exist on a spectrum; they aren't binary states**. Just because you've eliminated metadata-based coupling, it doesn't mean there's no coupling at all.

This doesn't mean DI is not a useful technique to reduce coupling, but you must understand what type of coupling it can reduce and **which one it can't**.

11.3 DI Works with Modular Design

DI is only useful if your code is modular. If you've worked in a few Salesforce orgs, you probably know most Salesforce orgs don't have modular code or API-like libraries as we discussed in the preceding chapter. In most orgs, everything is thrown together in huge classes, long methods, duplicated code, etc.

If you do use modular design or are working toward it, DI can be useful to manage dependencies between objects and reduce their metadata-based coupling, which in turn has other benefits such as easier testing and flexibility, which we'll explore later.

If you don't have any modularity in your org, you will not be able to use DI and experience its benefits.

11.4 What Is a Dependency?

A dependency is any other object that a class needs in order to carry out its functionality. Consider Figure 11-1 which shows a screenshot of an Apex class (in pseudocode).

```
15   public class StageUpdateRules implements TriggerAction.BeforeUpdate {
16
17       private final FeatureFlags flags = new FeatureFlags();
18
19       public void beforeUpdate(...) {
20
21           Logger.info('Validating opportunity updates');
22
23           if (flags.evaluate('enhancedOpportunityRules').isEnabled()) {
24
25               List<Opportunity> closedWonOpps = (List<Opportunity>)
26
27                   Collection.of(newList)
28                       .filter(Opportunity.StageName).equals('Closed Won')
29                       .getList();
30
31               for (Opportunity opp : closedWonOpps) {
32
33                   if(OpportunityValue.isHigh(opp)){
34                       opp.addError('Must have an Amount of at least $10,000'
35                   }
36               }
37           }
38
39           Logger.saveLog();
40       }
41   }
```

Figure 11-1. *An apex class with multiple modular dependencies*

Here, StageUpdateRules depends on

- FeatureFlags
- Logger
- Collection
- OpportunityValue

These are very clear-cut dependencies as those objects have completely different responsibilities. A dependency can also be something that **we choose to make a dependency**. In the example from earlier,

CHAPTER 11   DEPENDENCY INJECTION AND BOUNDARIES

`LeadConversionUtil` was a dependency of `CustomLeadConversion` but only because **we chose** to split the class into two classes.

Dependencies can also be subtle. Consider the following method:

```
protected override Boolean shouldRunAgain() {

    Boolean shouldRun =  [SELECT COUNT() FROM Account WHERE
                          Processed__c = false] > 0;
    if(!shouldRun) {

        throw new Exception('No more accounts to process');
    }
}
```

Here, `shouldRunAgain` has an **implicit dependency** on the ability to query the database, which is provided to us natively simply by using the SOQL keywords. Furthermore, the query itself depends on the `Processed__c` field. If this field doesn't exist in the org, the class cannot be deployed.

Now, should all dependencies be injected? Should I modify `StageUpdateRules` to take an instance of `FeatureFlags`, `Logger`, `Collection`, and `OpportunityValue` via the constructor? Should I also make all those classes implement an interface? How about implicit dependencies like inline SOQL queries? Should those be somehow injected as well?

To answer that, we must understand that not all dependencies are equal.

11.5 Not All Dependencies Are Equal

As we've seen, it's normal for objects to depend on other objects. In fact, that's the whole premise of modularity. If objects do one thing, they must be composed together to achieve bigger things and that will inevitably create dependencies.

CHAPTER 11 DEPENDENCY INJECTION AND BOUNDARIES

However, not all dependencies are equal. Some dependencies exist to provide general infrastructure concerns, such as logging, DML operations, async processing, etc.

Consider another example:

```
public with sharing class MassLeadConversion {
    private MyLogger logger = new MyLogger();

    ...
```

Here, `MassLeadConversion` depends on `MyLogger` for the purposes that are not related to business logic. Logging is a separate concern, and one that is cross-cutting, meaning it's a concern that applies to the entire system.

On the other hand, other dependencies exist to compose higher-level logic from smaller modules. For example, consider this pseudocode:

```
public class StageUpdateRules {

    ...
        if(OpportunityValue.isHigh(opp)){
            opp.addError('Too low!');
    ...
    }
}
```

Here, `StageUpdateRules` depends on `OpportunityValue` because it provides specialized behavior that is required to satisfy the business requirement. It's unlikely that `OpportunityValue` is reused *outside* non-opportunity-related modules.

There's a significant difference between these two types of dependencies:

- **Infrastructure Dependencies**: These provide application-wide services that are unrelated to specific business logic, such as logging or async processing.

- **Domain-Specific Dependencies**: These encapsulate specialized behavior required to satisfy specific business requirements within a given domain.

Infrastructure dependencies are more likely to be good candidates for dependency injection because they are likely to change for unrelated reasons. For example, the behavior of `MyLogger` can change for many reasons that have nothing to do with lead conversion.

We may also want different loggers that provide specialized behavior. In our example:

```
public with sharing class MassLeadConversion {
    private MyLogger logger = new MyLogger();

    ...
```

The `MassLeadConversion` class directly references `MyLogger` and is responsible for creating an instance of it. This means it isn't possible to provide a different implementation or provide a dummy implementation during tests. Additionally, any change to `MyLogger` could break `MassLeadConversion`. For these reasons, this is a good candidate for DI.

Again, to make this DI-friendly, we just have to do three things:

- Put `MyLogger` behind an interface.
- Make `MassLeadConversion` depend on the interface and not the specific implementation.
- Make `MassLeadConversion` take a reference to the interface in the constructor.

CHAPTER 11 DEPENDENCY INJECTION AND BOUNDARIES

The end result:

```
public with sharing class MassLeadConversion {

    // MyLogger is behind the IMyLogger interface
    private IMyLogger logger;

    // We inject the dependency
    public MassLeadConversion(IMyLogger logger) {
        this.logger = logger;
        logger.log('Starting MassLeadConversion');
    }
}
```

So, now what? Well, now, if we ever have a different type of logger, we can pass it to `MassLeadConversion` without changing `MassLeadConversion`. For example:

```
// declare variable with the interface type
IMyLogger logger;
Id userId = UserInfo.getUserId();

if(getUserType(userId) == UserType.STANDARD) {
    //assign the value with a specific implementation
    logger = new MyLogger();
}
else if(getUserType(userId) == UserType.GUEST) {
    //same here
    logger = new AnonymizedLogger();
}

// inject the polymorphic dependency
MassLeadConversion conversion = new MassLeadConversion(logger);
```

292

CHAPTER 11   DEPENDENCY INJECTION AND BOUNDARIES

In the above example, we can change the type of logger based on the user type. We can add more types, and `MassLeadConversion` doesn't have to change at all. All it cares about is that the `logger` adheres to the contract.

This is only possible because `MassLeadConversion` is not responsible for instantiating `MyLogger`. It delegates that responsibility to some other code while also not caring what the logger actually does. This separation of concerns ensures that `MassLeadConversion` can focus solely on its own functionality, without being tightly coupled to the details of the logging implementation.

Additionally, in a test, I can pass a dummy implementation that does nothing, which helps ensure I'm only testing the behavior I care about. Consider this pseudocode:

```
@IsTest
...

IMyLogger logger = new MockLoggerDoesNothing();

MassLeadConversion conversion = new MassLeadConversion(logger);
```

This flexibility makes DI particularly useful for infrastructure dependencies like `Logger`. However, this dynamic is less likely to occur with domain-specific classes.

Going back to our classic example:

```
public class CustomLeadConversion {

    //the policy uses the detail for lower level operations
    private LeadConversionUtil utils = new
    LeadConversionUtil();

    ...
}
```

CHAPTER 11 DEPENDENCY INJECTION AND BOUNDARIES

It's unlikely that we'll ever need another version of LeadConversionUtil that changes at runtime. So, the DI-enabled version of the same code

```
public class CustomLeadConversion {

    private ILeadConversionUtil utils;

    public CustomLeadConversion(ILeadConversionUtil utils) {
        this.utils = utils;
    }
}
```

is likely unnecessary unless we know beforehand that there are different versions of ILeadConversionUtil.

This doesn't mean that domain-specific classes are never good candidates for DI. There are cases where domain classes have variations that should change based on the context of the org, the user, or even runtime conditions. This is especially true when there's a clear **boundary** in our application.

Let's talk about that.

11.6 Boundaries

A boundary is **the point where one responsibility or domain ends and another one begins**. It's a point where control, data, or responsibility is handed off to another system, domain, or module. These handoffs mostly involve unknowns or complexities that go well beyond the scope of the current module.

Not all module interactions are considered boundaries. For example:

```
DateTime dt = DateTime.newInstance(2004, 1, 27, 4, 1, 2);

Time expected = Time.newInstance(12, 1, 2, 0);

System.assertEquals(expected, dt.timeGMT());
```

CHAPTER 11   DEPENDENCY INJECTION AND BOUNDARIES

Here, we are interacting with three modules, `DateTime`, `Time`, and `System`. The interaction is very simple, and the modules are simply working together to achieve a specific goal.

Contrast this with the following pseudocode:

```
@AuraEnabled
public static void importData() {
    try {
        List<Contact> contacts = (List<Contact>)
        fetchJsonFromGitHub(
            githubContacts
        );

        List<Experience__c> experiences = (List<Experience__c>)
        fetchJsonFromGitHub(
            githubExperience
        );

        Database.insert(contacts);
        Database.insert(experiences);

....
```

Here, there are two example boundaries.

The `importData` method gets `contacts` and `experiencies` by using the GitHub API. We have no idea what happens inside of `fetchJsonFromGitHub`. There's probably a lot of code to make sure the user is authenticated, to handle errors, etc. Furthermore, there's logic literally being executed in a different software, GitHub. This is a clear boundary because `importData` **loses control over what happens** inside `fetchJsonFromGitHub`.

Second, and probably less obvious, are the calls to `Database.insert`. What happens when these two lines execute? A whole set of operations will be triggered as per the order of execution: triggers, flows, validation

295

CHAPTER 11 DEPENDENCY INJECTION AND BOUNDARIES

rules, duplicate rules, etc. Basically, at this point, the `importData` method releases control of the logic and passes it to someone else (the `Database` module).

If we were to impersonate `importData` just before we call the `Database` class, we would probably say *"ok, whatever happens happens."* We can't control what happens next.

Boundaries can make or break our application. If the GitHub API is down, `importData` will not work. Also, if GitHub significantly changes the API, our logic will break too. Similarly, if the DML operation causes a validation rule on an unrelated object to fire, this could cause a cascading failure which eventually causes `importData` to fail as well (see Chapter 7 on cascading failures).

Boundaries are needed to reduce complexity as we saw on the preceding chapter, but they can also make our code harder to reason about and test. For example, if we find a bug in `importData`, is it our code, or is it something inside of `fetchJsonFromGitHub`? Is it our code, or did something fail in an unrelated trigger handler after we called the database? This is exactly what makes boundaries good candidates for DI.

Why? Because if those dependencies are injected behind an interface, we can mock them or supply a dummy implementation during tests. This allows us to test our code with full confidence that if something isn't working, **it's us and not them**.

In this particular example, I could hide the GitHub API behind an interface (`IGitHubAPI`) and pass it directly to the method (dependencies can also be injected in methods, not just constructors):

```
@AuraEnabled
// inject the GitHub API as an interface
public static void importData(IGitHubAPI gitHub) {
    try {
```

CHAPTER 11 DEPENDENCY INJECTION AND BOUNDARIES

```
    // use it here
    List<Contact> contacts = (List<Contact>) gitHub.
    fetchJsonFromGitHub(
        githubContacts
    );
```

Then, in a test, I can provide a dummy implementation of `IGitHubAPI`:

```
// MockGitHubAPI doesn't make any real HTTP calls
// and "always works"
IGitHubAPI github = new MockGitHubAPI();
```

This way, I can test `importData` assuming that the GitHub API works as expected. If something goes wrong during testing, I know who's at fault: me.

With all this said, we can go back to our original example.

```
public class CustomLeadConversion {

    private ILeadConversionUtil utils;

    public CustomLeadConversion(ILeadConversionUtil utils) {
        this.utils = utils;
    }
}
```

Is the interaction between `CustomLeadConversion` and `ILeadConversionUtil` really a boundary? Does `CustomLeadConversion` completely lose control and "whatever happens happens"? In this hypothetical example, not really. But in your Salesforce org, maybe. It really depends on the use case.

The goal of this section was to help you understand not all dependencies and interactions are the same. Dependencies within the same domain often share a common purpose and are tightly related. For example, in a lead conversion module, all dependencies are likely working toward the same goal. In contrast, dependencies across different domains, such as a GitHub API or DML operations, **represent a shift in responsibility or control**.

Now that we understand this distinction, it's easier to give some concrete guidelines on when to inject and when not to.

11.7 Better Injected or Better Hard-Coded

How do we know if a dependency is better injected or better hard-coded on a specific class? Here are some rough guidelines.

Clarification The term "hard-coding" often carries a negative connotation, such as hard-coding record IDs, credentials in CI configurations, or magic numbers (see Chapter 2). These practices are typically considered poor design

In this context, however, "hard-coding" refers to directly instantiating a dependency within a class. This is not inherently bad—it's a normal design choice. The key is to decide when to inject a dependency versus when to hard-code it.

Consider **injecting dependencies** when

- The external module represents a shift in responsibility or control. In other words, the interaction represents a real boundary and not just a collaboration

- The interaction between your module and the external module is so complex that you want to test your own module's logic in isolation (which would require you to supply a dummy implementation of the external module during tests)

- There are variations of the external module, such as different flavors of a logger, different shipping services behind a `IShippingService` interface, etc.

- You want to be able to swap out the implementation of the module at runtime based on user preferences, org-level configuration (such as custom metadata types), etc.

- You are splitting your org into different `sfdx` packages and you want the external module to live in a different package

- That module is the `Database` class. We'll explore why in the next chapter

Consider **hard-coding dependencies** when

- The external module is a simple utility with no variation, such as a `Collections` class

- You have no concrete evidence that there will ever be a variation of the external module

- The module is simple to instantiate

- The interaction between your module and the external module is simple; there's no significant loss of control or shift in responsibility

Again, these are guidelines and not rules, but they should be useful enough for you to use as a checklist when deciding whether to use DI.

11.8 Late Binding

As I hinted in the first section of this chapter, DI moves the responsibility of instantiating objects *somewhere else*, but I didn't specify where. Consider our classic example:

```
public class CustomLeadConversion {
    private ILeadConversionUtil utils;
    public CustomLeadConversion(ILeadConversionUtil utils) {
        this.leadConversionUtil = utils;
  }
}
```

We said that now `CustomLeadConversion` can take any implementation of the `ILeadConversionUtil` without knowing which implementation it is. But for this statement to be true, it means we need the following code somewhere else:

```
ILeadConversionUtil utils = new SpecificUtilImplementation();
CustomLeadConversion conversion = new CustomLeadConversion(utils);
```

And this code, ironically, knows how to instantiate the specific instance of `ILeadConversionUtil`, and it's also coupled to it at the metadata level. So, while we freed `CustomLeadConversion` from those constraints, we just moved them somewhere else.

There are two solutions to this problem. First, we may decide that is ok for this higher-level module to have this knowledge. Perhaps, this is the trigger handler or some sort of orchestrator that is considered a "core" module. This couples this module to a lot of other classes, but the coupling stops there. Other classes who consume the specific instances will never know what those instances really are. This is a way to **limit the scope** of the coupling.

CHAPTER 11 DEPENDENCY INJECTION AND BOUNDARIES

A more elegant solution is to use late binding. Late binding is a technique that allows us to dynamically instantiate a class without ever knowing its name or without having a direct reference to it.

Consider the following example where I have an interface that allows me to interact with any Git provider:

```
public interface IGit {
    void doCommit(String message);
}
```

I have specific implementations for GitHub and Bitbucket:

```
public  class GitHubAPI implements IGit {

    public void doCommit(String message){
        System.debug('Committing to GitHub: ' + message);
    }

}

public class BitbucketAPI implements IGit {

    public void doCommit(String message){
        System.debug('Committing to Bitbucket: ' + message);
    }

}
```

Then, I have a `GitOperations` class that can work with any Git provider, without knowing which one it is:

```
public class GitOperations {

  IGit gitApi;

  public void init(String provider){

    gitApi = (IGit) Type.forName(provider+'API').newInstance();
```

301

CHAPTER 11 DEPENDENCY INJECTION AND BOUNDARIES

```
    gitApi.doCommit('Initial commit');
  }
}
```

Here, the `init` method takes a simple string, such as `GitHub` or `BitBucket` . Then, using this name, it dynamically generates the Apex class name by adding `API` to it and using the `Type.forName` method to get a hold of that class. Finally, the `newInstance` method creates an instance of that class, without ever knowing what class it is.

```
GitOperations git = new GitOperations();
git.init('GitHub');// << just a string!!
```

This is called late binding because the act of binding (assigning a concrete reference to a variable) **happens at the last minute at runtime and not during compilation.**

The string provider could come from a user preference, from a custom metadata type, an API call, etc. This is the ultimate metadata-based decoupling mechanism because now the actual names of the classes are nowhere to be found in the code.

Of course, if you pass a string that is not an actual class name, an exception is thrown, so late binding brings additional complexity. To counter this, you can use the `ApexTypeImplementor` to validate that the string provided corresponds to a class that implements the interface you are working with. For example:

```
SELECT ClassName FROM ApexTypeImplementor
WHERE InterfaceName = 'IGit' AND IsConcrete=true
```

This returns both `GitHubAPI` and `BitbucketAPI`. So, before passing the string to `Type.forName()`, you can validate that the string provided is returned by this query. You could even wrap this functionality in a simple utility method:

CHAPTER 11   DEPENDENCY INJECTION AND BOUNDARIES

```
public class Interfaces {

    public static Boolean implement(String apexClass, String
    targetInterface){

        List<ApexTypeImplementor> subTypes =  [SELECT ClassName
                    FROM ApexTypeImplementor
                    WHERE InterfaceName = :targetInterface
                    AND IsConcrete=true
                    AND ClassName = :apexClass];

         return subTypes.size() > 0;
    }
}
```

And then:

```
String provider; //populated via custom metadata type, etc

if(Interfaces.implement(provider,'IGit')){
    //use Type.forName() safely
}
```

Late binding is often used with DI, but it's not mandatory. You should consider using this technique when you want maximum flexibility, such as having dependent classes live in different packages that can be deployed independently or swap out the implementation based on configuration or user preferences.

11.9 Inversion of Control

We already covered the Inversion of Control Principle (ICP) in Chapter 9. Here, I just want to clarify why ICP is usually conflated with DI. The simple answer is that when you hide an implementation behind an interface, you make **your module and the external module both depend on the same interface**. For example:

```
public class CustomLeadConversion {

    private ILeadConversionUtil utils;

    public CustomLeadConversion(ILeadConversionUtil utils) {
        this.leadConversionUtil = utils;
  }
}
```

Here, both `LeadConversionUtil` (who implements the interface) and `CustomLeadConversion` depend on the `ILeadConversionUtil` interface and not on each other. That's the premise of the ICP.

However, as we saw earlier, the real benefit of the ICP is somewhat philosophical. In this case, it's `CustomLeadConversion` who defines the interface and tells `LeadConversionUtil` what to do, rather than depending on it directly. If this isn't clear, there's a bigger explanation on Chapter 9.

Ultimately, you can practice DI without the ICP, but they usually play well together.

11.10 Conclusion

Dependency injection is a good tool for reducing (certain types of) coupling, improving flexibility, and enabling better testing when our modules interact with boundaries. It helps decouple classes by delegating the responsibility of creating dependencies.

CHAPTER 12

Unit Tests, Stubs, and Mocking the Salesforce Database

No code sits unintegrated for more than a couple of hours.

—Kent Beck

This chapter is the whole reason I wrote this book.

If you are familiar with my work, you may know that I've been deeply involved in the Salesforce DevOps space for some years. I've created courses, written extensively about continuous integration and continuous deployment (CI/CD), and worked at two major Salesforce DevOps vendors, Salto and AutoRABIT.

At some point, I had to face an uncomfortable truth: **You cannot practice real CI without writing clean code.** Salesforce DevOps tools can be incredibly helpful to automate manual steps and simplify deployments, but true CI is a reflection of clean code practices. It's not something you can buy and implement in your org.

CHAPTER 12   UNIT TESTS, STUBS, AND MOCKING THE SALESFORCE DATABASE

> **Note** Continuous integration (CI) is the practice of running all tests every time you commit a change to a shared branch in version control. The goal is to catch issues early by frequently running tests alongside your colleagues' changes, which will increase your confidence that nothing is broken.
>
> For example, if you create a new validation rule and all tests pass, you know the change is safe. If some tests fail, you know some rework is needed.
>
> More importantly, CI is meant to happen continuously—not just at the end of a sprint or before deployment.

However, there's a big elephant in the room: CI relies on fast-running tests. And if your tests are slow (as they are in most Salesforce orgs I've worked with), running all tests with every small change becomes impractical. I've seen orgs where running all tests takes 40 minutes or more. In shared sandboxes, where other developers are also running their tests, the delays become unmanageable (and incredibly frustrating).

Without fast tests, CI simply isn't feasible. No matter how good your tools or processes are, you need tests that run quickly to ensure every change is safe to deploy.

For the past few years, my mission has been to help the Salesforce ecosystem adopt DevOps practices. I've realized that this mission cannot be fulfilled unless developers know how to write tests that run fast enough to enable real CI. And to make the problem worse, I eventually learned that one of the most effective ways to achieve this is by implementing advanced techniques for mocking the Salesforce database during tests.

This is a very complex topic, and it's hard to explain without a solid foundation in modularity, dependency injection, object-oriented programming, and the other concepts we've explored throughout this book.

CHAPTER 12   UNIT TESTS, STUBS, AND MOCKING THE SALESFORCE DATABASE

That's why I couldn't just write an article about it and call it a day. Most Salesforce developers aren't trained in these concepts, and the topic requires a lot more context to truly understand. So, I had to write everything you've read so far to prepare for this chapter. If you've read this book in order, **congratulations for making it this far**. You now have a solid foundation to tackle one of the most challenging aspects of Salesforce development.

This book exists to help you write cleaner code, not as an end in itself, but so you can use those principles to unlock advanced design patterns, write faster tests, and practice CI the way it's meant to be done. And that, in turn, is what will unlock the real power of Salesforce DevOps.

That said, we can't jump straight into mocking the Salesforce database. We need to cover some basics first to ensure we are on the same page.

12.1 Why Bother with Testing

A few years ago, I wrote the code for HappySoup.io, a NodeJs app that helps you understand dependencies in a Salesforce org (like where a field is used). The app became a hit very quickly, and at the time of this writing, it has 4,000 monthly active users.

I didn't write a single unit test for it. Not even one.

Why didn't I write tests? At the time, I was learning NodeJs, JavaScript, Heroku, Git, etc. while also writing the code. That's a lot of work, and it took me ten months of daily work during evenings and weekends (this was before the AI era). Writing tests was just another thing to learn and implement, and it simply wasn't a priority for me at the time. I also had no idea the app was going to become so popular. Today, I do write tests for all my NodeJs projects.

What's interesting is that the lack of tests has not made the product any worse. It still works, it's used daily by hundreds of people, and for all intents and purposes, it's thriving. The app wouldn't magically be more successful just because I wrote unit tests for it.

The problem though is that **I have zero confidence in my ability to make changes to it without breaking it**, especially considering I wrote the code years ago and no longer recognize it. If I had to change to core API today, I'd have to manually do a lot of regression testing, which is very time-consuming. I basically can't make a simple change and walk away quickly with the confidence that I didn't break it.

And that's exactly why I should've written tests for it and why you should do it too. Plus, let's not forget that Salesforce requires 75% code coverage anyway, so you don't really have a choice (insert wink emoji).

Tests are sort of insurance policy. They help us make changes with confidence. They are meant to make ours jobs a little easier.

I once worked in a Salesforce org where I had no confidence whatsoever about the changes I was making. I wouldn't know if the code I'd written was actually going to work until I hit production and was run with real production data. I didn't enjoy being a Salesforce developer in that company.

So, the real value of writing tests is not to satisfy Salesforce's code coverage requirement but to help us write code with confidence and less stress. Being a Salesforce developer isn't easy, and we should find ways to make it less hard.

However, to write tests, we first need to know some basics, and as you'll see shortly, most people are unable to agree on some of the basics, which makes the topic more complicated than it needs to be.

12.2 Nobody Knows What a Unit Test Is

Ask ten people what a unit test is, and you'll get ten different answers.

One of the most influential books on unit testing is *The Art of Unit Testing* by Roy Osherove. In the first edition, Osherove said a unit was a method. By the third edition, he'd changed his mind—now he says a unit is a unit of work (I'll explain shortly what that means). That's a pretty big shift, and it shows how even experts with bestselling books can change their views over time (we saw in Chapter 9 how Robert C. Martin also changed his mind twice about the SRP).

And here's the problem with that: people who only read the first version are probably still out there telling everyone that **a unit is a method**. And people who read the third version are now probably saying **a unit is a unit of work**. And people who didn't read neither version but instead read the book *Unit Testing* by Vladimir Khorikov are probably out there telling everyone that **a unit is a unit of behavior.**

Which one is it?

The truth is there's no single, universal definition. It's all subjective, based on experiences, opinions, and what made sense to someone at the time. Even this book you're reading right now is just another opinion.

I bring this up not to criticize other authors for their work or anyone that is willing to admit their previous ideas where incomplete but to emphasize that there are conflicting definitions about what a unit is and that unlike other industries; there isn't a single authority that can impose that definition on us.

One definition I particularly like is Martin Fowler's:

> *Object-oriented design tends to treat a class as the unit, procedural or functional approaches might consider a single function as a unit. But really it's a situational thing -* ***the team decides what makes sense to be a unit*** *for the purposes of their understanding of the system and its testing.*

In a way, this is a no-answer answer, because it's telling us that it's up to us to decide what a unit is. And that's probably the best answer. However, if we want to decide what a unit is in our context, it's helpful to explore some common definitions.

CHAPTER 12   UNIT TESTS, STUBS, AND MOCKING THE SALESFORCE DATABASE

12.2.1 Unit As a Method

This definition states that any method is a unit. So to do unit testing, you have to test the methods of a class.

This definition is problematic because it implies testing the internal implementation of a module, not its behavior. This breaks encapsulation and causes your abstraction to leak. If you later refactor the internal structure of the class, the tests will break, even if the behavior of the class did not change.

I suspect this is the reason Osherove changed his mind in subsequent editions of his book.

12.2.2 Unit As a Unit of Work

In the third edition of his book, Osherove gave the definition of a unit as a unit of work. A unit of work in this context does not refer to the Unit of Work pattern for DML operations. Instead, it refers to a use case.

A use case has inputs and outputs. Suppose you have a method that creates an account record based on a name and a phone number:

```
public AccountCreationResult createAccount(String name, String phone) {

        AccountCreationResult result =
        new AccountCreationResult();

        validateNotNull(name, phone);

        name = formatName(name);
        phone = formatPhone(phone);

        result.account = new Account(Name = name, Phone = phone);
```

```
    try {
        Database.insert(result.account);
        result.success = true;
    } catch (Exception e) {
        result.supportCase = createSupportCase(
                name,
                e.getMessage()
        );
        result.success = false;
    }

    return result;
}
```

The unit of work here is that given a name and a phone number, you will get back a `AccountCreationResult` variable, which can be used to determine if the account was successfully created. How the method achieves that is irrelevant; it could use other methods or other classes.

So, using the unit of work definition, a unit test would test the behavior of `createAccount`, without caring about how the internals work.

Note however, that `createAccount` happens to be a method. That's just a coincidence. Osherove explains that a unit of work can be composed of several classes or methods.

12.2.3 Unit As a Unit of Behavior

In the book *Unit Testing*, Vladimir Khorikov gives yet another definition of a unit. In this definition, a unit is a unit of observable behavior.

A unit of behavior is something that is meaningful to the problem domain and something that a business user would probably recognize as valuable. This is not too different from the unit of work definition.

Imagine you are testing whether a new lightbulb is working. How would you tell your partner the way you will test it?

When I flip the switch on the wall, I expect the light to come on.

vs.

When I flip the switch, I expect it to close a circuit, allowing electricity to flow from the breaker panel through the wiring to the light fixture, where the bulb heats up and emits light.

Clearly, the first one is the observable behavior that is meaningful to us. The details are irrelevant. I find this a good definition because it helps us focus on the "what," not the "how." Tests that focus on the "what" are more likely to continue to work even when refactoring the internals of a module.

12.2.4 Unit As Unit of Code

In a blog post titled *Introducing apex-mockery, a Unit Test Mocking Library* Ludovic Meurillon and Sebastien Colladon say that unit tests are meant to test the **smallest amount of code** of a project.

The article also states that unit tests must only rely on pure logic and be completely decoupled from their dependencies (other classes) and boundaries (other services, such as data storage or web services).

While I'm a huge fan of Colladon and Meurillon's work, this definition is problematic because it can be misinterpreted as a unit being a method, which we already saw can lead to leaky abstractions and break encapsulation.

The latter part of their definition, in which they argue unit tests should be completely decoupled from their dependencies, is mostly true, with exceptions. As we saw in the previous chapter, not all dependencies should be treated equal, and it's acceptable for some dependencies to be hard-coded (this is a dangerous statement if taken out of context; please read the previous chapter for more details).

> **Note** Regardless of the correctness of the definition, the apex-mockery library is very flexible is not limited to testing units of code.

12.2.5 Which One Is It?

As we saw in the previous sections, all definitions are different, and some are even contradictory. My opinion is that the **unit of behavior** is probably the most practical one for several reasons:

- It aligns the unit tests with business requirements.
- It keeps the focus on the high-level abstraction and not the details (no leaks!).
- It's resistant to refactoring.
- It can work as documentation for your project or specific classes.

That doesn't mean that units of behavior should be tested with all their dependencies and boundaries. We can still test the behavior in isolation of its dependencies if we use proper dependency injection techniques and mocking (which we'll explore soon).

One potential challenge with this definition is that it's easy to confuse it with integration tests. I will talk about integration tests shortly. For now, we can break out of this conflict by focusing on the properties of a good unit test, which I find more useful than obsessing over the definitions.

12.3 Properties of a Good Unit Test

For the remainder of this chapter, when I say "unit tests," I'm referring to **units of behavior** that we want to test because they are valuable to the business. These tests focus on **observable behavior** rather than implementation details.

As I mentioned in the previous section, it's more productive to focus on what makes a unit test *good* than to dwell on conflicting definitions. This list of properties was written by Kent Beck, and because it's so good, I'm just going to provide it as is. A good unit test is

- **Isolated**: Tests should return the same results regardless of the order in which they are run.
- **Deterministic**: If nothing changes, the test result shouldn't change.
- **Fast**: Tests should run quickly.
- **Writable**: Tests should be cheap to write relative to the cost of the code being tested.
- **Readable**: Tests should be comprehensible for the reader, clearly explaining the motivation for writing the test.
- **Behavioral**: Tests should be sensitive to changes in the behavior of the code under test. If the behavior changes, the test result should change.
- **Structure-Insensitive**: Tests should not change their result if the structure of the code changes.
- **Automated**: Tests should run without human intervention.

- **Specific**: If a test fails, the cause of the failure should be obvious.
- **Predictive**: If all tests pass, the code under test should be suitable for production.
- **Inspiring**: Passing the tests should inspire confidence.

If we focus on these properties, we can write unit tests that are useful and that eventually enable CI. This should be possible regardless of what definition of "unit" you choose to follow.

12.4 Integration Tests and Interactions with the Database

An integration test checks how different components of a system work together. Unlike a unit test, which focuses on testing a single behavior in (mostly) isolation, an integration test ensures that **interactions between modules work as expected when combined.**

12.4.1 Salesforce Tests Are Integration Tests by Default

Here's where things start to get a bit interesting. In traditional software development, it's generally accepted that a unit test does **not** interact with the database, because the database is considered a nondeterministic and external dependency. Because of this, you'll often find that traditional literature explains that **only** integration tests should interact with the database, because you want to test if the unit of behavior also works well when combined with external dependencies (like the database).

CHAPTER 12   UNIT TESTS, STUBS, AND MOCKING THE SALESFORCE DATABASE

This may be a strange concept to get your head around because Salesforce has taught us to write integration tests from day one. All the tests that we write interact with the database and can trigger the order of execution, other triggers, flows, etc. Of course, the data is actually rolled back, and nothing is committed after the tests finishes, but it's common knowledge that in a Salesforce test, you can safely insert, update, and query any data you want.

Let's see an example to put things into perspective. Consider the example code we saw earlier, which creates an account record:

```
public AccountCreationResult createAccount(String name, String phone) {

    AccountCreationResult result =
    new AccountCreationResult();

    validateNotNull(name, phone);

    name = formatName(name);
    phone = formatPhone(phone);

    result.account = new Account(Name = name, Phone = phone);

    try {
        Database.insert(result.account);
        result.success = true;
    } catch (Exception e) {
        result.supportCase = createSupportCase(
                name,
                e.getMessage()
        );
        result.success = false;
    }
```

CHAPTER 12   UNIT TESTS, STUBS, AND MOCKING THE SALESFORCE DATABASE

```
        return result;
    }
```

Here's how Salesforce taught us to test this behavior:

```
@IsTest
public static void account_created_successfully(){

    //arrange
    String newAccountName = 'Test Account';
    String newPhone = '123-456-7890';

    //act
    Test.startTest();

    AccountApproval.AccountCreationResult result =
    new   AccountApproval().createAccount(
            newAccountName,
            newPhone
    );

    Test.stopTest();

    //assert
    Assert.areEqual(true, result.success);

    Account accountFromDB = [SELECT Name, Phone
    FROM Account WHERE Id = :result.account.Id];

    Assert.areEqual('TEST ACCOUNT', accountFromDB.Name);
    Assert.areEqual('1234567890', accountFromDB.Phone);

}
```

We call the system under test (the thing we are testing) between `Test.startTest` and `Test.stopTest`. We expect that between these two statements, the `Database.insert` call was actually made inside of createAccount. To further prove it, we query the database and confirm that the account was inserted and that the name and phone number were formatted correctly.

This is how most Salesforce tests are written, and in theory, there's nothing wrong with it.

However, when I run this test, here's what I get:

```
AccountApprovalTests.account_created_successfully

Fail
System.AssertException: Assertion Failed:
Account name should be in uppercase.
Actual: Test Account:
```
Expected: TEST ACCOUNT
Actual: Test Account

=== Test Summary

NAME	VALUE
Outcome	**Failed**
Tests Ran	1
Test Run Id	707Wy00000DV0sU
Test Setup Time	0 ms
Test Execution Time	**3412 ms**
Test Total Time	3412 ms

The test failed, and not only that, it took 3,412 milliseconds to run, which is 3 and a half seconds. That may not sound like much, but this was literally **one test method**. If you had 1,000 tests methods that took 3 seconds, that's 50 minutes. Imagine having to wait for 50 minutes every time you run all tests after you commit a small change. As I said earlier, with this setup, it's impossible to practice CI.

CHAPTER 12   UNIT TESTS, STUBS, AND MOCKING THE SALESFORCE DATABASE

Let's look at the failure. We passed `Test Account` as an input, and we expected to receive an account with the name in all caps, `TEST ACCOUNT`. This behavior is achieved by the internal private method `formatName` which is called inside of `createAccount`:

```
private string formatName(String name) {
    return name.toUpperCase();
}
```

This is such a simple method (in fact, a pass-through method; which we called out as an antipattern earlier in the book) that it would be silly to unit test it. It's highly unlikely that `String.toUpperCase` suddenly doesn't work.

But then, how do we know what caused the name to not come back in upper case? What is a flow? A trigger? Or was it something in our code? The fact that we even have to ask these questions means that this is an integration test. Our intention was to test this unit of behavior, but in reality, we are testing its interaction with the entire ecosystem of automation that exists in the org. **That's not a pure unit test.**

12.4.2 Integration Tests Are Not Evil

In the previous section, we saw how a simple method doesn't work as expected, and we suspect it's due to its interaction with the database. In other words, when we insert the account, it's likely that there's another trigger or flow that is undoing the change to the account name.

At this point, some schools of thought would argue that this is the problem with integration tests: they allow external factors to influence our unit of behavior. Advocates of this approach would typically demonstrate how to create a pure unit test for this method, one that doesn't interact with the database.

CHAPTER 12 UNIT TESTS, STUBS, AND MOCKING THE SALESFORCE DATABASE

Here's a **terrible** example of how one might do this (I'll explain shortly why this is an antipattern):

```
name = formatName(name);
phone = formatPhone(phone);

result.account = new Account(Name = name, Phone = phone);

try {
    if(!Test.isRunningTest()){
        Database.insert(result.account);
    }
    result.success = true;
} catch (Exception e) {
    ...
}
```

Basically, before we insert the account, we ensure that this is not a test. If it's a test, then the insert doesn't happen. Notice however, we still return the `result` variable which has the result of the operation.

Then, I simply need to remove the SOQL queries from the test and do the assertions against the `result` variable.

```
//act
Test.startTest();

AccountApproval.AccountCreationResult result =
new AccountApproval().
                    createAccount(
                    newAccountName,
                    newPhone
            );
Test.stopTest();
```

320

CHAPTER 12 UNIT TESTS, STUBS, AND MOCKING THE SALESFORCE DATABASE

```
//assert
Assert.areEqual(true, result.success);

Assert.areEqual('TEST ACCOUNT', result.account.Name);
Assert.areEqual('1234567890', result.account.Phone);
```

Now, when I run the test, here's what I get:

```
=== Test Summary
NAME                              VALUE
_____       _____

Outcome                           Passed
Tests Ran                         1
Pass Rate                         100%
Test Execution Time               60 ms
Test Total Time                   60 ms
```

Sixty milliseconds compared to 3.5 seconds—and the test passed. This confirms that the code itself works as intended. The slow runtime and the failure to transform the account name were caused by external factors.

And there you have it: a pure, fast unit test. You could deploy this to production, call it a day, and rejoice in the fact that now you can practice true CI.

Now, back to the real world. That all sounds great in theory, but here's the thing: **integration tests are much closer to reality than pure unit tests**.

What's the value of testing units of behavior without their dependencies if they break in production because of those very dependencies? (I'll explore this question—and the trade-offs of integration tests—at the end of the chapter.) Integration tests are still required to ensure our logic works in the real world, not in a vacuum. This is especially true in Salesforce development because…

12.4.3 Salesforce Is a Database-Driven System

In traditional software development, the database is considered an external dependency. It's widely accepted that you should wrap the database with an interface, so that you can mock it during tests and just in case you later decide to switch providers (e.g., from MySQL to PostgreSQL). Additionally, the database needs to exist on each developer's machine (or at least in a Docker image), which can lead to the infamous "*it works on my machine*" problem if the database isn't properly configured.

For these reasons, mocking the database is a widely accepted practice as it allows developers to test logic in isolation, ensuring speed and avoiding dependency-related failures.

But Salesforce isn't a traditional piece of software. As much as we might wish it behaved like one, **it doesn't**. Salesforce, and Apex in particular, is completely tied to the database. The following automation components all depend on database transactions:

- Triggers
- Flows
- Validation rules
- Duplicate rules
- Field constraints (e.g., unique values, length)
- Assignment rules
- Auto-response rules

And many more. Ignoring this reality and pretending all business logic resides in code, as it does in traditional applications, would be naive. Furthermore, all these components can and will interact with our code, often in ways we can't predict (like those admins creating validation rules in production...).

If we test our logic without actually performing DML operations, we're testing a behavior in isolation—even though in reality, it won't run in isolation.

This is where we find two opposite forces: a good unit test should be isolated from its dependencies, but in Apex, those dependencies have much more impact than they do in traditional software.

However, one good reason to skip the database is it helps us understand quickly if failures in the test are because of our code or external dependencies. For example, if I had started with the code that skips the database during tests and the test had failed, I'd immediately know where to look: my code. This can be make debugging a lot easier and helps you get fast feedback, another property of a good unit test.

So, there is value in testing our logic without the interaction with the database, and that's exactly what I intend to teach you in this chapter.

But you must understand the trade-off of doing this: you are testing a behavior in a way that is completely different to how it will actually run in production. That difference could be business critical for many use cases.

Later, we'll see how we can combine both unit tests and integration tests.

12.4.4 Integration Tests Are Slow

Another reason advocates of the "pure unit test" school of thought argue against integration tests is that they can be slow. In my example, a simple test ran for almost four seconds. This is likely because inserting the account triggered hundreds of flows, validation rules, triggers, and other automation—all of which add up. Removing the database from the equation becomes an appealing shortcut to improve test speed.

On the other hand, some argue that if a test takes four seconds to run, it's likely **your users are also waiting four seconds when they insert an account**. Rather than pretending the database doesn't exist, this school of thought suggests you should focus your time and energy on refactoring your code to make it more performant.

This is a valid concern, and performance optimization is a topic worth exploring. However, I won't go into that here. If you're struggling with Apex performance issues, I highly recommend the book *Mastering Apex Programming* by Paul Battisson, which dedicates four chapters to the subject.

12.5 Mocking DML Operations

Let's summarize our discussion so far:

- **Pure unit tests** focus on logic, not interactions with boundary-level dependencies (like the database).
- They are **much faster** than integration tests.
- The tests we've all been taught to write are **integration tests.**
- Integration tests are closer to reality than pure unit tests.
- However, they can be slower and make debugging harder because the source of failures isn't always clear.
- We haven't yet discussed how to balance the two: how many tests should be unit tests vs. integration tests? (We'll explore this later.)

With all that said, I will now show multiple techniques for skipping the database, ranked from worst to best. My focus will be on patterns, not production-ready code—though I'll share some library recommendations toward the end.

For now, I'll focus on DML operations for now and will later talk about mocking SOQL queries.

CHAPTER 12   UNIT TESTS, STUBS, AND MOCKING THE SALESFORCE DATABASE

Finally, I want to acknowledge a big concern: if you skip DML operations, then you cannot use SOQL queries later in your tests to verify that the records were inserted. You have to do something entirely different, which I will cover later.

12.5.1 Brute Force

The worst way to skip the database is the (anti)pattern we saw earlier:

```
if (!Test.isRunningTest()) {
    Database.insert(result.account);
}
```

The reason this is bad is because it pollutes business logic with testing needs. In my experience, this is unfortunately a widely adopted practice. Another variation of this antipattern is also used to test exceptions.

In the same code, we have a bit of exception handling:

```
try {
    if (!Test.isRunningTest()) {
        Database.insert(result.account);
    }
    result.success = true;
} catch (Exception e) {
    ...
}
```

A common challenge is how to test the exception path. One pattern I've seen a few times is to also use Test.isRunningTest, like this:

```
try {
    if (Test.isRunningTest() && forceException == true) {
        throw new Exception('Test exception');
    }
```

325

```
        Database.insert(result.account);
        result.success = true;
} catch (Exception e) {
    result.supportCase = createSupportCase(name,
e.getMessage());
    result.success = false;
}
```

Here, `forceException` is a private boolean variable that is made visible to the test code:

```
@TestVisible
private Boolean forceException = false;
```

Then, in the test, you set this to true, which when combined with `Test.isRunningTest()` forces the exception to be thrown.

This is a worse antipattern because now you also have variables that only exist for the purpose of testing different scenarios. I will come back to this scenario later and explain how to properly test exceptions.

12.5.2 Testing the Internals Without the Database

Another way to skip the database is to decompose the logic of the class under test into smaller private methods and then test those methods in isolation. **This is also an antipattern.**

For example, I could make all the `private` methods visible to test code by using `@TestVisible`:

```
@TestVisible
private string formatPhone(String phone) {
    return phone.replace('-','');
}
```

```
@TestVisible
private string formatName(String name) {
    return name.toUpperCase();
}

@TestVisible
private Case createSupportCase(String accountName, String
error) {...
```

Then, I can test those methods individually, without ever testing the public method createAccount, which is where the DML operation happens:

```
@IsTest
public static void test_internal_implementation(){
        //arrange
        String newAccountName = 'Test Account';
        String newPhone = '123-456-7890';
        AccountApproval accountApproval = new
        AccountApproval();

Assert.areEqual(
    'TEST ACCOUNT',
    accountApproval.formatName(newAccountName)
);

Assert.areEqual(
    '1234567890',
     accountApproval.formatPhone(newPhone)
);

accountApproval.validateNotNull(newAccountName, newPhone);

}
```

CHAPTER 12   UNIT TESTS, STUBS, AND MOCKING THE SALESFORCE DATABASE

Now, I'll admit this made the test a lot easier and simple, but that's only temporary. As soon as I change how any of the internal methods work, the test is bound to break. As we discussed earlier, this is similar to considering methods as a unit, which causes our abstraction to leak and creates coupling between the test code and the internals of the module.

This should be avoided and I'm only showing here as an example of what not to do. Always aim to test the **observable behavior of your code**, not its internal implementation.

12.5.3 Simple Context-Aware Wrapper

The next pattern to skip the database is to wrap DML operations in a thin wrapper that knows whether it's running in a test or not, for example:

```
public class DatabaseOps {

    public static void doInsert(SObject record){

        if(Test.isRunningTest()){
            record.Id = FakeId.getFrom(record.getSObjectType());
        }
        else{
            Database.insert(record);
        }
    }

}
```

Here, `DatabaseOps` wraps `Database.insert` with `doInsert`, which toggles between test and production behavior. If the code is being called during a test, we simply assign a fake Id to the record using the `FakeId` class (you can find examples of this pattern online). If we are not in a test, we call the real `insert` method.

This is a little better because at least now the test vs. nontest behavior is encapsulated into this class. Then, our class under test can use this as a drop-in replacement to the `Database` class, for example:

```
try {
    DatabaseOps.doInsert(result.account);
    result.success = true;
} catch (Exception e) {
    result.supportCase = createSupportCase(name,
    e.getMessage());
    result.success = false;
}
```

In this example, the dependency is hard-coded (i.e., I'm not using dependency injection), which means you can't replace it with a mock version during tests. However, that's the point—the wrapper already knows if it's running in a test, so mocking isn't necessary.

While this is better than the previous two, it doesn't provide as much flexibility as the next few patterns.

12.5.4 Dependency Injection

This next pattern uses traditional dependency injection (DI). We start by creating a simple interface that defines the DML operations that we want to support:

```
public interface IDatabaseOps {
    void doInsert(SObject record);
}
```

CHAPTER 12   UNIT TESTS, STUBS, AND MOCKING THE SALESFORCE DATABASE

Then, we create two classes, one for production code:

```
public class DatabaseOps implements IDatabaseOps{
    public void doInsert(SObject record){
        Database.insert(record);
    }
}
```

And another one to use during tests:

```
public class MockDatabaseOps implements IDatabaseOps {
    public void doInsert(SObject record){
        record.Id = FakeId.getFrom(record.getSObjectType());
    }
}
```

Then, the class under test will take a reference to the interface in its constructor:

```
private IDatabaseOps dbOps;

public AccountApproval(IDatabaseOps dbOps){
     this.dbOps = dbOps;
}

....
   try {
       dbOps.doInsert(result.account);
       result.success = true;
   }
 ...
```

330

Finally, during a test, we can pass the mock version of the interface:

```
IDatabaseOps mockDB = new MockDatabaseOps();
//act
Test.startTest();
AccountApproval.AccountCreationResult result = new
AccountApproval(mockDB).
    createAccount(
        newAccountName, newPhone
);
Test.stopTest();
```

This is very similar to the previous except here we have a clearer separation of concerns. We can implement the mock version with all sorts of test utilities, without polluting `DatabaseOps` with those details. We may also have different implementations of the interface which allows us to add new behavior without changing the code (remember the Open/Closed Principle from Chapter 9), for example, you may pass an implementation of `IDatabaseOps` that has additional logging which may be needed only for certain classes.

12.5.5 Test Doubles and the Stub API

Finally, one of the best versions of this pattern is to use the **Stub API** in Apex. First, let's clarify the term "stub" (as a nonnative English speaker, this term has never made much sense to me in the context of unit testing).

A stub is a piece of a larger thing, kind of like a leftover. In other contexts, it's a placeholder. In the world of unit testing, a stub is a simplified implementation or a placeholder for a dependency. Its purpose is to provide controlled behavior during a test without relying on the actual implementation.

CHAPTER 12   UNIT TESTS, STUBS, AND MOCKING THE SALESFORCE DATABASE

You may be thinking that this is the definition of a mock, and you'd be forgiven to think that. There are conflicting definitions, and in some programming languages, testing frameworks combine the concepts of stubs and mocks into one, even though they are different.

First, you must understand that both mocks and stubs are considered test doubles. This is an umbrella term to represent anything that "looks like the real thing." The term comes from using doubles in movies when filming action scenes. In our example earlier, `MockDatabaseOps` is a sort of test double for the real thing: `DatabaseOps`.

The difference between a stub and a mock is how you intend to use them. A stub typically provides canned or predefined responses to methods. For example, when we call `doInsert` in `MockDatabaseOps`, what happens is already defined: we do nothing other than providing a fake Id. Really, I should have called this `StubDatabaseOps`.

A mock, on the other hand, is used when you want to test the interactions between modules and confirm that certain methods were called, how many times, in which order, etc. I appreciate this isn't the clearest explanation, but this isn't the time to show the differences, I will come back to this later. For now, you just have to remember that a stub provides predefined responses, whereas a mock is used to verify the interactions between modules.

Anyway, back to the Stub API. The stub API comprises the `System.StubProvider` interface and the `System.Test.createStub()` method. None of these are meant to be used directly; instead, they are meant to be used to create mocking frameworks: frameworks that abstract all the details of how to create mocks and that allows users to create predefined responses (stubs) and test specific method interactions (mocks).

It is out of the scope of this book to show you how to create a mocking framework. For now, I will show you how to create a very naive, non-production-ready one just to understand the basics, and later, I will provide some recommendations for mocking frameworks.

Chapter 12   Unit Tests, Stubs, and Mocking the Salesforce Database

It may be easier to see the end result first. Here's what our test will look like:

```
DatabaseOps stubDB = (DatabaseOps)new Stub(DatabaseOps.class).
                    when('doInsert').doNothing().create();
//act
Test.startTest();
AccountApproval.AccountCreationResult result = new
AccountApproval(stubDB).
                        createAccount(newAccountName, newPhone);
Test.stopTest();
```

Notice how I no longer use the `IDatabaseOps` interface. Instead, I use the `Stub` class (which we'll create together in a moment) to define that when `doInsert` is called, nothing should happen. Then, I pass the instance of `DatabaseOps` class to the constructor of the class under test.

This is the ultimate flexibility. In other classes, I could define that when `doInsert` is called, something should indeed happen. Also, since I no longer need an interface just for the purposes of mocking, this reduces complexity in our code base.

Finally, I can dynamically determine what should happen when certain methods are called. This is much powerful than hard-coding some logic with the help of `Test.isRunningTest`.

To create the `Stub` class, first, I need to implement the `StubProvider` interface:

```
public class Stub implements System.StubProvider
```

Then, we can define some private properties that tell us which class and which method we are stubbing:

```
//i.e doInsert
private String methodToStub;
```

333

//i.e with which arguments?
private Object argumentToMatch;

//i.e what should doInsert return
private Object returnValue;

//i.e what class are we mocking: DatabaseOps
private Type typeToMock;

Then, using the fluent interface pattern, I can create setters for these properties:

```
public Stub(Type typeToMock) {
    this.typeToMock = typeToMock;
}

public Stub when(String methodToStub) {
    this.methodToStub = methodToStub;
    return this;
}

public Stub with(Object argumentToMatch) {
    this.argumentToMatch = argumentToMatch;
    return this;
}

public Stub thenReturn(Object returnValue) {
    this.returnValue = returnValue;
    return this;
}

public Stub doNothing() {
    this.returnValue = null;
    return this;
}
```

Finally, the `create` method creates the stub or mock for the class in question:

```
public Object create() {
    return Test.createStub(typeToMock, this);
}
```

These methods combined allow for the fluent interface pattern we saw earlier:

```
DatabaseOps stubDB = (DatabaseOps)
        new Stub(DatabaseOps.class).
        when('doInsert').doNothing().create();
```

Finally, the `System.StubProvider` interfaces requires us to implement the `handleMethodCall` method. This method is called when our real method is called (i.e., `doInsert`). **It intercepts the method and changes its behavior and return value based on whatever rules we define.**

In our case, I created a simple and naive implementation that checks if the method being called and the arguments match what we passed on the fluent interface:

```
public Object handleMethodCall(
        Object stubbedObject,
        String stubbedMethodName,
        Type returnType,
        List<Type> listOfParamTypes,
        List<String> listOfParamNames,
        List<Object> listOfArgs)
{

        //if the method called matches the method we said
        we wanted
        //to stub, we return the value we said we would return
```

```
        if(stubbedMethodName == methodToStub && listOfArgs[0] ==
        argumentToMatch) {
            return returnValue;
        }
        return null;
}
```

If your head is spinning, it's because this API isn't meant to be used directly. It's designed for creating mocking libraries or frameworks, which is a very advanced topic. Unless you're confident in what you're doing, I recommend using an existing mocking framework instead of building one from scratch.

That said, I encourage you to try recreating this example. Writing my own (naive) framework was the only way I truly understood the Stub API.

12.6 Libraries for Mocking DML Operations

As we saw in the previous section, creating a mocking library with the Stub API is not trivial. For that reason, I recommend that you use one of the following libraries created by the community.

There are two types of libraries:

- General-purpose mocking libraries: These assume you are using a wrapper around the `Database` class. With the library, you mock the responses of that wrapper.

- Drop-in replacements for the `Database` class: In this model, you simply use the library-provider wrapper as a replacement for the `Database` class. The libraries contain utilities for mocking DML statements.

Every library is different, and their approach may change over time, so I will leave it up to you to research them and figure out which fits your needs better. With what you have learned so far, their value proposition should be clear.

12.6.1 General-Purpose Mocking Libraries

In this category, I recommend **Amoos** (which stands for "Apex Mock Objects, Spies and Stubs") created by Robert Baillie and **Apex-mockery** by Ludovic Meurillon and Sebastien Colladon.

You should use a general-purpose mocking library if you already have a wrapper for DML operations but don't have a way to easily mock it during tests. Also, this library can also be used to mock any other class that you define. I highly recommend either of them for general-purpose testing needs.

12.6.2 Drop-In Replacements for the Database Class

For a drop-in replacement, I recommend Google's **ditto-mocks** library or **Moxygen**, created by Zackary Frazier.

If you have never done any DML mocking, then I recommend starting with a drop-in replacement, as it makes the learning curve much shorter.

12.7 Mocking DML Statements Affect SOQL Queries

So far, we've focused on mocking DML operations. However, database operations aren't one-sided. If we skip persisting data to the database, our queries will return empty results. This creates a challenge for tests that assert observable behavior based on queried records. For example:

```
Account accountFromDB = [SELECT Name, Phone FROM Account
                         WHERE Id = :result.account.Id];
Assert.areEqual('TEST ACCOUNT', accountFromDB.Name);
Assert.areEqual('1234567890', accountFromDB.Phone);
```

In this case, the query will return nothing because no data was actually inserted into the database.

This forces us to assert behavior using only the in-memory representation of the record. While this may work, it doesn't reflect the reality of how the record will interact with other automation in the org, such as triggers, flows, or validation rules.

So, when mocking DML operations, you must consider this trade-off.

12.8 Mocking SOQL Queries

One of the most painful experiences I've had as a Salesforce developer is that of creating test data in a test class for a given class. I once worked in an org where the data model was so complex that to create a case record, you had to first create at least ten records first, all of which had their own dependencies, their own validations rules, etc.

It was so bad that I would often run out of governor limits just while preparing the data set, and I had to use a combination of `Test.startTest` and a few other tricks to disable certain triggers. And most of the times,

CHAPTER 12   UNIT TESTS, STUBS, AND MOCKING THE SALESFORCE DATABASE

all I needed was a few case records to be there because a deeply nested `if` condition required cases to be extracted with a SOQL query.

We've been taught that to allow our queries to execute in a test context, we have to use `@TestSetup` along with data factories.

Consider the following simplified example:

```
public Account transferAccountOwnership(
        Id accountId,
        Id newOwnerId
){
        Account account = [SELECT Id, OwnerId
        FROM Account WHERE Id = :accountId];

        User newOwner = [SELECT Id,IsActive
        FROM User WHERE Id = :newOwnerId];

        //we could have filter this out with SOQL.
        //I did it on purpose to add complexity to the example

        if(!newOwner.IsActive) {
            throw new DmlException('New owner is inactive');
        }

        account.OwnerId = newOwnerId;
        update account;
        return account;
    }
```

Here's how we would think of testing this:

```
@IsTest
static void testTransferAccountOwnership() {
        Account account = new Account(Name = 'Test Account');
        insert account;
```

339

CHAPTER 12 UNIT TESTS, STUBS, AND MOCKING THE SALESFORCE DATABASE

```
    User user = new User(LastName = 'Test', IsActive
    = true);
    insert user;

    AccountOwnershipRules rules =
    new  AccountOwnershipRules();

    Account updatedAccount = rules.transferAccountOwnership
    (account.Id, user.Id);

    Assert.areEqual(user.Id, updatedAccount.OwnerId);
}
```

We insert the data and then test our logic with that data. But just as it used to happen to me all the time, it turns out this code actually doesn't compile. I get this dreaded error message:

```
System.DmlException: Insert failed.
First exception on row 0; first error: REQUIRED_FIELD_MISSING,
Required fields are missing: [Username, Email, Alias,
TimeZoneSidKey, LocaleSidKey, EmailEncodingKey, ProfileId,
LanguageLocaleKey]
```

That's right. Just to create a simple user, I'm forced to come up with a username, a profile, a short alias, etc. And so we resort the data factories, to complex csv files, etc. My opinion at the time of this writing is that these are all antipatterns when you work with a complex-enough org.

So, how can we create test data to allow our queries to return the correct data in a test context, without spending hours figuring out how to create that data? Mocking.

12.8.1 How to Mock SOQL Queries

Mocking SOQL queries is similar to mocking DML operations. You have to use a sort of wrapper around your queries, and you mock the results. Really, the correct term here should be "stub," because all we want to do is to give a predefined response without actually querying the database.

At a high level, mocking SOQL queries involves wrapping the SOQL query in a class or method that you can stub, either manually or using something like Apex-mockery or Amoss. In other words, to mock SOQL queries, **you will have to stop using inline SOQL queries**. Queries must be wrapped by either a class or a method that you can intercept during a test. I will show you two ways of doing this.

12.8.2 Moving SOQL into Methods

Using the examples above, you'd have to move the queries to their own methods, like this:

```
public Account transferAccountOwnership(
        Id accountId,
        Id newOwnerId
){
        Account account = queryAccount(accountId);

        User newOwner = queryUser(newOwnerId]);

        //we could have filter this out with SOQL.
        //I did it on purpose to add complexity to the example

        if(!newOwner.IsActive) {
            throw new DmlException('New owner is inactive');
        }
```

CHAPTER 12   UNIT TESTS, STUBS, AND MOCKING THE SALESFORCE DATABASE

```
        account.OwnerId = newOwnerId;
        update account;
        return account;
}
```

Then, with Amoss, Apex-mockery, or your own implementation of the Stub API, you can intercept those methods are provide canned responses.

```
//populate the list with some accounts without inserting them
List<Account> accountsToReturn = new List<Account>();

//then
AccountOwnershipRules rules = (AccountOwnershipRules)
        new Stub(AccountOwnershipRules.class).
            when(queryAccount).returning(accountsToReturn).
            create();
```

This way, when `queryAccount` is called internally, the `accountsToReturn` will be returned.

12.8.3 Use a SOQL Wrapper

This pattern involves creating a general-purpose SOQL wrapper that among other things provides ways to intercept queries and provides predefined responses during a test. There are some libraries out there, but I'm going to focus on **SOQL Lib** by Piotr Gajek.

Here, instead of using queries directly, we use a fluent interface, like this:

```
public Account transferAccountOwnership(Id accountId, Id newOwnerId) {

        Account account = (Account) SOQL.of(Account.
        SObjectType)
```

CHAPTER 12   UNIT TESTS, STUBS, AND MOCKING THE SALESFORCE DATABASE

```
    .with(Account.Id, Account.OwnerId)
    .whereAre(SOQL.Filter.with(Account.Id).
equal(accountId))
    .mockId('transferAccountOwnership.queryAccount')
    .toObject();

    User newOwner = (User) SOQL.of(User.SObjectType)
    .with(User.Id, User.IsActive)
    .whereAre(SOQL.Filter.with(User.Id).equal(newOwnerId))
    .mockId('transferAccountOwnership.queryUser')
    .toObject();

    if(!newOwner.IsActive) {
        throw new DmlException('New owner is inactive');
    }
    account.OwnerId = newOwnerId;
    update account;
    return account;

}
```

Personally, I'm not a fan of fluent interfaces for queries, because in my mind, this

```
[SELECT Id, OwnerId FROM Account WHERE Id = :accountId]
```

is orders of magnitude easier to mentally parse than this

```
Account account = (Account) SOQL.of(Account.SObjectType)
        .with(Account.Id, Account.OwnerId)
        .whereAre(SOQL.Filter.with(Account.Id).
equal(accountId))
        .mockId('transferAccountOwnership.queryAccount')
        .toObject();
```

However, I do find that mocking these types of fluent queries is much more straightforward and a joy to eye. You will notice that for both queries, I've set a property called `mockId`, which is whatever string I want to use to identify the queries.

Then, in my test class, I simply need to specify which query should return which data, using the same Id:

```
@IsTest
static void testTransferAccountOwnership() {

    Account fakeAccount = new Account(Id = FakeId.getFrom(Account.SObjectType));

    User fakeUser = new User(Id = FakeId.getFrom(User.SObjectType), IsActive = true);

    SOQL.setMock(
        'transferAccountOwnership.queryAccount',
        fakeAccount
     );

    SOQL.setMock(
        'transferAccountOwnership.queryUser',
         fakeUser
     );

    Test.startTest();
    AccountOwnershipRules rules = new AccountOwnershipRules();
    Account result = rules.transferAccountOwnership(fakeAccount.Id, fakeUser.Id);
    Test.stopTest();

    Assert.areEqual(fakeUser.Id, result.OwnerId);

}
```

When the fluent interface runs in a test context, it'll check if any of the queries have been stamped with an Id, and if that Id is found in `SOQL.setMock(id, data),` the results are intercepted and provided as predefined responses (stubs).

12.9 Should You Mock the Database?

All the techniques we've explored in this chapter can help you decrease test execution times and simplify test setup, both of these are enablers of CI as I mentioned earlier. The remaining question is whether you should actually do this?

It's possible that your org is relatively small, and tests run in under ten minutes, in which case I'd argue you don't need to do this (yet). Perhaps you work in a large team and introducing these patterns would dramatically increase complexity (temporarily) and you are not willing to pay that price.

I also haven't answered the question I posed earlier: What is the value of testing units of behavior in isolation, if they may break in production?

The answer is rather disappointing: we should have a combination of **both unit and integration tests, as they both have their place**. No number of unit tests will ever get close to reality as integration tests do. With this in mind, I recommend the following:

- Test the observable behavior of a module with at least **one** integration test that covers the "happy path"
- Test **all other variations** of the behavior with pure unit tests

This would naturally lead to a high percentage of unit tests and a lower percentage of integration tests. However, this means that for integration tests, you'll still have to resort to creating "real" test data with data factories and the like. In other words, the techniques I described here will not completely remove the pain points I described earlier.

However, the key is to have less integration tests so that the complexity of them doesn't overwhelm you and to have more unit tests so that you can get fast feedback and practice real CI.

12.10 Conclusion

Mocking the database can make CI a reality for many teams. However, you must understand it comes a cost. That cost is high complexity and, to some extent, less accurate tests, as they don't consider other automation that will impact how your code behaves.

My goal of this chapter was to introduce the necessary concepts for you to think if this can indeed be of benefit. If you are considering following the approaches discussed here, you should make it a team-wide decision.

Finally, consider implementing a gradual approach. You don't need to refactor all your tests to mock the database. Focus on the ones that are causing the most performance issues during test execution and start using these patterns for all new code.

CHAPTER 13

The Apex Well-Architected Framework

> *Simplicity is a great virtue but it requires hard work to achieve it and education to appreciate it. And to make matters worse: complexity sells better.*
>
> —Edsger W. Dijkstra

This chapter aims to serve as a conclusion to the book and to bring it all together in a cohesive way (pun intended).

As of the time of this writing, there isn't an agreed approach to structuring Apex code and organizing files and modules. Most orgs organically grow into a big ball of mud, where it's impossible to untangle anything without frustration. Other orgs early on adopt a framework like FFLIB (a.k.a. Apex Enterprise Patterns), created by Andrew Fawcett. And other orgs achieve some level of modularity with unlocked packages and internal libraries.

CHAPTER 13   THE APEX WELL-ARCHITECTED FRAMEWORK

My goal with this chapter is to propose a new way to structure an Apex code base and to provide opinionated recommendations on what libraries and tools you should use. You should be aware that this will be the most opinionated chapter of all, and many of my recommendations are based purely on personal preference and experience. **At no point do I claim that this is the best way to do things.**

Also, my recommendations will be compared against the FFLIB framework. If you've never heard of this framework, some of the discussions may not resonate too much with you, but I'll try to generalize my arguments as much as possible.

13.1 A FFLIB Recap

FFLIB was created by Andrew Fawcett over a decade ago as of the time of this writing. The framework originated from his experience building FinancialForce (now called Certinia), a popular managed package in the AppExchange. The framework is also known as Apex Enterprise Patterns because the patterns are a direct implementation of the techniques shown in the canonical book *Patterns of Enterprise Application Architecture* by Martin Fowler.

The framework proposes that we split our Apex code in three layers, as depicted in Figure 13-1.

CHAPTER 13   THE APEX WELL-ARCHITECTED FRAMEWORK

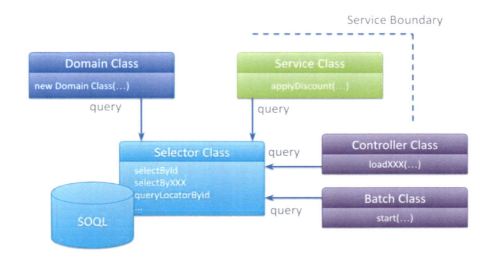

Figure 13-1. *The three layers and how other classes use the layers. (Source* https://andyinthecloud.com/category/design-patterns/*)*

At a high level, this how each layer works:

- **Domain Layer**: Handles business logic and enforces rules for specific objects. This is where things like validations, triggers, and calculations live. It's the go-to place for managing how an object behaves.

- **Service Layer**: Manages use cases that involve multiple objects or external systems. This layer takes care of more complex business processes that span across different parts of the system.

- **Selector Layer**: Takes care of data retrieval by wrapping SOQL queries for specific objects. This helps keep things consistent, avoids duplicate queries, and makes the code easier to maintain.

349

So, in theory, you'd have an Opportunities class that handles all opportunity logic, an OpportunityService class that orchestrates logic and exposes common services, and an OpportunitySelector class where all opportunity-related queries are stored.

Application-level code (triggers, batch classes, queueable classes, etc.) should call the service class. This is depicted in Figure 13-2.

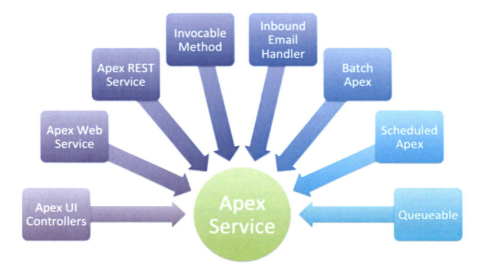

Figure 13-2. *Different contexts reuse the service layer. (Source https://andyinthecloud.com/category/design-patterns/)*

This framework has become incredibly popular in the Salesforce community and for good reason. Many developers credit FFLIB with simplifying their work and reducing headaches, and it continues to be a trusted framework for structuring Apex code. We, as an ecosystem, owe Andrew Fawcett and his contributors our gratitude for introducing proven software design principles to Salesforce development. We clearly need more of that.

However, no framework is without its drawbacks. In the next section, we'll examine some of the challenges associated with FFLIB and explore why a new way of thinking may be warranted.

13.2 The Challenges with FFLIB

One of the primary challenges with this framework is how it positions itself as a solution for achieving "separation of concerns" (SoC). The messaging around SoC is so emphatic that it even tells us there are scenarios where you might choose **not** to implement SoC. For instance, at the time of writing, the Trailhead module on this topic includes a section titled **"When You Don't Need SoC on Salesforce,"** suggesting that SoC is both binary and optional.

Assuming you've read all the chapters in this book, you probably know that SoC is not something you can directly implement; it's an outcome. It emerges from applying the principles of modularity, coupling, and cohesion we've explored throughout this book. Furthermore, SoC is not binary; it doesn't simply exist or not exist. Like coupling, it operates on a spectrum, and it is a degree (low coupling vs. high coupling).

The issue isn't just the inaccurate terminology. My concern is that this way of thinking might discourage developers from critically engaging with the principles of SoC. Instead, they may blindly follow patterns, treating them as prescriptive rather than adaptable.

I would much rather see a team of Salesforce developers engaging in ongoing discussions about modularity in their org—debating where responsibilities should lie and how to maintain cohesion—than simply adding a method to the service class because the framework dictates it.

With that said, let's now look at some more specific concerns I have with FFLIB.

13.2.1 Narrow View of the Platform

I believe FFLIB thrives in a managed package environment, where the objects you operate on are owned by the package and finite in scope. For example, if the package provides specific functionality for the `Opportunity` object, it's logical to have an `OpportunityService` class to encapsulate its functionalities. Similarly, when developers working for the company that owns the package need to add new queries, centralizing them in an `OpportunitiesSelector` class makes sense, as all developers are likely focused on the same functionality.

In other words, this framework is well-suited for building a well-defined product with clear boundaries, such as an AppExchange package. Managed package development typically involves controlled data models and cohesive teams, which I think makes FFLIB a great fit. In fact, the framework originated from the lessons learned when building managed packages (plus Martin Fowler's teachings).

However, this isn't the reality for most development teams. In a typical enterprise company, developers and consultants come and go, and many different departments shape how Salesforce is used. Take the `Opportunity` object, for example. It might serve marketing, sales, and customer support, each with its own unique logic and requirements. Cramming all of that into a single `OpportunityService` class is exactly what the Single Responsibility Principle (SRP) encourages us to avoid.

Just as a reminder, SRP tells us that if the same module can change for different reasons—like different requests from marketing, sales, or support—it's better to split them up. Otherwise, changes in one area could have unintended consequences in another, making the code harder to maintain and more error-prone.

In short, the idea that you can put all logic in three classes (the service, the domain, and the selector) does not fit the reality of teams who are **not** building managed packages.

13.2.2 Selectors Are Shallow Modules

FFLIB encourages us to include all SOQL queries in a single selector class, like `OpportunitiesSelector`. The argument for doing this is to have consistency on the "shape" of your SObjects and prevent runtime errors. For example:

```
Opportunity oppty = [SELECT Id FROM Opportunity LIMIT 1];
if(oppty.name == 'hello'){
    //error!
}
```

When I run this, I get the dreaded error:

```
System.SObjectException: SObject row was retrieved via SOQL without querying the requested field: Opportunity.Name
```

This occurred because I didn't include the `Name` field in the query.

The FFLIB literature suggests that by centralizing all queries in a single class, you can ensure all records come back with the same set of fields (i.e., the same "shape"), and thus, you prevent the above error message. But really, all you need to do to prevent this error is to include the field in your query. You should be able to discover the error during testing, add the field to the query, and move on. This shouldn't take more than two minutes, and it doesn't warrant having all queries in the same class. For example, I can fix the above error with this:

```
Opportunity oppty = [SELECT Id, Name FROM Opportunity LIMIT 1];
```

Problem solved. It took me longer to write this sentence than to add the field to the query.

Aside from that, the main problem is that queries are often highly specific to particular requirements. As a result, selector classes can quickly grow to include dozens of methods, each serving a unique purpose or slight variation of a similar query. For example, a selector class might look something like this (in pseudocode):

```
public class OpportunitiesSelector {

    queryById()
    queryByIndustry()
    queryByField(field...)
    queryWithAllFields()
    queryWithTheseFields(fields...)
    queryWithBinds()
    queryWithLineItems()
    queryWithParentOpportunity()
```

When every method becomes this specific, the pattern doesn't encourage reusability. Instead, it often leads to developers creating new tailored methods or modifying existing ones, at the risk of breaking other classes that depend on them. As the class grows, it becomes harder to come up with meaningful and descriptive names (see Chapter 2).

In other words, the selector ends up exposing a **complicated interface while offering limited value**. As we've seen many times throughout this book, this is the textbook definition of a shallow module.

In my opinion, the main benefit of this approach is to enable mocking of the queries during tests, as we discussed in the previous chapter. However, there are other techniques for mocking queries that are much more lightweight and don't require a centralized selector.

13.2.3 Over-engineering

Because FFLIB is not a way of thinking but rather a specific implementation, it comes with a lot of baggage. There are numerous interfaces to implement, which adds complexity. As we discussed in a previous chapter, the goal of modularity is to reduce complexity, not increase it. Similarly, the YAGNI principle reminds us to build for today's needs, not for hypothetical future scenarios, though, of course, there are exceptions.

I've come across entire YouTube channels and GitHub repositories dedicated to explaining these patterns, which, to me, signals that the patterns themselves are not simple. They require convoluted explanations and a deep understanding of how all the pieces fit together. In other words, **the framework is not progressive**.

A progressive framework grows with your code base. You start small, using only what you need, and as your system scales, you add more functionality to manage the complexity. FFLIB, on the other hand, takes an all-or-nothing approach.

13.2.4 Not Built for Salesforce

Finally, FFLIB is based on Martin Fowler's work on enterprise patterns. His book was written in 2002 and is based on his experience working with old Java applications, not modern architectures. That on its own is not a problem; after all, I wrote an entire chapter on OOP even though many of its concepts are much older and there are often better alternatives today. I also believe there's a lot of value in taking **inspiration** from other realms of software design and applying those ideas to Salesforce. In fact, if you think about it, that's what this book is all about.

CHAPTER 13   THE APEX WELL-ARCHITECTED FRAMEWORK

The problem is that when Fowler came up with these patterns, he wasn't working with Salesforce in 2025. He was solving problems in old, monolithic Java applications; systems that had full control over business logic, state, and execution flow.

He wasn't dealing with validation rules breaking his code or case assignment rules undoing ownership changes made in Apex. He wasn't designing for a platform where governor limits dictate how many DML operations you can commit in a single transaction. His patterns were designed to solve **his problems**, problems that made sense in the context of the software he was working on.

If Fowler were working with Salesforce today, you can bet he wouldn't have written the exact same patterns. He would've considered the event-driven nature of the platform, the mix of declarative and programmatic logic, and the constraints imposed by multitenant architecture. That's why **we can't just take patterns from a different era and a different problem domain and apply them blindly**. Instead, we should understand the principles behind them and **adapt them to fit the unique constraints of Salesforce development.**

As I've mentioned before, Salesforce is a database-driven system: not a traditional piece of software, no matter how much we might wish otherwise.

Some may argue that this mindset is just an excuse for poorly structured Apex or that Fowler's patterns are timeless. But the truth is, the patterns themselves are **not** timeless; the **underlying principles are**.

So, what is at the core of these patterns? Modularity. For me, it's much more valuable to learn the principles of modularity than to blindly apply patterns that were created for a completely different architectural domain and a different era.

13.3 Gratitude

After spending the last few sections critiquing FFLIB, I want to take a moment to emphasize that this is not a critique on its creators or collaborators. The framework has brought immense value to the Salesforce community, and our ecosystem is undeniably better because of it. Few people will ever match the inspiration, vision, and technical expertise of Andrew Fawcett, and for that, we owe him our gratitude.

Critique is necessary if we want to move forward, even if it's uncomfortable. With that said, the responsibility now falls on me to propose an alternative.

13.4 What's the Alternative?

As much as I'd like to propose a drop-in replacement for FFLIB, that's not what I want to propose here. Instead, I want to propose **a set of guiding principles that can be implemented differently based on team size and org complexity**. I will also provide some opinionated recommendations for some libraries that you should consider.

Based on my experience, I don't think the Salesforce ecosystem is ready for a batteries-included framework that developers can start using from day one. I've seen firsthand how valuable such frameworks can be outside of Salesforce development. For example, when I built HappySoup, I used `express.js` for the back end and followed its recommendations. This let me focus on what I wanted to build, instead of how to build it. I can't overstate how helpful that was.

Salesforce development, though, is different. Many Salesforce developers come from nonengineering backgrounds, and most teams are a mix of admins and developers. On top of that, there's much more to Salesforce than just Apex; you can build an entire application without writing a single line of code.

CHAPTER 13   THE APEX WELL-ARCHITECTED FRAMEWORK

There's also the reality that Salesforce orgs tend to operate in enterprise environments with tight controls. It's not easy to get approval to use a library that affects every part of how you write Apex. What happens if the library maintainers abandon it? Or if a bug in the library blocks a critical deployment? In traditional software development, these concerns are smaller because there are many more developers, and for every library, there are usually multiple alternatives. That's just not the case with Salesforce.

Instead of creating an implementation framework, I believe we should focus on **principles**. Principles give us the flexibility to adapt to our specific needs, whether we're a small team working on a simple org or an enterprise team managing a highly complex environment. This way, we're not locked into a single approach but can still draw on proven ideas to write modular, scalable, and maintainable code.

What we need is a Well-Architected Framework for Apex.

13.5 Apex Well-Architected Framework

The **Apex Well-Architected Framework** is meant to provide guiding principles and specific recommendations for structuring your Apex code base. I'll refer to it as AWAF for simplicity (and yes, for marketing purposes too). It shouldn't be a surprise that all the recommendations are based on what we've learned in this book.

Note   I see the irony in critiquing the concept of a framework only to propose another. The difference is that FFLIB is an implementation framework that dictates where to put your code because "that's how the framework works." AWAF, on the other hand, is a **principles-based framework** that provides guidelines to help you think about software design.

CHAPTER 13   THE APEX WELL-ARCHITECTED FRAMEWORK

My vision is that every team can implement AWAF, yet each implementation can be completely different. In a way, **no one should be able to tell you what an org using AWAF *looks* like; instead, they should be able to tell you what working in such an org *feels* like**. A developer may work on two completely different code bases, yet the experience should feel the same.

I'd like to imagine a future where teams who follow AWAF are constantly engaging in discussions about modularity, coupling, cohesion, and testability, where decisions are driven by principles, not dictated by a framework. Instead of simply adding code where the framework tells them to, they would do so based on their desire to balance multiple design forces.

It's my hope that this way of thinking inspires you to not only adopt these principles but to share them with your colleagues and friends in the Salesforce ecosystem. Now, let's look at AWAF in detail.

Note   The following sections will be more prescriptive in nature. Throughout the book, I've avoided saying "you must" or "you should" as much as possible, focusing instead on presenting information and letting you decide what applies to your environment.

In this chapter, however, I'll take a more assertive approach. Take everything I say with a grain of salt and adapt it to your unique context.

CHAPTER 13 THE APEX WELL-ARCHITECTED FRAMEWORK

13.6 Use Salesforce DX Folders

You should use Salesforce DX folders to organize your code into features, use cases, and business units. At the time of this writing, Salesforce DX has been in place for years, and there's no excuse anymore not to make the most out of it. Gone are the days of ANT and the Force.com IDE, with outdated Metadata API format.

Teams should be using the Salesforce DX source format, as seen in Figure 13-3.

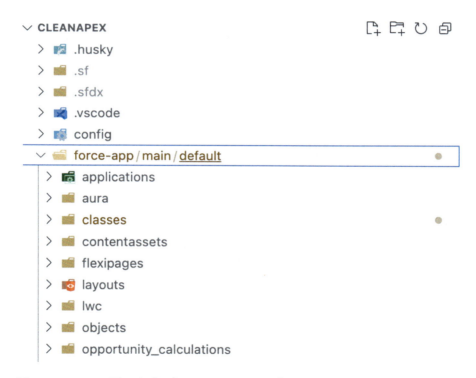

Figure 13-3. *The Salesforce DX source format*

CHAPTER 13   THE APEX WELL-ARCHITECTED FRAMEWORK

The source format allows for the creation of custom folders. Your team should make an effort to organize metadata in folders that make the architecture of your org very clear. Figure 13-4 shows an example of what such a project could look like.

***Figure 13-4.** Custom folders to represent business units or problem domains*

Notice how under `force-app/main`, we have a `customer_support` folder. Here, we can see different use cases for that business unit, such as logic and custom fields related to case closure or calculating SLAs.

This is an example of what's known as a screaming architecture. The architecture is "screaming" at you, telling you exactly what it does. This term originates from Robert C. Martin's Clean Architecture, and it reflects an architecture where structure and intent are immediately obvious to anyone looking at the code base.

Before Salesforce DX, it made sense to encapsulate all these use cases in a single class like `CasesService`, as FFLIB would dictate. This was necessary because there was no other way to organize units of logic while keeping them close to each other (cohesion). But with the advent of Salesforce DX folders, this is no longer needed, and I now consider it an antipattern.

A code base using AWAF uses Salesforce DX source folders to represent the architecture of the org.

361

CHAPTER 13   THE APEX WELL-ARCHITECTED FRAMEWORK

13.7 Where to Place Business Logic

One of my personal challenges with FFLIB has always been the separation between the Service and Domain layers, which I find somewhat artificial. According to the theory, the Service layer is meant to expose API services for a particular object, such as opportunities.

> **Note** Here, I'm using the term API to represent a service or an internal API that a module exposes, not a REST or SOAP API. Think of it as the interface of the module, as we've discussed in other chapters.

Here's an example from the Trailhead module:

```
public with sharing class OpportunitiesService {
    public static void applyDiscounts(
        Set<Id> opportunityIds,
        Decimal discountPercentage)
    {
```

Here, the `OpportunitiesService` class exposes an API to apply discounts to certain opportunities. But I encourage you to pause and think why couldn't this logic exist in the Domain layer? For example:

```
//this is the domain layer according to fflib
public class Opportunities {
    public static void applyDiscounts(
        Set<Id> opportunityIds,
        Decimal discountPercentage)
    {
```

CHAPTER 13   THE APEX WELL-ARCHITECTED FRAMEWORK

I can't think of a reason this logic should sit in a Service layer. In fact, I'd argue for creating a class called `OpportunityDiscount` that encapsulates all the logic required to calculate discounts. Then, I would place this class in the respective Salesforce DX source folder for that business unit and use case.

The theory on Trailhead tells us that the Domain layer (e.g., the `Opportunities` class) should only handle logic related to trigger events and input validation. In my humble opinion, this is an entirely artificial separation. If calculating discounts for opportunities is such an important functionality, why should it be separate from the Domain class?

Also, both classes above are exactly the same. The only difference is in the name. If I add the word "service" to it, it magically becomes a Service class. Without it, it's a Domain class. Again, in my opinion, this is an artificial separation.

Two points are at the center of this critique. First, the Service vs. Domain pattern **does not provide concrete guidance on when to keep logic together or when to keep it apart**. The guidelines I provided in Section 10.4 are much more straightforward and applicable. As a reminder, a desire to reduce complexity should be the driving force of this question.

Second, **FFLIB offers little guidance on where to put business logic**. Should business logic reside in the Service layer? Or in the Domain layer? Should it be split between the two (which decreases cohesion)?

For AWAF, I want to provide concrete guidelines that answer three questions:

- What is business logic?
- What is not business logic?
- Where should business logic go?

13.7.1 What Is Business Logic?

Business logic becomes easier to define when we first consider what **is not** business logic. Here are some examples of nonbusiness logic:

- Retry logic for queueable Apex
- Bypass logic in trigger handlers
- Governor limit logic (e.g., delegating to an async handler when nearing the DML limit)
- Pure database transaction logic (e.g., catching exceptions, retrying, aggregating records into a list)

From these examples, we can deduce that business logic is the logic that our users care about, like, *"when an opportunity is closed/won, a default contract should be created."* The infrastructure in which that logic runs (whether a trigger, queueable, or platform event) is irrelevant to the business.

13.7.2 Business Logic Should Be Written from the Inside Out

Some schools of thought advocate for creating a clear separation between business and infrastructure logic. For example, in the **imperative shell, functional core** architecture, business logic is completely decoupled from infrastructure logic, making the business logic easier to test. Figure 13-5 depicts this architecture style.

CHAPTER 13 THE APEX WELL-ARCHITECTED FRAMEWORK

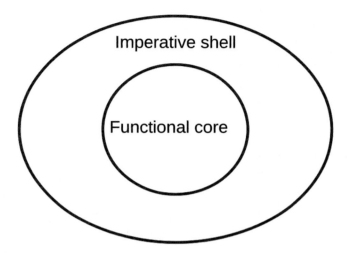

Figure 13-5. *The functional core represents the pure business logic. The imperative shell wraps it and provides infrastructure services*

In this approach, when we have a business requirement (like creating a contract for a closed opportunity), we model that logic in a way that's completely decoupled from external dependencies like the database or governor limits. This layer is called the functional core—it contains the pure business logic that can be easily unit-tested.

Here's what it might look like:

```
public class ClosedOpportunity {

    public Decision createContract(Opportunity oppty){
        if (oppty.StageName == 'Closed Won') {
            return Decision.CREATE_CONTRACT;
        }
        return Decision.DO_NOTHING;
    }
```

CHAPTER 13 THE APEX WELL-ARCHITECTED FRAMEWORK

```
    public enum Decision {
        CREATE_CONTRACT,
        DO_NOTHING
    }
}
```

Notice how the method `createContract` simply returns a decision, either "create a contract" or "do nothing." This logic reflects how the business would describe the requirement, without any mention of DML operations or infrastructure concerns. And in fact, it should be incredibly easy to unit-test this.

The imperative shell is then a wrapper class responsible for interacting with the database and other dependencies. It takes the decision from the functional core and performs the actual interactions with the database:

```
public void createContract(Opportunity oppty) {

    ClosedOpportunity.Decision decision =
    new    ClosedOpportunity().createContract(oppty);

    if (decision == ClosedOpportunity.Decision.CREATE_
    CONTRACT) {
        // Perform the actual DML operation
    } else {
        // Do nothing
    }
}
```

Again, advocates of this approach argue that the functional core's purity makes it easier to test and maintain.

However, if you've read this book in order, you probably suspect that I'm not a huge fan of this approach. The imperative shell is almost a mirror of the functional core, except it handles infrastructure logic. This causes high coupling between the two classes and adds complexity and maintenance overhead.

So, if I don't agree with this approach, why spend so much time discussing it? Because I believe one of its core ideas is valuable: **we should build business logic from the inside out.**

Rather than starting with infrastructure concerns (e.g., triggers or platform events, comparing `Trigger.new` against `Trigger.old`, etc.), we should begin by modelling the core logic in a way that's somewhat agnostic to how it's called. For example, the method in the functional core accepts an `Opportunity` object directly—it doesn't care whether the opportunity came from `Trigger.new` or a batch class. This is not so different from a recommendation I made earlier in the book: aim to create somewhat general-purpose modules, as they are deeper.

13.7.3 Concrete Guidelines for Business Logic

With all this said, let me now give some concrete guidelines as per the AWAF model:

- Always consider building business logic from the inside out. This enables easier testing and reusability.

- Where possible, decouple the business logic from the infrastructure logic by using plain and simple dependency injection. For example, consider injecting a wrapper around the `Database` class, so that you can unit-test the pure business logic.

- Trigger handler classes are considered infrastructure and should contain only the minimal business logic required to route records to the correct class. The bulk of the logic should be inside "functional core" classes. This ensures that business logic remains reusable, testable, and independent of trigger contexts like `trigger.new`.

- Focus your efforts on identifying where in the Salesforce DX hierarchy a class should be. It should be in a place where its intent, purpose, and business value become obvious.

- Where to put business logic should be influenced **by a desire to increase cohesion**.

In short, rather than prescribing, *"business logic should go in this layer because my framework says so,"* I'm encouraging you to follow the above principles. They will guide you in making decisions that fit your specific org, team, and use cases.

13.8 Filtering Logic in Trigger Handlers

In the previous section, I mentioned that trigger handlers should only contain minimal business logic and route records to the correct class. However, because triggers are so central to Salesforce development, I want to expand on this a bit more and give clear guidance.

A question I had for several years was where should you place filtering logic. Consider this example in the `OpportunityTriggerHandler` class:

```
//oldOpptys is trigger.old
//newOpptys is trigger.new

List<Opportunity> closedOpptys = new List<Opportunity>();

for(Opportunity newOppty : newOpptys.values()){

    Opportunity oldOppty = oldOpptys.get(newOppty.Id);

    //filtering logic
    if(
      newOppty.StageName == 'Closed Won' &&
      oldOppty.StageName != 'Closed Won')
```

CHAPTER 13   THE APEX WELL-ARCHITECTED FRAMEWORK

```
    {
        closedOpptys.add(newOppty);
    }
}
if(!closedOpptys.isEmpty()){
    //call the "functional core" class
    new ClosedOpportunities().createContracts(closedOpptys);
}
```

Where should this logic be? Should it be inside the trigger handler class? Also, is this considered business logic?

In my opinion, this is business logic because if you were to create a contract for every opportunity that was updated, regardless of whether the stage changed to `Closed Won`, the business will surely complain. However, this is business logic that is inevitably tied to the infrastructure: we must compare `trigger.new` against `trigger.old` to determine if we should proceed. That's why I said in the previous section that it is acceptable for trigger handlers to contain minimal business logic.

Now, let me expand on that statement: **Trigger handlers can contain business logic if that logic relates to filtering the records that must be processed by a "functional core" class.**

One problem with this recommendation is that it assumes the functional core can really work without knowing anything about its environment. Suppose that to check if a `Contract` must be created, we also must check if the `Opportunity` has `line items` with an approved status. If we do the subquery inside the trigger handler, we are implicitly saying that the `ClosedOpportunities` class will expect a list of opportunities and their line items. What if we forget to run the subquery? What if other contexts pass the opportunities without the line items?

What we are seeing here is that there's coupling between the filtering logic and the pure business logic, but that coupling has a long distance. Some part of the business process is in the trigger handler, while other

CHAPTER 13   THE APEX WELL-ARCHITECTED FRAMEWORK

parts are in the "functional core" class. That distance is the opposite of cohesion. If modules are inevitably coupled, then we must shorten that distance between them and make the coupling more obvious: that is cohesion.

To achieve this, we could add a method on `ClosedOpportunities` that is responsible for filtering opportunities that meet the precondition, for example:

```
//inside of ClosedOpportunities.cls
public static List<Opportunity> getClosedWonOpportunities(
        Map<Id, Opportunity> newOpptys,
        Map<Id, Opportunity> oldOpptys)
    {
        List<Opportunity> closedOpptys = new List<Opportunity>();
        for(Opportunity newOppty : newOpptys.values()){
            Opportunity oldOppty = oldOpptys.get(newOppty.Id);

            if(
              newOppty.StageName == 'Closed Won' &&
              oldOppty.StageName != 'Closed Won')
            {
                closedOpptys.add(newOppty);
            }
        }
        return closedOpptys;
    }
```

This method simply returns a list of closed opportunities based on the values of `trigger.newMap` and `trigger.oldMap` (without referencing the trigger context directly). With this, we could have the following code in the trigger handler:

```
List<Opportunity> closedOpptys = ClosedOpportunities.getClosedW
onOpportunities(newOpptys, oldOpptys);
if(!closedOpptys.isEmpty()){
    new ClosedOpportunities().createContracts(closedOpptys);
}
```

This way, the dependency between the state of the opportunities and the `createContracts` method becomes obvious.

That said, I'm not suggesting you do this with every scenario. The official AWAF guidance is: **filtering logic should reside in trigger handlers. If lack of cohesion becomes a problem, considering moving that logic to the same "functional core" class that the trigger routes the records to.**

13.9 Domain Classes

In the FFLIB model, domain classes are meant to encapsulate business logic related to a specific object, including methods for trigger events like `beforeInsert()` and `afterUpdate()`. I see the benefit of this approach: having trigger handler methods and other object-related logic in the same class increases cohesion.

However, in my opinion, one domain class per object only works for very small domains. As soon as you have different use cases for the same object, often from multiple business units, the domain class (e.g., `Opportunities`) becomes a "god class." It becomes a catch-all for all logic related to that object, deviating from the both the Single Responsibility Principle (SRP) and the modularity principles we explored in Chapter 10.

CHAPTER 13   THE APEX WELL-ARCHITECTED FRAMEWORK

"God" classes are also a source of merge conflicts and awkward workarounds. If two developers need to make changes to the same class for different reasons, this often leads to merge conflicts later in the CI/CD pipeline. Even worse, sometimes, one of those requirements needs to be removed from the release because of failures during UAT, leading to developers commenting out the code or having to recommit changes. All this could be avoided if developers were working on different classes.

To avoid the problems of these monolithic domain classes, I recommend using domain classes that **represent a meaningful state of the object, if that state is relevant to the business.**

The most common example of a meaningful state is record types or special status fields like `Opportunity.StageName` or `Case.Status`.

For instance, record types represent subtypes of the main object, similar to subclasses in OOP. Imagine you have opportunities with a Partnerships record type and others with a Customer record type. These subtypes often drive business-specific behavior, such as showing different UIs (via page layouts) or filtering records in flows, triggers, etc.

This leads to code like the following:

```
if (oppty.RecordType == 'Partnerships') {
    // Do something
}
```

How many methods in your org are filtering by record type? In a large org, it could be hundreds. This often results in deeply nested if/else statements and methods that do more than one thing.

In AWAF, **you create a class that represents the record type of the object and encapsulate all related logic there.** For example:

```
public class PartnershipOpportunities { ...

public class CustomerOpportunities { ...
```

CHAPTER 13 THE APEX WELL-ARCHITECTED FRAMEWORK

The constructor for these classes can take care of filtering out irrelevant records, like this:

```
public class PartnershipOpportunities {

    private List<Opportunity> partnerOpptys;

    public PartnershipOpportunities(
        List<Opportunity> opportunities)
    {
        this. partnerOpptys = new List<Opportunity>();

        for (Opportunity opp : opportunities) {
            if (opp.RecordType == 'Partnership') {
                this. partnerOpptys.add(opp);
            }
        }
    }

    public void notifyNewOwner() {
        // Do something with partnerOpptys
    }
}
```

In the trigger handler (or other contexts), you simply pass a list of opportunities to the class and execute the relevant logic:

```
... partnerOpptys = new PartnershipOpportunities(opptys);

partnerOpptys.notifyNewOwner();
```

This approach avoids the need for scattered `if/else` statements across your code base and keeps related logic together in one place.

This idea shouldn't be limited to record types. **Any meaningful state can be represented this way.**

For example, consider closed cases. The business might have specific logic for handling cases that are closed, like notifying customers or generating reports. Rather than putting all this logic in a generic `Cases` class, you could create a `ClosedCases` class to encapsulate it.

```
public class ClosedCases {
   // logic specific to closed cases
}
```

I'm not suggesting that every record type or picklist value has a counterpart Apex class. If the state of an object is meaningful, then the state should be represented by a class. That state may be represented with a record type, a custom picklist field, or something else.

When in doubt, remember the YAGNI principle.

13.10 Internal Libraries

Even though AWAF is meant to be about principles, I recognize the value of plug-in solutions that "just work." In this section, I will make recommendations for what libraries you should strongly consider to speed up development in Salesforce.

I'm confident in recommending these libraries because their creators have a proven track record of actively supporting the code, helping users, and building a community around their projects. Many of these libraries have multiple contributors, which should ease any worries about using someone else's code in a production environment.

As far as AWAF is concerned, these libraries are inherently part of the framework because they embody the principles AWAF stands for. If better libraries emerge in the future, I hope the community embraces them as part of AWAF, continuing to evolve the framework as needed.

That said, as I stated earlier, you must be careful when using external libraries as authors may stop supporting them or may not be available to fix bugs that could impact critical functionality in your org. You use them at your own risk.

13.10.1 Trigger Handlers

I recommend the **Trigger Actions Framework** by Mitch Spano and the team at Google. This library is widely used by large enterprises, including Google itself, and provides a configuration-based framework for organizing trigger actions and defining their order of execution.

The framework models each trigger actions as a small class, which makes testing easier and can help reduce merge conflicts.

This approach can come at the cost of cohesion as related actions may be split across multiple classes; however, you can address this by organizing the classes within the appropriate Salesforce DX folders, as we discussed earlier.

If you are not able to switch trigger frameworks, then I recommend that you try to model your trigger handler logic in a way that supports modularity, cohesion, and a reduction in merge conflicts.

13.10.2 Apex Logging and Observability

Using `System.debug()` is fine for quick troubleshooting or Apex performance profiling during development. However, for production support, it's the worst possible solution. It requires setting up debug logs for the affected user, retrieving the log, and dealing with potential size limits where the part you actually care about gets trimmed.

For a better solution, I recommend **Nebula Logger** by Jonathan Gillespie. Nebula Logger is an observability framework that integrates with Apex, Lightning Components, Flow, OmniStudio, and external integrations. The library has strong community support and has been featured at many events, including Dreamforce.

13.10.3 Continuous Delivery with Feature Flags

Continuous Delivery (CD) is a set of practices designed to ensure that your code base is always in a deployable state. But what does that actually mean?

If you're using version control (and if you're not, talk to your manager ASAP), you probably have an integration branch where all changes from all developers are merged and tested. This branch is likely connected to a sandbox as well.

At some point, most teams run into a situation where a particular change cannot be deployed further down the CI/CD pipeline and it needs to be pulled out. How do you handle this? Some teams resort to commenting out the code (an antipattern we discussed earlier) or using Git revert to remove the unwanted change (or whatever DevOps tool they are using).

But what if you could deploy the integration branch to production even if a feature isn't ready? What if you could do this without impacting the business? If this were possible, **your integration branch would always be deployable.** Deploying would become simpler because you'd only need to push a single branch to production instead of cherry-picking individual changes.

Feature flags let you hide a specific feature behind a toggle that can be turned on or off via configuration. Here's an example:

CHAPTER 13   THE APEX WELL-ARCHITECTED FRAMEWORK

```
// some of code here, and then:

FeatureFlags flags = new FeatureFlags();

if (flags.evaluate('enhancedQuoteEditor').isEnabled()) {
    // run the logic for the enhanced quote editor
}
```

In this example, all the logic for the enhanced quote editor is encapsulated within the `if` statement. The `FeatureFlags` class checks if there's a custom metadata record (or custom permission) for the `enhancedQuoteEditor` feature and determines whether the feature should be active.

This allows you to safely deploy the changes inside the `if` block to production while the feature is still in progress. The logic won't run because the feature is disabled in the configuration. Once the feature is ready, all you need to do is deploy the latest version of the integration branch and enable the feature in production.

This approach is supported by the **feature-flags** library, which I created. The library has become popular in recent months and was also featured at TrailheadDX.

In short, teams using AWAF actively try to keep their integration branch in a deployable state, avoiding messy workarounds later in the pipeline. This library supports that goal.

Note The library only supports Apex and LWC. It's not possible to hide configuration metadata behind a feature flag, such as new fields, permission set changes, etc.

13.10.4 Selector Classes

A big part of FFLIB is the selector classes, which are used to encapsulate all SOQL queries. As explained earlier, these classes quickly become shallow modules.

However, one advantage of selector classes is that because the query is wrapped with a class, you can mock that class during tests. We saw that this can be orders of magnitude easier than inserting dozens of records and trying to pass all validation rules in a test class.

As an alternative to FFLIB selectors, I recommend **SOQL Lib** by Piotr Gajek. We saw this library in action in the previous chapter:

```
Account account = (Account) SOQL.of(Account.SObjectType)
      .with(Account.Id, Account.OwnerId)
      .whereAre(SOQL.Filter.with(Account.Id).
      equal(accountId))
      .mockId('transferAccountOwnership.queryAccount')
      .toObject();
```

The library has good community support and, most importantly, provides one of the quickest and simplest way of mocking queries.

Finally, unlike object-specific selectors, SOQL Lib is a general-purpose module. As we've explored in earlier chapters, general-purpose modules are inherently deeper and provide more value across the code base.

13.10.5 General Utilities

Apex Libra by Piotr Kożuchowski provides general Apex utilities that almost every org will eventually need. For example, the library comes with a lot of built-in methods for dealing with collections:

```
Map<Id, Opportunity> opportunityByAccountId = (Map<Id,
Opportunity>)
    Collection.of(opportunities).mapBy(Opportunity.AccountId);
```

There are also utilities for easily working with picklists in Apex:

```
Picklist p = new Picklist(Account.Type);

String default = p.getDefaultValue();
String[] values = p.getValues();
SelectOption[] options = p.getSelectOptions();//(VisualForce)
Picklist.Entry[] entries = p.getEntries();//(Aura Enabled)
```

There are many other utilities as well such as mocking, HTTP callouts, etc.

Finally, Apex Libra also provides general principles and recommendations for structuring Apex code, such as how and where to store constants.

13.11 Other Principles

There are many other principles that are implicitly part of AWAF and that are covered throughout this book. Basically, everything I've recommended throughout this book is part of AWAF. This includes the following:

- Keep public methods deep.
- Methods should do one thing on the same level of abstraction.
- Use guard clauses or early returns to reduce nested `if/else` logic.
- Don't spread a single business process across multiple trigger handlers.

- Use exception handling on the entry points of your application (LWC controllers, trigger handlers, etc.). Sometimes, it's fine to let an exception bubble all the way up.
- Use OOP where it makes sense; sometimes, functional code is best.
- You must always balance coupling with cohesion.
- Test the observable behavior of your code.

Two different code bases following these principles would feel the same, even if they are completely different as to how they implement them.

13.12 Conclusion

AWAF is not meant to replace FFLIB. In fact, I believe teams using FFLIB can build on it by adopting AWAF principles. The two approaches don't need to compete; they can complement each other.

I'm also aware that AWAF isn't a complete framework, and that's intentional. It's not here to solve every problem you'll face in Apex development. Instead, it's a foundation for thinking about your code differently. I believe this is better than a set of rules that you must follow without thinking.

If there's one thing I hope you take away from this book, it's a new way of thinking about Apex development. My goal isn't just for you to write better code but to help you build something that simplifies your work and your life as a developer.

Thank you for reading.

Index

A

Abstract classes, 223–229
Abstraction, 61–64, 66, 69, 74, 80, 160, 162, 204, 209, 252, 270, 277, 286
Abstract *vs*. actual distinction, 199
Acceptance criteria, 25
accessLevel parameter, 72
AccountDomain class, 17
AccountOwnership class, 174
Account records, 4
Account trigger handler, 9
allOrNone parameter, 67, 70
allowPartialSuccess parameter, 70
Antipattern, 52, 54, 125, 130, 205, 319, 320, 325, 326
ApexDoc, 128, 129
Apex Enterprise Patterns, 47, 347
Apex Libra, 378, 379
Apex logging, 375
Apex-mockery, 337, 341
Apex Mock Objects, Spies and Stubs (Amoss), 337, 341
ApexTypeImplementor, 302
Apex Well-Architected Framework (AWAF), 358, 359
  guidance, 371
  principles, 379, 380
  record type, 372
AppExchange package, 352
Architectural map, 62
Artificial encapsulation, 206
Asynchronous processing
  CDC, 179–182
  definition, 177
  platform events, 182–184
  queueable processes, 178, 179
Atomicity, 173
Atomic operations, 170–173
Atomic *vs*. partial operations, 70
AutoQueueable, 228
AutoRABIT, 130

B

Bank transaction, 198
Bitbucket, 301
Boolean arguments, 70–72
Boolean logic, 139
  annual revenue, 15
  evaluation criteria, 14
  example, 13, 34
  extracting, 15
  for loop, 13
  formula fields, 31, 32

INDEX

Boolean logic (*cont.*)
    hiding, 32
    if statement, 16
    isPartnerAccount and
        isGoldTier, 16
    methods, 18
    page layout, 32
    redundant expression, 14
    requirement, 15
    supplier field, 13, 15
    trigger handler, 35
    valid names, 35
    wrapping, 33
Boolean parameters, 67–70
Boolean variables, 142, 143
Boundary
    complexity, 296
    definition, 294
    example, 294
    execution, 295
    goal, 297
    hard-coding dependencies, 299
    implementation, 297
    importData method, 295
    injected dependencies, 298, 299
    modules, 295
    pseudocode, 295
Brute Force, 325, 326
Bugs, 209
Business domain, 50
Business logic, 30, 213
    API services, 362
    createContract method, 366
    critique, 363

    definition, 364
    external dependencies, 365
    functional core
        architecture, 364–366
    guidelines, 367, 368
    logical grouping, 276
    modularity, 265
    and route records, 368
    Trailhead module, 362
Business processes, 170–173
Business units, 361
Business users/personas, 236

C

Calling methods, 136
Cascading failures, 184
Certinia, 348
Change data capture
    (CDC), 179–182
Chinese philosophy, 271
Class *vs*. instance, 198–200
Clean code, 42
    boolean logic, 13–16
    definition, 2
    Don't Repeat Yourself, 19–23
    example, 2–4
    explanation, 24
    formatting, 6–9
    learning, 52
    method signature, 9, 10
    naming, 56
    refactoring, 23
    reusable, 17–19

INDEX

reusing domain class, 25
side effect, 25
steps, 4, 5
structure, 4
using names, 11, 12
Clean code philosophy, 96–100
Cleanliness, 2, 6
Clean validations, 162, 163
Cognitive load, 99, 148
Cohesion, 351, 359, 370, 375
    definition, 272, 273
    methods, 272
    Salesforce development, 275, 277–279
    subelements, 273, 274
Collection class, 253
Colonization, 193
Comments
    Aha!, 122
    ApexDoc, 128, 129
    dead code, 126, 127
    funny, 127
    implementation, 134
    pop-up, 129
    reasons, 122–125
    reference, 133
    to-do comments, 129–132
    types, 124
    version control, 120–122
Compilers, 115
Concept-oriented programming, 196
Configuration-based framework, 375

Continuous delivery (CD), 376, 377
Continuous deployment (CD), 305
Continuous integration (CI), 305, 306
Conversion status, 37
Coupling, 62, 351, 359, 369
    complexity, 269
    custom fields, 271
    definition, 268
    HttpRequest and HttpResponse classes, 268
    metadata, 270, 278
    polymorphism, 269, 271
    smaller methods, 107, 108
CPU time consumption, 146
createMarketingCase method, 237
createPartnerAccountTask() method, 23
Cross-object operations, 174–176
Custom fields, 271
CustomLeadConversion class, 245, 247, 248, 250, 269, 282–285

D

Drop-in replacements, database class, 336, 337
Database.Batchable class, 245
Database.Batchable interface, 244
Database-driven system, 322, 323
Database.insert() method, 78
Database tables, 200
Database transactions, 322
Data storage, 312

INDEX

Date class, 259–261, 273
deactivateAccount method, 117
Dead code, 126, 127
Debug logs, 146, 181, 212, 213, 375
Decoupling, 176, 177
Deep *vs.* shallow modules, 106, 107
Dependency
 Apex class, 287, 288
 definition, 287
 domain-specific classes, 293
 example, 290
 implicit, 289
 infrastructure, 290
 loggers, 291, 292
 logging, 290
 method, 289
 pseudocode, 290, 293
 responsibilities, 288
 result, 292
 types, 290
 version, 294
Dependency injection (DI), 108, 245, 249, 281, 306, 329, 331
 coupling, 283, 285, 286
 decouple classes, 282
 definition, 282
 implementation, 284, 285
 modular design, 287
 responsibility, 284
Dependency inversion principle (DIP), 245–251
Deployment-time decoupling, 176
Designing errors out of existence, 255, 256

Ditto-mocks, 337
DMLExecutable class, 239
DMLExecutable interface, 88, 208
DMLExecutable variable, 149
DML operations
 Brute Force, 325, 326
 DI, 329, 331
 discussion, 324
 empty list, 146
 enum, 81
 fluent interface pattern, 73
 implementation, 78
 interfaces, 218, 219
 libraries
  drop-in replacements, database class, 337
  general-purpose mocking libraries, 337
  types, 336
 multiple boolean parameters, 75
 simple context-aware wrapper, 328, 329
 SOQL queries, 325, 338
 test doubles and stub API, 331–336
 testing internals without database, 326, 328
DMLOperations class, 73
Domain Builder library, 43
Domain classes, 371–374
Domain layer, 349, 362, 363
Domain-specific dependencies, 291

Do Not Repeat Yourself
 (DRY), 252–254
Don't repeat yourself too much
 (DRYTM), 252
Dreamforce, 376
Duplication, 64

E

Empty, 141, 142
    list validation, 145–149
    reasons, 145
Encapsulation, 193, 197
    in Apex, 205, 206
    Apex transactions, 203
    deep modules, 203
    definition, 203
    JavaScript function, 204
    macro level, 204
    modifiers, 203
    OOP paradigm, 204
Enterprise patterns, 355
Enums
    advantage, 82
    definition, 76
    DML class, 80
    execute() method, 81
    features, 82
    Operation enum, 80
    problems, 80
    trigger contexts, 76
    version, 77
Exception handling, 166–170, 182,
 184, 185, 325

Exception management, 118
executeDML function, 86
External dependencies, 315, 323
External documentation, 125
External libraries, 375

F

Facade design pattern, 104
Feature flags, 126, 265, 376, 377
FFLIB
    challenges
        narrow view of platform, 352
        over-engineering, 355
        Salesforce, 355, 356
        selector class, 353, 354
        SoC, 351
    domain layer, 349
    framework, 347, 348
    layers, 349
    recap, 348–351
    selector layer, 349
    service layer, 349
FinancialForce, 348
Fragility, 93
Functional programming, 192
Funny comments, 127

G

General-purpose mocking
 libraries, 336, 337
General-purpose module, 261, 262,
 264, 265

INDEX

getBaseTask() method, 21, 23
getCaseAge method, 237
getDefaultClient method, 45
getPopulatedFieldsAsMap()
    method, 160
getSupportCaseSLA method, 236
GitHub, 301
God classes, 372
Governor-limit decoupling, 176
Gratitude, 357
Guard clause, 139, 152–158

H

Hard-coding dependencies, 298, 299
High cohesion, 274, 275
High-level policies, 251
HTTP callout, 5

I, J

IDatabaseOps interface, 333
Implicit boolean expression, 38
Implicit dependency, 289
Individuality, 193, 197
Information hiding, 101, 102,
    204, 260
Infrastructure dependencies,
    291, 293
Inheritance, 201
    in Apex programming, 212–215
    bugs, 209
    composition, 215, 217
    definition, 208

Grasshoper class, 211
higher-level categories, 209
log method, 216
reuse behavior, 211
variations and
    commonalities, 215
Injecting dependencies, 298, 299
Integration tests, 313
    antipattern, 320
    database-driven system, 322, 323
    external factors, 319, 321
    performance optimization, 324
    recommendation, 345
    result variable, 320
    Salesforce, 315–319
    test speed, 323
    trade-offs, 321
Intentions, 36, 37
Interfaces
    in Apex, 221, 222
    definition, 217, 218
    DML operations, 218, 219
    execute method, 220
    implementation, 219–221
    setOperation method, 218
Interface segregation principle
    (ISP), 243–245
Internal business names, 12
Internal information, 101
Internal libraries
    Apex logging and
        observability, 375
    CD and feature flags, 376, 377
    general utilities, 378, 379

INDEX

plug-in solutions, 374
selector classes, 378
trigger handlers, 375
Inversion of Control Principle
(ICP), 304
isBypassed method, 102
isNotBlank() method, 142

K

keySet() method, 29
Knowledge-based coupling, 283

L

Lambda expressions, 86
Late binding, 300–303
LeadConversionUtil, 246, 248,
269, 282–285
LeadConvert class, 196
Limits.getDmlStatements()
method, 108
Liskov substitution principle
(LSP), 241–243
Logging, 118, 130
Longer methods, 104, 106
Loose coupling, 269
Low cohesion, 273, 274

M

Magic numbers, 52–55
Map.get(key) method, 161
Maps, 144, 145

MassLeadConversion class, 216,
291, 293
Math class, 195
Metadata-based coupling, 283, 284,
286, 287
MetadataTriggerHandler
class, 102
Method signature, 9, 10
Misleadingness, 116
MockDatabaseOps, 332
Modular design, 287
Modularity, 193, 197, 306,
351, 355, 356, 359, 371
Apex libraries, 262, 263
benefits, 258
business logic, 265
definition, 258
functions, 265, 266
guidelines, 267
information hiding, 259
Lego blocks, 258
negative consequences,
266, 267
properties, 259–262
pseudocode, 258, 264
users' business
requirements, 263
Moxygen, 337
Mulesoft, 204
Multiple boolean
parameters, 72–76
Multiple returns, 153–158
Multitenant
architecture, 356

INDEX

N

Naming
- boolean logic, 31–36
- clean code, 56
- code relevant, 40–42
- collection type
  - accountList or opportunityMap, 28
  - boolean variable, 29
  - conditions, 29
  - implementation, 30
  - instance, 30
  - List and Set variables, 28
  - Map convention, 30
  - partnerAccounts and inactiveAccounts, 30
  - sObject type, 31
  - variable declaration, 29
- context, 42–44
- for loop, 52
- intention, 36, 37
- lifespan, 53
- magic numbers, 53–55
- metadata elements, 27
- principles, 28
- problem domain, 50, 51
- programming constructs, 27
- pronounceable, 47, 48
- same type but different, 38–40
- searchable, 48–50
- team effort, 56
- validation rule, 27
- variables and classes
  - camel case, 46
  - coding, 44
  - custom data types, 45
  - Pascal case, 46
  - reusing class names, 46, 47
  - static and nonstatic context, 45

Nebula Logger, 118, 265, 376
NetSuite, 25, 49
Nonatomic operation, 170
Nonbusiness logic, 364
notifyAccountOwners() method, 25
Null, 135, 136
- list validation, 150–152
Null coalescing operator (??), 139–141
NullPointerException (NPE), 136–138

O

Object-oriented design, 309
Object-oriented programming (OOP), 87, 259, 306
- abstract classes, 223–229
- in Apex, 200–202
- challenges, 195–197
- class *vs.* instance, 198–200
- definition, 194
- encapsulation, 202–206
- history, 192, 193
- inheritance, 208–217
- interfaces, 218–222
- polymorphism, 207, 208, 229–231

INDEX

responsibilities and attributes, 194, 195
    sending messages, 195
Object relational mapping (ORM), 202
Observability, 375
Observable behavior, 314
One-liner methods, 104
One test method, 318
One thing method
    checklist, 67
    definition, 65, 66
    example, 59
    review, 65
    sample method, 66
    steps, 61
Open/closed principle (OCP), 84, 93, 238–241
Opportunities, 265
OpportunityDiscount class, 363
OpportunitySelector class, 350, 352
OpportunityService class, 350, 352, 362
OpportunityTriggerHandler class, 368
Osherove, 310, 311
Over-engineering, 355
Overloaded methods, 71

P

Page layouts, 372
Parent processes, 165
Partner account task, 5, 12

Pass-through method, 97, 319
Platform events, 182–184
Polymorphism, 201, 207, 208, 214, 229–231, 239, 250, 269, 271, 284
Principles-based framework, 358
Problem domain names, 50, 51
Problem domains, 361
Procedural programming, 192
Production deployment, 126
ProductMaster class, 43
Pronounceable names, 47, 48
Public methods, 108

Q

Queueable class, 222, 223, 226, 228, 240, 252

R

Random string, 62
reassignRelatedRecords method, 175
Record types, 372
Reference comments, 133
Regression testing, 270, 308
Return null, 159–162
Rolled back, 171, 172

S

Safe navigation operator (?), 136–139
Salesforce development, 275, 277–279, 350, 355–357, 368

389

INDEX

Salesforce DevOps, 121, 305, 307
Salesforce DX, 360, 361, 363
Salesforce tests, 315–319
Salesforce UI, 186
Screaming architecture, 361
Searchable names, 48–50
Selector classes, 18, 378
Selector layer, 349
Self-documenting code,
    19, 118–120
Separation of concerns (SoC), 351
Service class, 363
Service layer, 349, 350, 362, 363
Shallow module, 353, 354
Short methods, 95
shouldRunAgain method, 224
Side effect, 25
Simple context-aware wrapper,
    328, 329
Single responsibility principle
    (SRP), 93, 99, 235–238,
    352, 371
Smaller methods, 107, 108
Smalltalk programming
    language, 192
SObject type, 230
SObject.clone() method, 75
Software design principles
    description, 233, 234
    designing errors out of
        existence, 255, 256
    DRY, 252–254
    SOLID, 234–251
    YAGNI, 254

SOQL Lib, 342, 378
SOQL queries
    data model, 338
    DML statements, 338
    error message, 340
    example, 339
    inline, 341
    methods, 341, 342
    synchronous transaction, 54
    testing, 339
    wrapper, 342, 343, 345
Special-purpose module, 261
Stack, 186
Static methods, 199
Strategy design pattern, 87
Strings, 81, 99, 103, 142
Stub API, 331–336
StubDatabaseOps, 332
StubProvider interface, 333
Subprocesses, 165
Subtasks, 109–112
Switch statements, 82
    chain method, 77
    definition, 76
    design pattern
        adherence, 84
        coding, 84
        conditional logic, 84
        creating interface, 87
        DML.Operation values, 89
        executing, 89
        functions, 86
        languages, 86
        problem, 85

INDEX

resulting, 90–92
strategy, 87
executeX() method, 83
syncAccountWithNetsuite()
method, 25
System.StubProvider interface, 332
System.Test.createStub() method, 332

T

TaskAfterTriggerHandler class, 178
Task trigger, 187
Team sport, 56
Template method pattern, 229
Testability, 64, 65, 359
Test doubles, 331–336
Test utilities, 331
Thinking patterns, 177, 188
Threads, 165
Tight coupling, 268, 270
To-do comments, 129–132
toString method, 212
Traditional software development, 315, 322, 358
Trailhead module, 351, 362, 363
Trigger.AccountTrigger
execution, 169
Trigger actions framework, 101, 102, 240, 265
Trigger handlers
AWAF guidance, 371
ClosedOpportunities class, 369, 370
coding, 371

contexts, 373
internal libraries, 375
OpportunityTriggerHandler
class, 368
statement, 369
Trigger.OperationType enum, 76
Triggers
cross-object operations, 174–176
decoupling, 176, 177
exceptions, 184–188
Type-narrowing, 243

U

Unit of behavior, 311–314
Unit of code, 312, 313
Unit of work, 310, 311
Unit testing, 331
definition, 309
method, 310
properties, 314, 315
reasons, 313
unit of behavior, 311, 312
unit of code, 312, 313
unit of work, 310, 311
version, 309
Utils class, 273

V

Validation
booleans, 142, 143
empty, 145–149
maps, 144, 145

391

INDEX

Validation (*cont.*)
    null, 150–152
    parameters, 162
    strings, 142
Version control, 120–122, 126
Very short methods
    to explain, 100, 101
    to hide information, 101, 102
    name action, 103, 104
    to simplify API, 102
Violation, 233

W, X

Web services, 312
writeToDebugLog
    parameter, 69
Writing tests, 307, 308

Y, Z

YAGNI principle, 355
You aren't gonna need it
    (YAGNI), 254

Printed in the United States
by Baker & Taylor Publisher Services